Sex and Secularism

Joan Wallach Scott

PRINCETON UNIVERSITY PRESS
PRINCETON & OXFORD

Published by Princeton University Press,
41 William Street, Princeton, New Jersey 08540

In the United Kingdom: Princeton University Press,
6 Oxford Street, Woodstock, Oxfordshire OX20 1TR

press.princeton.edu

Jacket Illustration and design by Amanda Weiss

Library of Congress Cataloging-in-Publication Data

Names: Scott, Joan Wallach, author.
Title: Sex and secularism / Joan Wallach Scott.
Description: Princeton, New Jersey : Princeton University Press, [2018] |
Includes bibliographical references and index.
Identifiers: LCCN 2017015590 | ISBN 9780691160641 (hardcover : alk. paper)
Subjects: LCSH: Feminism. | Women—Social conditions. | Sex role.
Classification: LCC HQ1190 .S38 2018 | DDC 305.42—dc23 LC record available
at https://lccn.loc.gov/2017015590

British Library Cataloging-in-Publication Data is available

This book has been composed in Miller

Printed on acid-free paper. ∞

Printed in the United States of America

10 9 8 7 6 5 4 3 2 1

"If the relation between the sexes is an essential, if repressed, dimension of social change, taking it into account ought—by extending the field of our questions and our perceptions—to change our understanding of history."

—MICHELLE PERROT

"We should look, therefore, at the politics *of national progress—including the politics of secularism—that flow from the multifaceted concept of modernity exemplified by 'the West.'"*

—TALAL ASAD

CONTENTS

FOREWORD

THE PUBLIC SQUARE was founded to help eminent scholars bring significant issues of the day to our attention. Its books explore topics that have great impact, that resonate. In *Sex and Secularism* Joan Wallach Scott unravels, with her customary elegance and style, a pair of tightly knit concepts whose interplay has exerted great influence in arenas ranging from global affairs to local politics.

With perspicacity and acuteness, Scott explains how in recent decades, the questions of gender and secularism have been mingled in political discourse, producing "a vision that shapes and is accepted as reality." This is the vision that informs the "clash of civilizations" polemic. Yet this version of secularism, as "we now understand it," "misrepresents history" and is perhaps best understood as a veil concealing the Islamophobia that lies beneath it.

Scott shows that the civilizational polemic makes gender equality synonymous with secularism (and gender inequality synonymous with Islam). This association serves two purposes: first, it fuels Islamophobia, and second, it distracts attention from the way inequalities and gender asymmetry continue to abound, rippling across politics, economics, and the family in both the East *and* the West. The history of secularism in Western modernity, she points out, far from guaranteeing women's liberation, was based on a division of labor that made women subordinate to men.

Scott argues that secularism is not an abstract concept but a set of ideas that have been deployed in specific contexts. "To what effects," she asks, and "to what ends" has secularism been used? Only by tracing the historical circumstances and studying what conditions are connected with this concept can we understand how it "organizes" the way "we view the world" and "manages our perception."

With characteristic ingenuity, Scott finds the relevant historical circumstances in histories of religion, race, and colonialism written by second-wave feminists and scholars of postcolonialism. By synthesizing their scholarship, she tracks the way the distinctions public/private, political/domestic, and reason/passion were defined by their associations with masculine/feminine and men/women. She goes on to make the more radical claim that we cannot understand the formation of modern Western nation-states without taking gender into account. Gender is always part of the discourse of secularism, albeit in different ways.

In her final chapter, Scott addresses the current emphasis on sexual emancipation as a test of democracy and of Western superiority. The substitution of sexual desire for abstract reasoning as the common ground of the human draws attention away from inequalities that persist even when sexual democracy (the recognition of varieties of sexuality and diversities of gender identification) is said to prevail.

In her masterful book, Joan Scott gives us a new understanding of the way sexual difference has defined and troubled discourses of secularism. In this way she launches a conversation appropriate for the Public Square.

Ruth O'Brien
The CUNY Graduate Center
New York, New York

ACKNOWLEDGMENTS

I BEGAN THIS BOOK soon after I finished *The Politics of the Veil* (2007) because secularism seemed to me to need more and broader attention than I'd given it in that book. It has taken me some time to address the question, and I've had lots of help. A seminar on "Secularism" at the School of Social Science at the Institute for Advanced Study (IAS) in 2010–11 launched the project and brought together a group of scholars whose critical ideas and differences of approach taught me how to think better about the subject. They included Gil Anidjar, Kathleen Davis, Mayanthi Fernando, Elizabeth Shakman Hurd, Cécile Laborde, Tomoko Masuzawa, Mohammed Naciri, Laura Secor, Winnifred Fallers Sullivan, Anna Sun, and Judith Surkis.

Another seminar, this one on "Globalization and Social Change" at the Graduate Center of the City University of New York in 2015, made important suggestions about chapter 5 especially. I particularly appreciated the input from Gary Wilder, Massimiliano Tomba, Nadia Abu El Haj, Herman Bennett, and Duncan Faherty. Yet another seminar, this one for anthropology graduate students that I co-taught with Mayanthi Fernando at Berkeley in the fall of 2016, expanded my thinking even further at the final stages of writing. Brent Eng, Aaron Eldridge, Mohamad Jarada, Philip Balboni, and Basit Iqbal were terrific listeners and interlocutors. The comments from a reading group at IAS in 2016–17 that included Fadi Bardawil, David Kazanjian, Massimiliano Tomba, and Linda Zerilli enabled me to clarify arguments in the introduction and chapter 4.

Over the years, my critical insights have been sharpened by my conversations with and reading of the important books of Saba Mahmood. Along the way, Eric Fassin, Seth Moglen, Kabir Tambar, Noah Salomon, Katherine Lemons, and Gayle Salamon have offered perceptive comments, and their work has helped clarify my thoughts. Judith Butler and Elizabeth Weed, as usual, gave me more to think about than I sometimes wanted to hear—but listening made all the difference.

I can't now remember everyone who posed all of the terrific questions to me when I gave talks on sex and secularism, but those moments of critical engagement made a huge difference for the conceptualization of this book. One I do remember came from my colleague Didier Fassin, who suggested pointedly that what I was talking about was a *discourse* of secularism, not a fixed category of analysis. He was, as usual, exactly right. So was Brian Connolly, a former student who has become a good colleague and friend. Brian read the entire manuscript with attention and care; his comments pointed me to contradictions and shortcomings in my arguments that, I hope, have now been corrected. Wendy Brown and Joseph Massad read the manuscript for the press (they later revealed their identities to me), and their input made this book immeasurably better than it otherwise would have been.

I have not only benefited from the specific attention to the book from students, friends, and colleagues but also from the body of scholarship on which it is based. As I say in the introduction, this is a synthesis of long years of hard work by scholars working on feminism, gender, sexuality, race, class, and postcolonialism across the disciplinary spectrum. Without their research and analytic incisiveness, my own work would have been impossible. They are cited in notes and in the bibliography, but that can't express the enormity of my debt—our debt—to them.

Some of the chapters have material from previously published articles of mine: "The Vexed Relationship of Emancipation and Equality," *History of the Present* 2.2 (Fall 2012); "Sexularism," in Scott, *The Fantasy of Feminist History*, Duke University Press, 2011; "Secularism, Gender Inequality and the French State," in Jocelyne Cesari and Jose Casanova, *Islam, Gender and Democracy in Comparative Perspective*, Oxford University Press, 2017; "Laïcité et égalité des sexes," in Valentine Zuber, et al, *Croire, s'engager, chercher: Autour de Jean Baubérot*, Turnhout Brepols, Collection de l'Ecole des Hautes Etudes, 2017.

Although I am now professor emerita at the Institute for Advanced Study, I continue to enjoy the benefits of a place that values the life of the mind above all else. Here, not only faculty colleagues but a dedicated staff enable us to work unhindered by the usual details of existence. Nancy Cotterman has been my assistant for more years than either of us wants to remember; Donne Petito administers the School of Social Science with aplomb; Marcia Tucker runs a library like no other, assisted by Kirstie Venanzi and Karen Downing. They all, in one way or another, have made this book possible.

At Princeton University Press, Ruth O'Brien (the editor of the Public Square series) and Brigitta van Rheinberg have not only exemplified the highest forms of professionalism, they have been encouraging and supportive as well. Cathy Slovensky is a copy editor par excellence.

As my work has been sustained by colleagues and friends, so my life is enriched by my family: Lizzie and Eric, Tony and Justine, and their amazing children—my grandchildren—Ezra, Carmen, Henry, and Nadia. Although I fully appreciate that my thinking about the future is a product of the very discourse of secularism that I critically explore in these pages, I nonetheless hold out the hope that these children will find a way—against great odds—to contribute to the creation of a more just and egalitarian world. This book is for them.

SEX AND SECULARISM

INTRODUCTION

The Discourse of Secularism

ATTENTION TO SECULARISM has again entered popular discourse as part of the "clash of civilizations" rhetoric. Of course, there is a long history of academic study of secularization, the processes by which European states are said to have brought organized religion under their control, introduced bureaucratic management and technical calculation into their governing operations, and justified their sovereignty in terms of republican or democratic theory, that is, as representatives of the mandate of those considered citizens, not as the embodiment of God's will. Secularism has been taken to be synonymous with these processes; the historical triumph of enlightenment over religion. But in its recent usage, it has had a simpler referent as the positive alternative, not to all religion but to Islam. In this discourse secularism guarantees freedom and gender equality while Islam is synonymous with oppression.

Although some critics of Islam specify their target as political and/or fundamentalist Islam, most indict all of Islam in their condemnations. Thus, the idea of a "clash of civilizations," as articulated by the political scientist Samuel Huntington in

1993, posed Western Christianity against Islam in a conflict that, he maintained, "had been going on for 1300 years."[1] In the article, he soon referred to Western Christianity simply as "the West," and although secularism was not denoted as such, it was implicit in the contrasts that he offered between freedom and oppression. As the phrase "clash of civilizations" gained prominence, especially after 9/11, secularism and gender equality became increasingly emphasized as the basis for Western superiority to all of Islam. So in 2003, the head of the French commission recommending a ban on Islamic headscarves in public schools explained that according to the principle of *laïcité* (the French word for secularism), "France cannot allow Muslims to undermine its core values, which include a strict separation of religion and state, equality between the sexes, and freedom for all."[2] In the same year, the American political scientists Ronald Inglehart and Pippa Norris argued that "the true clash of civilizations" was about "gender equality and sexual liberalization."[3] The religious demands of Islam were said to deny both. Since then, the emancipatory effect of secularism on women has been so taken for granted that the American novelist Joyce Carol Oates expressed surprise at the criticism she got for tweeting that "the predominant religion of Egypt" was responsible for violence against women during the summer protests of 2013.[4] It seems never to have occurred to her that misogyny of the kind responsible for the domestic violence that she often chronicles in her novels might be at issue, and that her comment might be construed as Islamophobic, so self-evident did her opinion seem to her. Perhaps the most virulent attack on Islam in the name of secularism comes from a defiant French organization called Riposte Laïque (Secular Retort), which brings together groups from across the political spectrum to defend the republic from impending annihilation by the Muslim hordes. "When one is attached to the Republic, to democracy, to women's rights, to freedom, to secularism, one has the obligation to be islamophobic simply because Islam cannot tolerate emancipatory values."[5] Here, by definition, secularism is associated with reason, freedom, and women's rights, Islam with a culture of oppression and terror. In this formulation culture is reason's other—reason assures the progress of history while culture protects immutable tradition.

In this book I examine the ways in which gender has figured in the discourses of secularism. I revisit a large body of literature written by second-wave feminists, as well as by historians of religion, race, and colonialism. I synthesize this work and offer new interpretations based upon it. The literature allows me to document the uses of the term "secularism" and to identify its various meanings and contradictions. On the basis of this history, it is very clear that the gender equality today invoked as a fundamental and enduring principle of secularism was not at all included in the first uses of the term. In fact, *gender inequality was fundamental to the articulation of the separation of church and state that inaugurated Western modernity.* I go further to suggest that Euro-Atlantic modernity entailed *a new order of women's subordination*, assigning them to a feminized familial sphere meant to complement the rational masculine realms of politics and economics. When the question of Islam arose in the late twentieth century, along with a polemic about the "clash of civilizations," gender equality became a primary concern for secularism. And even now, what counts as that equality is difficult to define because its meaning is secured largely by a negative contrast with Islam.

The book's arguments can be briefly stated this way: first, the notion that equality between the sexes is inherent to the logic of secularism is false; second, this false historical assertion has been used to justify claims of white, Western, and Christian racial and religious superiority in the present as well as the past; and third, it has functioned to distract attention from a persistent set of difficulties related to differences of sex, which Western and non-Western, Christian and non-Christian nations share, despite the different ways in which they have addressed those difficulties. Gender inequality is not simply the by-product of the emergence of modern Western nations, characterized by the separation between the public and the private, the political and the religious; rather, that inequality is at its very heart. And secularism is the discourse that has served to account for this fact.

The Discourse of Secularism

The title of this chapter, "The Discourse of Secularism," is meant to signal that I am not treating secularism as a fixed category of analysis but as a discursive operation of power whose generative effects need to be examined critically in their historical contexts. This means that when I refer to secularism, it is not objective definitions I have in mind. Instead, following Michel Foucault, my approach is "genealogical," that is, it analyzes the ways in which the term has been variously deployed, and with what effects. This approach does not deny the reality of the institutions and practices said to embody secularism; indeed, I examine those closely in the chapters that follow. But instead of assuming that we know in advance what secularism means, or that it has a fixed and unchanging definition, I interrogate its meaning as it was articulated and implemented differently in different contexts at different times.[6]

This approach distinguishes my work from much of the vast literature on secularism that has emerged in this century—usually directly or indirectly in response to the clash of civilizations polemic. Whether written by anthropologists, philosophers, or historians, these studies either assume or attempt to pin down an ultimate meaning for the concept and the processes it connotes. They fashion an analytic category distinct from the actual historical usages of the word itself. They ask undeniably important questions about the impact of secularization on religion or the state, about what is entailed in the constitution of secular subjects, about whether and how secularity opens the way for nonnormative sexual practices, about the nature of belief in a "secular age." Secularism is understood, for this body of scholarship, either as the linear evolution of ideas and institutions that brought us modernity or as a conceptual and political formation with identifiable characteristics.[7] It is used as an analytic category, with a set of characteristics that are apparent to an observer even when the word itself is not being used by those whose lives are being studied.[8] In that work, *secular* (referring to things nonreligious), *secularization* (the historical process by which transcendent religious authority is replaced by knowledge that can only originate with reasoning humans), and *secularity* (a nonreligious state of being) tend to be conflated under the umbrella of secularism.

In this book I do not take secularism as an analytic category apart from the discourse that deployed it, nor do I accept the assertion that gender equality is an inevitable (though belated) feature of secularism's history. Here I am in disagreement with the philosopher Charles Taylor's progressive narrative of secularism. From his perspective, the implementation of secularism is synonymous with progress, emancipation, and modernity. Discussing "Locke's egalitarian imaginary," he notes that "[it was] at the outset profoundly out of synch with the way things in fact ran. . . . Hierarchical complementarity was the principle on which people's lives effectively operated—from kingdom . . . to family. We still have some lively sense of this disparity in the case of the family, because it is really only in our time that the older images of hierarchical complementarity between men and women are being comprehensively challenged. But this is a late stage in a 'long march' process."[9] I think this comment assumes a cumulative progress toward equality that simply hasn't been the case. It works with an idealized or reified notion of secularism as a transcendent phenomenon when, in fact, it is anything but that.

I am more in agreement with Talal Asad's critique of this idea of secularism (written before Taylor's book) as a "myth of liberalism"—and with his call for attention to its discursive construction, that is, to its genealogy. "The secular is neither singular in origin nor stable in its historical identity, although it works through a series of particular oppositions," among them the political and the religious, the public and the private.[10] To this list I would add the opposition between reason and sex, masculine and feminine, men and women. My focus is on the politics of the discursive articulations of secularism, particularly as they depend on references to gender. In that sense, I am writing on the history of the polemical uses of the term and their resonances for political, social, and economic institutions and policies.

But—readers be warned—this is not a conventional intellectual or social history of the word *secularism* and its associated practices. It is, instead, a set of arguments bound loosely by a periodization related to the emergence of modern Western nation-states (from the eighteenth century on); it juxtaposes examples from places with different histories and geographies, not in order to deny their specificity but to insist on what was common to their invocations of secularism and its effects. Some readers will find the juxtapositions to be unlikely; some will want more contextualization than I have provided. Some will chafe at what they deem to be overly sweeping transgeographic historical claims about gender, sexuality, secularism, state formation, and capitalism. These are inevitable objections, which nonetheless misunderstand my own polemical aim: to engage and discredit, with a broad brush and the provision of as many varied instances as I could find, the current representation of secularism as the guarantor of equality between women and men. A broad brush inevitably invites objections, qualifications, instances that don't fit the overall pattern I think I discern. If this book provokes others to pursue more detailed and precise histories, that is all to the good. My aim is to open—not to definitively close—a conversation about the place of gender equality in the discourse of secularism.

I think of this book as exemplifying what Foucault referred to as the history of the present: a history that critically examines terms we take for granted and whose meanings seem beyond question because we treat them as a matter of common sense. Certainly, secularism has had that status for many of us. It is the reason, I think, that many of my colleagues, when hearing about this book, have expressed surprise at my interest in critically examining the term. They ask: Are you questioning the value of the neutrality of the state in relation to religion and the principle of religious noninterference in the deliberations of politics? Isn't it dangerous to do that at this moment of evangelical religious revival the world over? Do you dispute the fact that there is more space in liberal secular societies for a diversity of views about such things as sex and politics, and for dissenting movements to emerge? No, I reply, I endorse those principles and agree that there may be more open spaces, more possibilities for variety and change in some societies rather than others, but I don't think that those openings can be attributed entirely to "secularism," and to the contrast with religion upon which it depends. Simply endorsing that contrast doesn't help me to understand the discursive operations of secularism, its history, and contemporary political uses. I think it is important to explore the history of this polemical term to see how it has delimited our notions of progress, modernity, and change. This is a form of critique as Saba Mahmood defines it: "To critique a particular normative regime is not to reject or condemn it; rather, by analyzing its regulatory and productive dimensions, one only deprives it of innocence and neutrality so as to craft, perhaps, a different future."[11]

The very periodization of modernity—its contrast with a feudal past—was produced by a discourse of secularism, according to the critique of it by Kathleen Davis. She calls it "the 'triumphalist' narrative," which "came to mark the conditions of possibility for the emergence of the political qualities designated 'modern,' particularly the nation-state and its self-conscious citizen."[12] She links it as well to colonial conquests: "The liberation of Europe's political, economic, and social life from ecclesiastical authority and religion was defined as the very basis of politics, progress and historical consciousness . . . Correlatively, Europe's 'medieval' past and cultural others, mainly colonized non-Christians, were defined as religious, static, and ahistorical—thus open for narrative and territorial development."[13]

Davis points out that the periodization established by the secularization narrative offers an idea of modernity that depends for its definition on a contrast with an invented regressive feudal past. Her description of the actual history of feudalism finds it characterized by many rational, juridical aspects not easily distinguished from what counts as "modern." From this perspective, the categorization of religion as a singular phenomenon is not the predecessor but the product of secularization; it serves to define retrospectively what modernity is not. It is in these terms that Tomoko Masuzawa understands "the invention of world religions" in the nineteenth century and the vast scholarly enterprise that made religion a new object of study, the means by which the secular and the modern were allied in the Western historical imaginary.[14]

In recent years, scholars have begun to question the historical account of the inevitable triumph of the secular. Asad points out that the simple story of the decline of religion is no longer tenable. "If anything is agreed upon, it is that a straightforward narrative of progress from the religious to the secular is no longer acceptable."[15] Jordan Alexander Stein adds that study after study has revealed the persistence and importance of religion in the very countries of the West in which it was supposed to have disappeared. "The history of secularism," he writes, "is the history of a story we told, not of a thing that happened."[16] This story offered an abstract, schematic representation and a periodization that ignored the particular details of different nations, instead providing a unifying rationale for a series of economic, social, and political developments with diverse causes and outcomes, not all of them the result of what might be called a secular frame of mind. But although it may not reflect the realities it claims to describe, the secularism story (secularization, secularity) does have an important influence on the way these realities are perceived. It is a story, moreover, that has served different purposes in the historical moments and contexts in which it is told. In the eighteenth and nineteenth centuries, secularism was deemed the progressive alternative to religion—the sign of the advance of civilization. In our current context it is portrayed as a practice threatened by the return of religion, specifically Islam, although the Islam it refers to is as much a manifestation of secular politics as it is of the spiritual qualities associated with religion. The point is that secularism is a political discourse, not a transcendent set of principles, or an accurate representation of history. Like all discourses, though, it has a purpose and a set of effects that produce a particular vision of the world—a vision that shapes and is accepted as reality, even as it misrepresents history.

Secularism's Genealogy

The word "secularism" has a recent history—dating back only to the nineteenth century. Since it was first coined in that period, secularism has been a weapon in the arsenal of what Edward Said famously designated "Orientalism"—the caricatured representation of "the East" by Western academics and "a very large mass of writers, among whom are poets, novelists, philosophers, political theorists, economists, and imperial administrators [who] have accepted the basic distinction between East and West as the starting point for elaborate theories, epics, novels, social descriptions, and political accounts concerning the Orient, its people, customs, 'mind,' destiny, and so on."[17] Today, secularism is at the center of arguments about immigrants being advanced by politicians on the right and the left in the countries of Western Europe.[18] In these debates, secularism is identified with Western practices and beliefs that are said to contrast dramatically with Islam; gender equality is offered as one of the defining characteristics of this secularism.

The word "secularism" is not new, but compared to the much older *secular* (which the *Oxford English Dictionary* [*OED*] dates to the thirteenth century), it is surprisingly modern.[19] It was initially used as a polemic during nineteenth-century anticlerical campaigns in England and France when it stood for free speech and the moral autonomy of individuals against the pressures of organized religion. George Holyoake, a founder of the British Central Secular Society in 1851, came up with the term *secularism* to describe an alternative value system, independent of religion but also of atheism, which would teach "the law of humanity, the conditions of human progress, and the nature of human duty."[20] For the French, who first used the word *laïcité* in 1871 (as the Third Republic was struggling against the parties of throne and altar), the point was to offer "a political conception implying the separation of civil society from religious society [in which] the state exercises no religious power and the church no political power."[21] The word was used in these instances as a challenge to the cultural authority of organized Christianity and to its ability to influence or rival state power.

Secularism in its nineteenth-century usage takes its meaning from the definition of the *secular* as this-worldly. In the *Encyclopédie* the first use of *séculaire* is tied to things that happen at the end of a century (*siècle*), suggesting its roots in earthly temporalities.[22] The *OED* finds allusions to *secular* as early as the thirteenth century, referring to "secular priests," that is, to members of the clergy who left the cloister for a life in the world. A second usage distinguished the world and its affairs from the church and religion. The term, we are told, was largely negative: nonecclesiastical, nonreligious, nonsacred.[23] The negative connotations of *secular*, in its earliest usages, testify to its placement within religiously centered discourses—the religious defined (positively) against the worldly.

The sociologist of religion, José Casanova, locates the notion of the secular squarely within Western European Christendom's "double dualist system of classification."[24] The double dualism referred first to the Augustinian distinction between the City of Man and the City of God, this world and the next. In addition, within the world of man, there was a secular and a religious sphere. "Both dualisms were mediated . . . by the sacramental nature of the church . . . simultaneously belonging to both worlds."[25]

As Casanova tracks the history, we see the secular acquiring increasingly positive connotations. First used to refer to the way in which once-cloistered monks became priests living among laypeople, it then referred to the expropriation of monasteries and other church properties after the Protestant Reformation. The *Encyclopédie* links the word to the settlement of the Thirty Years' War at Westphalia, when German princes "seized the property of bishops, abbés and monks that were situated on their estates."[26] By the time of the French Revolution, the secular referred to the state and its representatives in opposition to the church and the clergy. If once the secular had been subsumed within religious discourse (as its antithesis), now it was the other way around: the religious became the negative other of the secular. The dualism Casanova refers to remained, but the City of Man now reigned supreme, and politics rather than sacrament mediated the difference. Religion did not disappear. It was relegated to the realm of the private: private conscience, private practice, private affect. In this discourse, the very absence of religion in spheres of economy and politics defined them as secular, even when the realms of private and public were, in fact, more difficult to separate than this representation implied.

Casanova notes that the particularity of the Christian conception distinguishes it from other religions (Eastern ones, in particular) which endorse no such dualisms and have no ecclesiastical organization. The historical study of "the transfer of persons, things, meanings, etc. from ecclesiastical or religious to civil or lay use" is, he suggests, not the study of a universal process but of a process distinctively embedded in the history of Western Christian societies. Writes Asad, "This separation of religion from power is a modern Western norm, the product of a unique post-Reformation history."[27]

By the nineteenth century the secularism/religion opposition was framed in terms of another binary, that between men and women, masculinity and femininity. The City of Man was literally represented as a masculine domain; within its walls and subordinate to it was the feminized realm of religiosity. The implementation of this separation was different in different countries and at different times. In majority Catholic nations like France, there were direct attacks on church power; in Protestant England and America, in contrast, religious practice itself was secularized, but in all cases the association of women and religion was clear. This is not to say that the institutions of religion were in women's hands; to be sure, churches both Catholic and Protestant were profoundly patriarchal organizations. Rather, nineteenth-century secularist campaigns deployed the language of sex difference in order to disarm the power of religious institutions, not by abolishing those institutions but by feminizing them.

Since the nineteenth century there have been changes in the ways the discourse of secularism has been mobilized, using a familiar set of oppositions but attributing different meanings to them. "Political" and "religious" in the nineteenth century meant the nation versus institutionalized religion (state versus church), but also the Christian nation versus the "uncivilized" and "primitive" tribes in Africa and the Ottoman lands. "Public" and "private" separated the market and politics, instrumental rationality and bureaucratic organization from home and family, spirituality, affective relationality, and sexual intimacy. Men figured on the public side, women on the side of the private. These oppositions continued well into the twentieth century, although the use of the word "secularism" itself declined as a way of designating the modernity of Western nations.

Secularism emerged again as a key word toward the end of the twentieth century with the return of religion as a social and political force, and particularly with the substitution of Islam for Soviet communism as a threat to the West at the end of the Cold War. Our twenty-first-century discourse of secularism conceives of the realms of the political and the religious differently from its nineteenth-century antecedents. "Political" signifies liberal democracy; "religious" denotes Islam. Gender equality is portrayed in terms of the difference between uncovered and covered societies, the sexually liberated versus the sexually repressed. In this contrast both religion (once a matter of private conscience in Western democracies), and sex (once associated with the most private and intimate side of life) have entered the public domain. Christianity has become synonymous with democracy, and the asymmetrical complementarity between women and men that grounded nineteenth-century secularism's discourse has been reoriented as a contrast between the fate of women, West and East.

The meanings of secularism have shifted in accordance with shifts in the political and social aims of those who invoke the term. At the same time, the story itself has had enormous staying power. Our view of history is shaped by that story; political appeals to it gain persuasive influence from simplified lines of division between the traditional and the modern, the repressive and the emancipatory. In the eighteenth- and nineteenth-century versions of the discourse, gender *in*equality provided the template for the organization of nation-states, the allocation of citizenship, and the justification for imperial rule. In its current version, secularism has become synonymous with (an ill-defined) gender equality that distinguishes West from East, the Christian secular from the Islamic. The attribution to secularism of these enduring qualities gives it something of a religious aspect, as fundamentalist as the Islam to which it is counterposed. Why has secularism reentered our vocabulary when for decades the very concept was absent from the rhetoric of emancipatory movements—movements whose animating spirit was often deeply religious? How and when did women's equality become identified with secularism? In what ways have the varying invocations of secularism shaped policies, laws, and institutions, as well as our understanding of history? These are some of the questions I address in this book.

The Evidence from History

I began this project because I knew that the current claim about secularism—that it was necessarily synonymous with women's emancipation—was simply not true. As a student of gender and women's history in France, I was startled to hear politicians claim that gender equality was a primordial value of democracy, dating back at least to the French Revolution of 1789. My work, and that of many scholars inspired by second-wave feminism and postcolonialism, has demonstrated over and over again the ways in which women in the modern West were excluded from political participation and cast in decidedly subordinate roles in the family and the labor market. I've returned to that work in the course of this book. It shows, among other things, that gender equality is absent from the founding documents of Western democracies even as they invoke the universal principles of the Rights of Man. It was not that the difference of sex was ignored at these moments, but that its troubling presence was resolved by the exclusion of women from the public sphere. In France, as late as the 1990s, there was an outpouring of opposition, largely from male politicians, to the passage of what became France's law on parity—a law that sought to guarantee equal access for women to elected political office.[28] Even after passage of the law in 2000, the goal of equality remains far from attained; in the legislative elections of 2012, women won some 25 percent of seats—doubling their earlier representation—but male politicians have continued to find ways to impede the progress of women in their quest for political office. To hear these same politicians invoke women's equality as a primordial value is still surprising, to say the least. It can only be concluded that they are instrumentalizing the concept for very specific political ends.

Gender equality did not become a primordial value for French politicians until this century and then only in contrast to Islam. This became clear to me when I did some research on the law of 1905 that separated church and state in France. I was reviewing the rulings on applications of the law, offered from 1905 to 2005, by the French Conseil d'État (France's highest administrative court, whose task is to deal with the legality of actions taken by public bodies). From 1905 until 1987, the court assumed that the question of religion had little bearing on the "woman question."[29] Even when offering its first opinion about the legitimacy of banning Islamic headscarves in public schools in 1989, the court did not raise the question of gender equality. Rather, it framed its decision in terms of threats to public order and proselytizing in the schools. (In 1989 they found neither to be in evidence.) In 2004, on the eve of passage of the headscarf ban, a report by the court noted that its previous decisions had been less influenced than they now would be by "questions linked to Islam and to the place and status of Muslim women in society."[30] The issue of women's equality as a feature of the separation of church and state was a new one for this body that had been offering guidance for nearly a century on the meanings of the law of 1905. It came up only in the context of heated debates about the place of West and North African immigrants in French society.

The French case is not the only example of the way in which the sharp opposition between the West and Islam serves to conceal the persistence of inequality on the Western side. Discrimination based on sex is evident elsewhere historically and in the present. A Swiss federal court, ruling in 2001 against a teacher who wanted to wear a *hijab* to class, argued that "it is difficult to reconcile the wearing of the headscarf with the principle of gender equality—which is a fundamental value of our society enshrined in a specific provision of the Federal constitution."[31] In Switzerland access for women to the vote took until 1971, making it hard to see gender equality as "fundamental" in the sense of a long-standing principle.

Currently, there is no lack of documentation about discrimination against women in the countries of the West: on average women earn lower wages than men and have nowhere near parity in political representation; working-class and immigrant women are at the very bottom of wage scales, often confined to the "care" industry; race is an important factor in the differential treatment of women; glass ceilings still prevent elite women's rise to the top in corporations and bureaucracies; domestic violence against women in all classes continues at alarming rates; misogynistic attacks seem to be increasing; sexual harassment is a fact of life for many women at work, at school, and on the street; women's access to contraception and the right to abortion are being seriously challenged by religious fundamentalists and their political spokesmen in the United States and elsewhere. The list could go on and on. This is not to say that the difficulties confronting women are the same the world over, only that the idea that inequality exists solely for Muslim women is simply not true. The stark contrast between Islam and the West works to distract from those difficulties on the Western side, but also to obscure an older history in which (as I will demonstrate in the chapters that follow) secularists represented life in terms of idealized separate and unequal spheres—political/religious, public/private, reason/affect, man/woman. According to their accounts, the presumed natural difference between the sexes was the social foundation of modern Western nation-states; sexual difference secured the racial superiority of Western nations to their "others"—in Africa, Asia, and Latin America.

Christian Secularism as a Mark of Racial Superiority

I have been struck in the course of research for this book by the way in which—contrary to the stated terms of the religious/secular opposition—Christianity was included on the secular side. I have already cited Huntington's notion of a clash of civilizations in which Western Christianity confronts the proponents of Islam. The association of Christianity and Western democracy is a persistent feature of the contemporary discourse of secularism. Arguably, this is a legacy of the Westphalia Treaty of 1648 that ended the wars of religion in Europe and established the principle of state sovereignty (especially the right of each ruler to determine the religion of his territory) for all of Christendom. As a result, state sovereignty (whatever the form of governance) and Christian practice became inextricably intertwined.

The explicit linking of secularism to its Christian traditions has become ever more forceful in the twenty-first century. When, for example, the Grand Chamber of the European Court of Human Rights ruled in 2001 that crucifixes could be displayed in Italian public school classrooms, it did so (perversely it may seem to some of us) in the name of secularism. The court declared that the crucifix was a cultural symbol that represented the identity of "Italian civilization" and its "value system of liberty, equality, human dignity and religious toleration, and accordingly also of the secular nature of the state."[32] In 2006, Pope Benedict XVI identified Christianity with reason (a hallmark of secularism once seen by anticlericals as antithetical to Catholicism), attributed to it the development of Europe, and contrasted it (by citing the opinion of a fourteenth-century Byzantine emperor) with the irrational violence of Islam.[33]

When I began this study, I initially attributed the association of religion exclusively with Islam to the visibility Muslims had acquired as a result of the Iranian Revolution of 1979, the growing numbers of Muslims residing in the countries of Western Europe, and the September 11, 2001 attacks on the World Trade Center in New York City. But I've learned not only that Christianity—sometimes unmarked, sometimes asserted—inheres in the discourses of secularism, but also that there is a tradition of pointing to Arabs and Muslims as the others of Indo-European Aryans that long antedates this recent history and that is tied to the articulation of the identity of Western nations and their colonial outreach.[34] Edward Said often cited Ernest Renan, philologist and philosopher, as an illustration of Orientalism. Here is Renan in a lecture to the Collège de France in 1862:

> Islam can only exist as an official religion; it perishes when it is reduced to a free and individual religion. Islam is not only a state religion, the way Catholicism was in the France of Louis XIV, and as it is still in Spain; it is a religion that excludes the state. . . . Islam is the most complete negation

> of Europe; Islam is a fanaticism much worse than what was known in Spain at the time of Philip II and Italy at the time of Pius V.[35]

Tomoko Masuzawa, looking beyond France, writes that this view of history was crucial for establishing "the essential identity of the West" through a contrast with its religious others.[36] "In the course of the nineteenth century, Islam . . . came to acquire a new alienness. Instead of being begrudged as the luxuriantly overbearing dominion of Eastern infidelity, the rule of Islam was now condescendingly viewed as narrow, rigid, and stunted, and its essential attributes were said to be defined by the national racial, and ethnic character of the Arabs, the most bellicose and adversarial of the Semites."[37] Gil Anidjar notes that in this period "religion is the Orient, the imperial realm to be governed and dominated, bombed, reformed and civilized."[38] In his view, the discourse of secularism always already included Christianity on its side against an Islamic other. But even if this was not everywhere the case, the important point is that there was an anti-Muslim aspect to the discourse of secularism that could be drawn on—as it has been recently—whenever the concept was invoked.

There is a connection between the secularism discourse's insistence on gender equality today and its anti-Islamic stance that has roots in this colonial history. As imperial powers conquered Arab lands, they pointed to the "barbaric" mistreatment "native" women received at the hands of their men. Moreover, they conflated race and religion in the figure of the Arab Muslim. Islam was the sign of Arab inferiority as Christianity was the mark of white superiority. So Lord Cromer, the local agent of the British after its occupation of Egypt in 1882, wrote that "the position of women in Egypt is a fatal obstacle to the attainment of thought and character which should accompany the introduction of European civilization."[39] The civilizing mission was justified as a means of elevating Arab/Muslim women's status, a status that was portrayed as degraded in contrast to white women's—even when white women did not enjoy citizenship or equal treatment under the law. While Islam was said to brutally repress women, secular Christians promoted the relationship between women and men as one of asymmetrical complementarity. The superiority of the Western organization of the difference of sex was confirmed by its contrast with the benighted East, represented as a region of racial (and thus social, political, economic) inferiority—if not permanently (biologically) so, then far behind on the evolutionary scale. Darwinian notions were taken up to explain progress in terms of the survival of the fittest. White skin was associated with "normal" gender systems, dark skin with immaturity and perversity. In this way, the inequalities of gender and the inequalities of race served to justify one another; they were taken to be the indisputable facts of natural history.[40]

Representations of racial difference were invariably sexualized, albeit in different ways. The Antillean psychiatrist Frantz Fanon offered this explanation for the "biological danger" that he saw whites associate with colonial subjects. "For the majority of white men the Negro represents the sexual instinct (in its raw state). The Negro is the incarnation of a genital potency beyond all moralities and prohibitions."[41] This man of dark skin (Fanon is talking about Arabs as well as black Africans) is depicted as the repudiated alternative to, literally the dark side of, the libidinal repression required by civilization. If he is also terrifyingly attractive, it is because he expresses the fantasy of "the civilized white man," his "irrational longing for unusual eras of sexual license, of orgiastic scenes of unpunished rapes, or unrepressed incest. Projecting his own desires on to the Negro, the white man behaves 'as if' the Negro really had them."[42]

In Fanon's understanding of it, desire served as a nexus for gender and race in the psychic politics of Europeans; gender distinctions were the product of the complex entanglements of family, race, and nation. Ann Laura Stoler reminds us that "race was a primary and protean category for colonial capitalism and managing the domestic was crucial to it."[43] In this mix, race was not only sexualized (as Fanon describes it), but it was also given a religious connotation. Christianity was the sign of white superiority; Islam was represented as one of the "other" religions practiced by inferior peoples of color. Conversion to Christianity was offered as a way of civilizing so-called backward peoples—for this reason missionaries were often dispatched to the colonies by the otherwise secular leaders of nations. But religions were also ranked by their treatment of women: the place of women in each of these different systems became a telltale sign of the superiority of one (Christianity), and the inferiority of the other (Islam, spiritism, polytheism).

The Utility of Gender

Gender is at the very heart of the secularism discourse.[44] The representation of the relationship between women and men has provided a way of articulating the rules of organization for emerging nations; in turn, those rules established the "truth" of the difference of sex. To put it another way, gender and politics were co-constitutive, the one establishing the meaning of the other, each providing a guarantee of the otherwise elusive and unstable grounds on which each rested. Gender referred its attributions to nature; politics naturalized its hierarchies by reference to gender.

How did this work? The social rules that announce and enforce the meanings of the difference between women and men insist that they refer to the timeless truth of anatomical genital differences. But the only truth there is about these differences is that their ultimate meanings are impossible to secure. Anthropologists and historians have shown that the traits and roles attributed to men and women have varied across cultures and time; sociologists remind us that they vary according to race and class, even within a single space and time; philosophers have grappled with the ways in which perception informs the lived experience of a material body; and psychoanalysts have taught us to be skeptical of the power of normative regulation to contain the unruly operations of the unconscious.

Gender, psychoanalysts insist, does not reflect the dictates of bodies. Rather, the difference of sex is the place where the relationship of mind and body, nature and culture is confounded. Writes Alenka Zupančič, it is the zone "where the two realms overlap; i.e., where the biological or somatic is already mental or cultural and where, at the same time, culture springs from the very impasses of the somatic functions which it tries to resolve."[45] Gender, from this perspective, does not base its social roles on the imperatives of physical bodies; rather, it is a historically and culturally variable attempt to provide a grid of intelligibility for sex. In the process, its rules extend beyond, even as they invoke, bodily references.

Those who fashion myths and offer religious or scientific explanations for differences of sex do so in the language of social organization; this language is not only about men and women but about hierarchy, lineage, property, community, and—perhaps most significantly—that other "natural" category, race. There are many differences among scholars about whether gender or race is the primary category for establishing hierarchies of difference. Sylvia Wynter, for example, argues powerfully for the primacy of race ("the ultimate mode of otherness") in what she calls the "totemic system" of difference—in it sex and class are "subtypes of otherness."[46] Those who call for analyses of "intersectionality" insist that all forms of otherness be taken into account, too often without asking how sex, race, or class establish specific kinds of identities and what the actual intersections consist of.

In my readings of the discourse of secularism, gender and race operate differently in the articulation of the national identities of Western European nation-states. The difference of race works to establish the outsider status of those others who aren't part of the presumed homogeneity of the national body—they are not only others but outsiders. The difference of sex poses another set of problems. It is a difference that can't be extruded; indeed, it is necessary for the very future of the nation.[47] Women may be men's others, but they are intimate and necessary others. Their standing as insiders, as members (and reproducers) of the national body, elevates them above racial outsiders; their subordination is not of a piece with the subordination either of race or, for that matter, of class. If secularism is a discourse about the articulation of the sovereign identity of Western European nation-states, then a racialized gender (the attribution of meaning to the difference of sex) is at the heart of that discourse. It is a problem of difference that is not external to the national body, but whose conceptualization nonetheless affects the way all outsiders are perceived, how their handling of differences of sex and sexuality establish their place on the evolutionary scale of civilization.

When the lines of gender distinctions hardened, as they did in the course of the eighteenth and nineteenth centuries, they enabled a new vision of politics (one I will discuss at greater length in chapter 3). With the advent of the democratic revolutions (in France and the United States) at the end of the eighteenth century, the absolute monarch no longer served as the embodiment of political authority. In his place were "the people" and their representatives, whose ultimate authority was uncertain at best. Who ruled and in whose name? Democracy, in the words of political theorist Claude Lefort, brought with it a regime of indeterminacy and uncertainty.[48] In this context, Foucault deemed sexuality "a dense transfer point for relations of power."[49] "Transfer point" is the key term here, for it can suggest the mutually constitutive nature of gender and politics that I want to evoke. At the same time, it suggests a certain separation that is not exactly the case. It's not that gender and politics as established entities come into contact and so influence each other. Rather it's that the instability of each looks to the other for certainty: political systems invoke what is deemed the immutability of gender to legitimize asymmetries of power; those political invocations then "fix" differences of sex, in that way denying the indeterminacy that troubles both sex and politics. When we ask how the roles and relationships of women and men figure in representations of modernity, we gain insight into the way whole societies—their politics and cultures—are being conceived.

Secularism—the polemical word first uttered in the nineteenth century—built on notions of differentiation that came into increasing prominence a century before. Its repudiation of religion as a relic of the traditional past followed from idealized distinctions between spheres of public and private, political and religious, modern and traditional, state and family, West and East, masculine and feminine, male and female. These distinctions had nothing in them of gender equality; rather, they were marked by a presumption of gender *in*equality. This was not simply a matter of refiguring gender distinctions that had existed from the earliest times, but of making the difference of sex a more central feature for explaining social and political organization.

Scholars have pointed repeatedly to an increased emphasis on the lines of sexual difference with the rise of capitalism and nation-states from the eighteenth century on. Kevin Floyd notes that "Capital's enforcement of a strong differentiation of public from private . . . is based on its naturalization of private property, but is also ultimately inseparable from an ongoing differentiation of social labor including a gendered division of labor, a division between manual and intellectual labor, and an atomizing, disciplinary specialization of knowledge itself."[50] Nancy Armstrong examined English conduct books that, she says, by the end of the eighteenth century "transformed the female into the bearer of moral norms and the socializer of men." They also offered techniques for regulating desire "aimed at nothing so clearly as producing gender-differentiated forms of economic behavior."[51] Denise Riley writes of "the increasing sexualisation, in which female persons become held to be virtually saturated with their sex which then invades their rational and spiritual faculties; this reached a pitch in eighteenth century Europe."[52] G. J. Barker-Benfield notes that gender distinctions "hardened" in England during the course of the eighteenth and nineteenth centuries.[53] Historian Isabel Hull refers to the impact of the growing emphasis on "civil society" in late eighteenth-century Germany: "Where once gender differentiation had ordered the private, nonstate world and created at most symbolic echoes in the public, it was now supposed to organize both. Thus as society swelled in importance, so did gender differentiation."[54] Historians of the American and French Revolutions have reached the same conclusion. Susan Juster sums up their work this way: "An emerging ruling class insinuated itself into the crevices of power by claiming masculine prerogative over an effeminate ancien régime. In each case, the anxieties borne of peripheral status—anxieties that, at bottom, were rooted as much in sexual as political insecurity—were resolved by a shrill association of manly valor among aspiring elites."[55] Elizabeth Maddock Dillon, discussing the place of women authors as producers of nineteenth-century American fiction, notes that "liberalism relies on a binary model of sex and gender: liberal doctrine both creates and sustains a rigidified opposition between male and female bodies and subjectivities."[56]

The logic of the narrative that associated increased gender differentiation with modernity is evident, too, in the countries of the non-West, where it was either imposed by colonial powers, usually in the form of family law, or imported and adapted in local practice by those seeking to live up to Western models. Writing about nineteenth- and twentieth-century Iran, Afsaneh Najmabadi notes that "the heteronormalization of eros and sex became a condition of 'achieving modernity.' "[57] There were, to be sure, differences in the experiences of postcolonial nations and their imperialist predecessors, but there were also important continuities, and a more rigidified gender differentiation was one of them.

Despite challenges from individuals and social movements, the sharp distinction between the sexes has endured, albeit with changes that are important to note. It is not change that I want to deny; it is the ahistorical equation in contemporary discourse of a reified secularism with gender equality—and the racism associated with that equation—that I think needs to be challenged. The current depiction of the evils of Islam in opposition to the unqualified good of the secular, with gender equality as its central feature, has served to distract our attention from the fact that sexual difference is an intractable problem for the nations of the secular Christian West, as it is for their counterparts elsewhere.

Plan of the Book

Since the current references to secularism presume that there are unchanging principles of gender equality at its core, I devote the first three chapters to challenging that presumption. By looking at the ways women in Western Europe, Britain, and the United States were associated with religion (chapter 1) and reproduction (chapter 2), and at how these activities were said to preclude engagement in politics (chapter 3), I summarize a huge scholarship that has long made that case. The aim is to remind us of the relevance of that work for current debates about secularism and, in so doing, to insist that secularism is a discourse with a history in which tensions and contradictions abound.

I then move away from that nineteenth- and early twentieth-century material to a moment when explicit references to secularism faded from view in the West, losing their political relevance in the context of the Cold War. In chapter 4, I argue that in the second half of the twentieth century, the old public/private distinction was dissolved in the realms of both religion and sexuality, putting into place concepts that prepared a new discourse of secularism in Western Europe and the Anglo-American world—one in which Islam took the place of Soviet communism as a threat to social order. In this new discourse, the secular and the Christian were increasingly considered synonymous, and women's sexual emancipation became the primary indicator of gender equality.

In the final chapter (chapter 5) I explore the complex uses of feminism and appeals to "sexual democracy" in the new discourse of secularism. The story is anything but straightforward and involves the insistence on sex as a public matter, and on women's sexuality (and by extension, nonnormative sexualities) as a right of individual self-determination. The emphasis on individualism is a part of what Wendy Brown has termed neoliberalism's rationality; it is not the same as its nineteenth-century antecedent.[58] At the same time, the difference of sex and its heteronormative claims has not disappeared, confusing woman's status as a desiring subject (free to determine her choices, both amorous and reproductive) with her status as an object of (male) desire. The contemporary discourse of secularism, with its insistence on the importance of "uncovered" women's bodies equates public visibility with emancipation, as if that visibility were the only way to confirm women as sexually autonomous beings (exercising the same rights in this domain as men). The contrast with "covered" Muslim women not only perpetuates the confusion between Western women as subjects and objects of desire, it also distracts attention from (or flatly ignores) persisting racialized gender inequalities in markets, politics, jobs, and law within each side. But more than that, it suggests homogeneity on either side of the divide—as if all Western women or all Muslim women had the same experiences, the same outlooks, the same lives. By conceiving of these women in starkly oppositional terms, we fail to see the difficulties that sexual difference poses in many contexts, and we then underestimate or mischaracterize the challenges those difficulties present to the achievement of the (perhaps ultimately utopian) goal of gender equality.

CHAPTER ONE

Women and Religion

THE ASSOCIATION OF WOMEN with/as religion was a hallmark of the secularism discourse. Writing in 1908, the French suffragist Hubertine Auclert refused the idea—regularly used to deny women the vote—that enfranchising women would mean more votes for the church party. The idea that religious sentiments disqualified women was "a bogeyman, as imaginary as the ones used to scare little children."

> Why are believing women treated more strictly than believing men? Men aren't asked for their philosophical ideas when they are given a ballot: priests, pastors, rabbis are treated no differently than free-thinkers.[1]

The attribution of innate religious sensibility to women as a group, she argued, was a pretext. Religious men were allowed to vote because they were men; women were denied the vote because they were considered inferior beings. The hypocrisy of self-proclaimed secularists on this issue infuriated her: they were perpetuating religious teachings about women's inferiority even as they refused the suffrage to women because of their supposed religious attachments. Auclert insisted that their hypocrisy extended to their toleration of forms of religion even more oppressive to women than Christianity. In Algeria, she wrote in her 1900 book, *Les femmes arabes en Algérie*, the recognition of Qur'anic law for matters concerning the family, marriage, and sexuality perpetuated the degradation of native womanhood. If French women were to be allowed to participate in the "civilizing mission" as citizens, they would bring enlightenment to French administrators and so to Algeria. As it was, the denial of the vote to "cultivated white women" while it was granted to "savage blacks" undermined the secular mission.[2] "To secularize France is not only to cease paying for the teaching of religious dogmas, it is to reject the clerical law that follows from these dogmas and that treats women as inferior."[3]

Auclert put her finger on the problem I address in this book: the fact that the discourse of secularism, despite its promise of universal equality, made women's difference the ground for their exclusion from citizenship and public life more generally. But I will suggest that it was not, as Auclert insisted, because religious ideas about women were left in place. Instead, the apostles of secularism, in France and elsewhere, offered what they took to be entirely new explanations for women's difference from men, rooting them in human nature and biology rather than divine law. Gender difference was inscribed in a schematic description of the world as divided into separate spheres, public and private, male and female. In fact, in this context the association of women with religion was not a relic of past practice but an invention of the discourse of secularism itself.

The notion of sharply differentiated spheres represented the public/private opposition as both spatial (the home and the church as opposed to the polis and the market) and psychological (an interior realm of affect and spiritual belief as opposed to the exterior realm of reason and purposive action). Public and private were, like a heterosexual couple, portrayed as complementary opposites. The world of markets and politics was represented as a man's world; the familial, religious, and affective domain was a woman's. Woman's role was to fill the void left by competitive individualism, to offer the moral glue that could cement individuals together in a national enterprise. Sexuality figured on both sides of the equation: women's morality must tame men's aggression; men's reason must bring women's passion under control. Sometimes—in what Elizabeth Hurd characterizes as Judeo-Christian secularism[4]—this meant that women's propensity to religiosity was seen in a positive light (the United States, England); in other instances, the attraction of women for religion was construed by secularists as dangerous (France, where laicism was the ideology, being the prime example). But either way, the sexual division of labor was taken to be the crux of the religious/secular divide. The counterpart to the reasoning male citizen was a woman whose piety was at once a brake on and a manifestation of her inclination to excessive sexuality. In this scheme of things, religion was privatized and feminized at the same time.

This was, to be sure, an idealized representation that universalized bourgeois norms and practices. As such, it excluded the lives and activities of multitudes of women, many of whom worked for wages, did not marry, and—if they did—exercised important influence inside and outside their families; it also excluded the lives and activities of those men who, for various reasons (race, dependency, lack of property), were deemed not to fit the category of the rational, abstract individual. Social historians have richly documented the distance between idealized norms and lived experience. But my point is that idealized norms still matter, not only in the expectations set for individual subjects, but because they set the terms for law, politics, and social policy.

Hurd has described two ways in which the regulation of the relationship between religion and politics has been conceived. The first, which she calls laicism, takes a strong stand about the absolute need to exclude religion from politics. The second, which she labels Judeo-Christian secularism, is more accommodating. It holds that the Judeo-Christian tradition provides the basis for the values of secular democracy.[5] The differences stem from the fact that in the nations of the Christian West, the versions of secularism differed depending upon the particular form taken by organized religion in relation to state power. Catholicism presented the greatest challenge to emerging nation-states; it was represented as an international force that undermined popular allegiance to the nation. Catholicism's hierarchical, patriarchal, and dogmatic ideology was denounced by secularists as antithetical to liberal values of individual freedom and belief. In states with Catholic majorities (France, for example) secularism was synonymous with republicanism and defined as anticlerical, an effort of male reason to salvage female credulity from the seductive wiles of Jesuit priests. At the same time, even in the stricter laicist regimes, there were nods to religion as a guarantor of morality and to women as the embodiment of the moral dimension of religious teaching and thus as the guardians of social cohesion and stability. Notes one historian, "most of the men who tried to separate the Churches from the State, wanted to make society more Christian even while they made the state more secular."[6] Properly tamed, religion could become an aspect of the national patrimony and an instrument of colonial rule. In states that were predominantly Protestant, in contrast (the United States and parts of Germany, for example), secularism was presented as an aspect of the Christian tradition, defined as the liberal alternative (the right of individual conscience), not only to Catholicism but to the oppressive religions of "the

Orient." Even as Protestant "free thought" seemed to provide openings for feminist claims, its proponents, for the most part, insisted upon gender distinctions based on the idea of separate spheres. Men were in the world, women at home, and this according to the laws of nature. Churches were subordinated to state law in different ways in different countries: disestablishment in the United States; establishment of a single state religion in England; redefinition of what counted as a legitimate, tolerated religion in France. There were also variations in things like state maintenance of church buildings, state certification of clerical competence, surveillance of educational curricula, and observance of religious holy days as state holidays. In all cases, however, the association of women with religion was the same. And the purported decline of religious influence over the course of the nineteenth century and into the twentieth did nothing to alter the way in which the relationship between women (emotional, inclined to superstition) and men (reasonable, practical) was conceived. If anything, religion was depicted as an increasingly feminized affair, an experience apart from and outside of history, identified this way not only by those who had little use for it but also by those who sought its consolations.

French Anticlericalism

The French Revolution was a critical moment in the reordering of the relationship between church and state. The role of the Catholic Church in legitimating the monarchy meant that a stark opposition between the religious and the secular structured revolutionary discourse and institutions. When it was permitted, religious practice was regulated by the state, which paid wages to priests who swore allegiance to the new regime.

Although the association of women and unreason was evident much earlier, it was the Revolution of 1789 that established the link in republican political discourse between women and religion. Writes historian Paul Seeley, "the Revolution's embodiment of the citizen as a rights-bearing and confessionally neutral male depended on a derogatory identification of religion with the female."[7] Like the female sex, religion was considered the source of the irrational and the violent; it was also the domain of the traditional and the hierarchical.

Historian Olwen Hufton noted that the actions of counterrevolutionary women in peasant villages, those who defended nonjuring priests and clandestinely practiced Catholic rituals for baptisms and burials, "provided the evidence for the politicians of the Third Republic [almost a century later] to withhold the vote from women."[8] During the dechristianizing campaign in year II of the revolution, the example of resistant village women became synonymous with women in general. So, while one comment from a *représentant en mission* was directed at a specific group of women ("And you, you bloody bitches, you are their [the priests'] whores, particularly those who attend their bloody masses and listen to their mumbo-jumbo"),[9] another extended the condemnation to women as a whole ("Remember, it is fanaticism and superstition that we will be fighting against; lying priests whose dogma is falsehood . . . whose empire is founded upon the credulity of women. These are the enemy").[10] In this view of things, women were the knowing consorts or the inevitable dupes of treasonous clerics. In either case, it was the greater emotional vulnerability of their sex that accounted for their actions. The opinion of a Dr. Moreau, writing in 1803, was widely shared: "Women are more disposed than men to believe in spirits and ghosts; . . . they adopt all superstitious practice more readily; . . . their prejudices are more numerous."[11]

Throughout the nineteenth century and into the twentieth, there was in France an intensifying struggle between clericals and anticlericals in which the question of women figured prominently. Secular republicans adorned their city halls with busts of Marianne (an idealized classical feminine figure)[12] in the same years that church authorities revived the cult of the Virgin Mary; historians of the Middle Ages produced what Zrinka Stahuljak calls "pornographic archaeology"—accounts of the perverted sexual escapades of supposedly celibate priests and nuns—even as Catholic recruitment of women religious grew by leaps and bounds.[13] The opposition between rational patriotic republican men and their unreliable, unreasonable women usually invoked statistical evidence on its behalf. And it is certainly true that the French Catholic Church drew increasing numbers of women to religious congregations and lay charitable activity over the course of the century. The ratio of men religious to women religious changed dramatically, from 3:2 in 1803 to 2:3 by 1878; and the number of nuns increased tenfold from about 13,000 in 1808 to 130,000 by the end of the century. Well after the removal of clerical teachers from public schools in the 1880s, the religious education of young children, particularly girls, remained in the hands of Catholic sisters. And the church recruited large numbers of married bourgeois women to its philanthropic associations, making (in the estimation of one historian) the "charitable lady . . . among the most ubiquitous public figures in the 19th century city [Paris] that most epitomized the modern age."[14]

Voluntary charitable activity, although performed in public, was considered an extension of women's familial and domestic role. The recruitment of women for this work was, to be sure, the result of a concerted effort on the part of church authorities to undermine the secularists, but it succeeded by appealing to exactly the image of women the secularists endorsed—one that emphasized their subordination to male authority, their role as agents and reproducers of morality, their self-sacrificing, caring maternal instincts, and their intuitive spirituality. It was in those terms that nineteenth-century bourgeois Catholic men described their faith—as inspired by the women in their lives. Both devout Catholic men and skeptical republicans, Seeley writes, "affirmed their political and religious identities by tying Catholic faith and ritual to a private female sphere."[15] In an odd inversion of causality, the stereotyping provided by republicans may well have helped to produce the very alliance they most feared. At the very least, it did little to counter the terms of the church's appeal to women. But that may have been beside the point. Importantly, the anticlerical portrayals of the religious inclinations of women worked to equate masculine identity with republicanism. On the one hand, anticlericals called upon republican husbands to turn their wives away from priestly influence; on the other hand, the depiction of women as inherently superstitious confirmed the natural division of labor between the sexes and justified the inequality that followed from it.

Nowhere is this more evident than in the writings of Jules Michelet, the great historian of the French nation and an ardent anticlerical. Michelet was born in 1798 in the waning days of the French Revolution; he died in 1874, in the early years of the Third Republic. In addition to vivid histories of the lives of kings and courtiers, revolutionaries and their enemies, he wrote inflammatory moralizing treatises on love, women, and the family, as well as denunciations of the perversities and evils of priests, confessors, bishops, and other representatives of the Catholic Church. In his quest for knowledge about women and their bodies, he attended lectures on gynecology and embryology at the Collège de France, and he obsessively monitored his young second wife's monthly rhythms with the persistent attention of an experimental scientist. His writings on these topics drew criticism as well as praise, and I don't offer them as evidence that all of France shared his opinions.[16] What they do illustrate is the way in which a great historian associated women and religion in secularism's polemical campaign.

Michelet's writings on women, the family, and the church were directed at husbands. *Du Prêtre, de la femme, de la famille* (1845) opens with a shocking announcement. "It was generally thought that two people were sufficient for a marriage, but that has changed. The new system . . . has three constituent elements." These are "the man, strong and violent; the woman, a creature weak by nature; the priest, born a man and strong, but who wants to make himself weak so as to resemble a woman . . . and so interpose himself between them."[17] As result of this invasion, "our wives and our daughters are raised and governed by our enemies" (14). These enemies are at once political—they represent the past and so are obstacles to progress—and personal: they are adept at the art of seduction, in effect cuckolding husbands whose distractions at work have made them strangers to their wives and children (309).

Most of the book is devoted to accounts of the machinations of priests, starting with Jesuit confessors in the sixteenth century, tracking the "ardent" letters exchanged between these men and the women they counseled, and ending in the nineteenth century, when the sons of peasants replaced the learned men of the religious orders of the past. If in the seventeenth century the likes of Fénelon and Bossuet charmed and seduced with their cultured intellects, the curés of the nineteenth century practiced the cunning and perseverance of the peasant cultures from which they came. In both cases, confessors manipulated the "soft and fluid natures of women," appealing to their passion, love of children, and need for affection. Intoning the language of devotion, they, in effect, became lovers: "you can't always tell who is speaking, the lover or the confessor" (69). In Michelet's fantasized scene of seduction, the two achieve an intimacy denied the rightful husband. In a dark corner chapel of the church, "this emotionally agitated man, this trembling woman, sitting so close to one another, talk in hushed voices of the love of God" (214). She is "on her knees," with head bowed before the priest as he listens to her confession. Learning her most intimate secrets, those unknown even to her husband, he achieves mastery, and thereby "recovers his manhood . . . and while she is weak and disarmed, he lays upon her the heavy hand of a man" (228). The relationship deepens and, inevitably, "for the soul to be truly yours, one thing is lacking . . . the body" (271). But the "voice of concupiscence" (270) is seemingly deflected by the priest onto love for God. "How fight against a man who disposes of paradise, and beyond that, hell, to make himself loved?" (279). How, in other words, claim power from this man who will go to any lengths to dispossess the republican husband of his wife? And, by extension, how rescue the secular state from the authority of the church?

In Michelet's stirring account, the man of God has insinuated himself into the republican husband's private domain of sex and family. Even if the conquest is only spiritual (and this scene conjures much more), the husband is compromised. The priest now has knowledge of the intimate details of the marriage, and "of your most secret weaknesses," which he most certainly shares with his colleagues. As he passes you in the street, humbly nodding at you, Michelet tells his reader, he turns away and silently laughs—such is the imagined humiliation visited on the husband betrayed (230). Himself less than a man, the priest nonetheless succeeds in emasculating the legitimate head of the household.

The priest who achieves his manhood in the company of other men's wives is a problematic figure. The celibate life is artificial ("absurd, impossible," against nature [27]) and the demeanor of these men (in skirts) is feminine. "The tactics of the confessor weren't all that different from those of a mistress" (34): they practiced tender flatteries and the arts of innocence (47); like women, Jesuits loved children (37). Fénelon, Michelet tells his readers, was "as delicate as a woman," tender and penetrating at the same time (142). Having studied women closely, these men become like them, crossing gender boundaries in unacceptable, even dangerous ways. The danger has many aspects, including the priest's "hatred" for women's natural roles as wives and mothers. He wants them only as lovers, lovers of God; for Michelet, this means the embrace not of life (with all of its reproductive possibilities) but of death (277, 241, 334). As the husband's rightful place is the defender of life, so the priest represents its mortal antithesis.

The full implications of this conquest of women for the church are nowhere more evident than in convents—the negative counterparts to the family home. There "the heart of a woman, of a mother, the invincible maternal instinct, which is the foundation of a woman, betrays itself" (253). The betrayal comes not only from the celibate life, but from its violations. Lurid stories of sex between priests and nuns detail aborted pregnancies and murdered babies, buried in clandestine graveyards. Ruled by the figure of a monstrous lesbian—a tyrannical woman, a devil incarnate, who imagines she can govern like a Bonaparte (260)—the nuns suffer enormous deprivation. Only the intervention of a male confessor alleviates their pain—restoring, in Michelet's depiction of it, something akin to an appropriate gendered division of labor. "Far from being opposed to the confessor in this place, my wishes are with him . . . in this hell, where law never penetrates, he is the only person who can offer a word of humanity" (260). Here the fraternity of men, representatives of the law, overcomes the nightmare of a domestic scene ruled entirely by women. The analogy is evident: only state rule can hold back the excesses of an unfettered religion. It is not the abolition of religion but its regulation (its "penetration" by state law) that is required.

What can be done to reclaim women for their husbands? How can the secular men to whom Michelet appeals turn their wives away from the lure of the church? The reasons for their inaction are clear: "victims of the division of labor, often condemned to a narrow specialization," modern men have become strangers to their wives and children, leaving the affective terrain to the Jesuits (301). But it is imperative that they now take heed: "Secularists, as we all are—magistrates, politicians, writers, solitary thinkers—today we must do what we haven't yet done: take in hand the cause of women" (xxiv). The "cause of women" is not their emancipation in political terms; rather, it has to do with acquiring intimate knowledge of the kind science offers. This knowledge reveals that woman is weak: she "is a sick person . . . a person wounded each month, and who suffers almost continually from the wound and its scar."[18] Effectively and repeatedly castrated, she is the victim of a cyclical biology that men are spared.

Men's time, for Michelet, is the linear time of history; women's, the time of eternal repetition. "History, which we so stupidly decline in the feminine, is a rude and savage male, a sunburnt, dusty traveler, Nature is a woman."[19] To rescue women from the lure of the church was not to alter their nature but to bring their difference into line with the needs of the republican state. Michelet appealed to husbands to change things by regaining control of the private side of their lives, studying their wives to better manage them. This control would be aided by laws against the clergy (which he consistently advocated) but also by implementing laws already in place—civil laws (based in France and elsewhere in Europe on the Code Napoléon), which made the family, and the father's supremacy within it, the cornerstone of secularizing nation-states. In this way the superiority of state regulation was established as natural and, reciprocally, the subordination of women to men was naturalized.

Michelet's call to action required concrete changes, but it also firmly secured the representation of women's leanings to religion as a persistent danger to the republic. This representation was evident well into the twentieth century, in socialist and syndicalist as well as parliamentary rhetoric. Republican legislatures repeatedly rejected bills for women's suffrage on the grounds that the female vote would inevitably enhance the power of the church. In 1922, the radical and anticlerical senator, Alexandre Bérard, argued that enfranchising women would be "sealing the tombstone of the Republic."[20] But at the same time, educational authorities debated the wisdom of removing religion entirely from girls' training. Françoise Mayeur reports that the 1880 law named for its sponsor, Camille Sée—a law aimed at replacing convent educations with public schools—called for including in the new curriculum the advice to teach girls their "duties toward God," presumably to provide them with the moral instruction they would transmit as mothers. The provision remained in place until 1923, Mayeur tells us, and then was only briefly rescinded.[21] We don't know how closely the new generations of republican teachers adhered to this advice, but it is telling nonetheless. In the eyes of some legislators and academics, lessons about God were apparently acceptable when transmitted by lay teachers, unacceptable when they came from the clergy.[22] Indeed, belief in the complementarity of the sexes was included in the curriculum with or without reference to God; women must be prepared to offer the moral and spiritual guidance that was the vocation of their sex. All of this suggests that the attribution of (dangerous or benign) religiosity to women was firmly in place in the discourses of republican France. It would take many generations of feminist objection such as Auclert's to unsettle, if not overturn, what had become an article of secularism's faith.

Protestant Secularism in the United States and Germany

Writing in 1888, Philip Schaff, a professor of church history, explained that the American Constitution was a preeminently Christian document:

> The First Amendment could not have originated in any pagan or Mohammedan country, but presupposes Christian civilization and culture. . . . Christianity alone has taught men to respect the sacredness of the human personality as made in the image of God and redeemed by Christ and to protect its rights and privileges, including the freedom of worship, against the encroachments of the temporal power and the absolutism of the state.[23]

Schaff's thinking was not exceptional. The work of historians John Lardas Modern, Susan Juster, Seth Moglen, and Brian Connolly show the extent to which discourses of secularism infused American Protestant thought from the 1760s onward. "America's God," Modern writes, "was not simply a theological product, but also a political effect of secularism."[24] (Here he echoes Max Weber's earlier assertion: "The separation of the 'private sphere' from the 'official sphere' is carried through in the church in the same way as in political, or other, officialdom."[25]) While Juster focuses on New England Baptists around the time of the revolution, Connolly on antebellum discourses of incest, and Modern on a variety of groups (Unitarians, liberals, evangelicals) in the 1850s, all maintain that despite the rhetoric of separation and the legal fact of disestablishment, there was no sharp break between "the religiosity of Protestantism and the secularity of the democratic nation-state."[26] In fact, the climate of secularity, with its attention to the political and technical agency of humans, as well as to the power of human reason to reveal "fixed laws," could work, according to Modern, to distinguish "true religion" from false. Connolly notes that in the arena of law, biblical prohibitions of incest were gradually replaced by prohibitions "grounded in natural law." Judges often saw no contradiction in replacing God's sovereignty with natural law discerned by reason, even as they insisted on Christian moral principles for sexual conduct and marriage. Writes Connolly, "The secular did not so much replace the sacred as it emerged alongside it."[27]

The important point for my argument is that these discourses of secularization brought with them new attention to gender difference and, as Philip Schaff's comment (cited above) suggests, it was a difference entwined with a racialized view of religion. In Juster's account, the first impact of politics was to raise the issue of the masculinity of the clergy. When, in earlier years, New England Baptists were a marginal dissenting sect, she says, women participated in church governance and theological debates, and were generally considered the equals of men. In the political crises leading up to the revolution, however, "the feminine nature of the church became a cause for concern among the evangelical leadership. . . . A politically vigorous and socially respectable religious society needed a more masculine image, and hence we see the emergence of patriarchal language and structure in Baptist churches after 1780."[28] As New England Baptists made a bid for the mainstream, siding with the patriots against the British, they took up the political language (of autonomy, independence, and virility) that would become the revolution's legacy. In what Juster refers to as "an almost archetypical reenactment of the Weberian evolution of a marginal religious society with charismatic origins to a rationalist, bureaucratic institution," the governance of churches moved from collective participation of women and men to "standing committees composed exclusively of men."[29] Once acceptable, interventions by women in doctrinal discussions became a sign of their "disorderliness," and trials of women so accused became more frequent by the turn of the century. Women's presumed propensity to disorder disqualified them from church governance even as it secured a vision of men as rational leaders. By 1810, a prominent denominational publication could state as entirely noncontroversial that Baptist churches "take for granted, that the duties and privileges of females in a Gospel Church differ from those of males."[30] "The politicization of religious dissenters in the revolutionary era," Juster concludes, "came about through a fundamental renegotiation of gender relations within the evangelical community. The political capacity of the evangelical clergy, in other words, did not (could not) fully emerge until they had essentially defeminized the evangelical polity and reclaimed for themselves a more masculine identity."[31] Significantly, as the masculine/feminine binary came to structure mainstream politics and the churches supporting it, prophetic visions of gender equality emerged from outsider religious sects, often led by women—and this is true not only in America but in Europe as well; such figures as Johanna Southcott, Mother Ann Lee, and Jemima Wilkenson were proponents of gender equality who did not take their lessons from secularist teachings.[32]

Moglen's work on Moravians in eighteenth-century Bethlehem, Pennsylvania, echoes Juster's findings about Baptists. In the early part of the century, in this charismatic, marginal religious movement, "women exercised an exceptional degree of leadership, both social and spiritual."[33] In 1760, as the leadership sought to accommodate criticism from outside the community, and to become more acceptable to political authorities, a new set of practices was introduced: "women were reinserted into the structure of the patriarchal family—and they lost most of the forms of power, leadership, material autonomy . . . that they had enjoyed in the first two decades of the city's history."[34] For Moravians, in other words, the process of secularization meant "radically reducing women's leadership and imposing sharp new forms of gender asymmetry and inequality."[35]

Modern writes about the 1850s, by which time disestablishment had weakened clerical institutions, making religion "the exercise of one's freedom in private" and secularism—with its connection to "machines and mechanized circulation"—an integral aspect of religious belief.[36] (Here, already, is an exception to the linear narrative of modernity that saw secularism as a replacement for religion.) Ann Douglas notes increasing competition among churches, anxieties about clerical impermanence in a new market-oriented star system, and the rise of sentimentalism as symptoms of "the feminization of American culture" in the nineteenth century. In her account, the lady and the clergyman form an alliance against what outsiders note was diminished public authority of the ministry.[37] Modern is less attentive to gender issues, but he does note the existence of a "trope of 'female influence,'" with multiple valences, all stemming from the purported "natural qualities of women."

These qualities were thought to make women more prone to seduction by evil forces but also more open to the workings of the Holy Spirit. Their influence could be either benevolent or deceptively dangerous.[38] It could be the basis for their subordination or for claims to women's rights.

Whether rhetorically or in practice, whether understood positively or negatively, women had become synonymous with religion by the mid-nineteenth century. Douglas offers many examples: the clergyman who writes to women that "religion is far more necessary to you than [to] self-sufficient men. In you it would be not only criminal, but impolitic to neglect it."[39] Yet it is precisely because men were not self-sufficient that they needed women's spiritual influence. The assertion of male superiority (in men's texts) made it possible to acknowledge the need for affective sustenance from women without admitting that men lacked it; women were more likely to point explicitly to their compensatory role. So it was that Eliza Farnham argued that women must reform men who were too committed to "position, fortune and connections"—the trappings of the "outer life."[40] And Sarah Josepha Hale wrote in 1830 of the wife's spiritual role as a corrective to the materialist values of her competitive-minded husband.[41]

Douglas notes that upper-class women and the clergy joined forces in the course of the nineteenth century to assert their emotional indispensability—through prayer and sentimental literature they performed a "redemptive mission" for society.[42] So pervasive was the association of women and religion, so overwhelming the presence of women in religious institutions, that the end of the century saw a move to promote a more "muscular Christianity" that would bring men back to the fold. The movement was more symptomatic than successful. It neither challenged gender stereotypes (granting, as it did, the muscularity of masculinity in opposition to the soft sensibility of femininity), nor dislodged women as the overwhelming presence in America's churches.

If, as Modern maintains, the secular imaginary "inflected how a range of Protestant subcultures felt themselves to be truly religious," it also brought with it a vision of separate spheres—private and public—that insisted on sharp distinctions between the capacities and sensibilities of women and men.[43] This was as true in the case of those eighteenth-century Baptists, who briefly claimed masculine prerogatives for the church and punished "disorderly women," as it was for the "feminized" nineteenth-century Protestant clergymen, who counted on the influence of women to sustain them and to nurture the religiosity that was considered (by clerics and politicians alike) the source of national morality in husbands and children.

The gendered division of labor was presented by these clergymen as a defining mark of modernity. In the teachings of liberal political theory, too, women's supposed innate preference for sentiment led them to voluntarily take up their domestic roles and in this, according to Elizabeth Maddock Dillon, they were symbolically associated with freedom of individual choice. "Within sentimental liberalism, the home is not simply an escape from the pressures and exigencies of market competition; rather it is the highest political good for both men and women: home is the location where freedom is ultimately instantiated."[44] Freedom in the sense of affective choice and fulfillment, experienced outside the constraints of politics and the market.

Christianity was a guarantee of this freedom, as was evident in contrasts to "others"—to vagabonds, slaves, and the unbelieving poor within the country, and especially to places where foreign religions prevailed. Connolly describes the way in which the antithesis between American matrimonial laws and so-called Hindoo marriages became a site for the consolidation of a homogenizing vision of national identity in antebellum America. While American marriage was depicted as consensual and subject to the rule of law, "Hindoos" were presented as hopelessly entrapped in primitive religious dogma and tribal kinship arrangements. This was said to be evident in the exploitation of girls as child brides, in the "barbaric" practice of widow immolation, and in the murder of unmarriageable daughters, to name just a few of the outrages described by missionaries and other visitors to those exotic lands. Representations of "the Hindoo," Connolly says, "did the work of making the Indian subcontinent wholly inscribed in religion."[45] Often it was Muslims who represented the antithesis of (Protestant) American freedom. When Thomas Jefferson used the hypothetical case of followers of the Qur'an to demonstrate the universality of the First Amendment's toleration of minority religions, he was reviled as a follower of Muhammad himself, therefore unfit to be a president of the United States![46]

A similar movement, ascribing modernity to civilized Protestant practices in contrast to the perpetual barbarities of Islam, has been described for the German state of Baden in the mid-nineteenth century. Historian Dagmar Herzog cites any number of dissenting ministers (apostles of free thought) who made the same claim. "What a beautiful lot, what a glorious sphere of activity women now have within Christianity and in comparison with those in the Orient and outside Christianity," said one.[47] Another celebrated "how the Occidental man brought trophies of victory to pay homage to the woman of his heart, while the Oriental man maintained the woman and maiden under an offensive yoke of slavery and did not allow her to recognize her own dignity."[48] Polygamy was an especially odious form of enslavement according to these German ministers, as it was for the US government, which granted freedom of religion to any number of Protestant sects but declared Mormons' practices unacceptable, despite the First Amendment (or, if Schaff's view was representative, because of it).

Another way the Protestant and the secular were equated was in contrast to Catholicism.[49] Here the antipathy was shared with French anticlericals, though from a different vantage. In the United States Catholicism was depicted as a false religion (as was Mormonism), its theological prescriptions denying the God-given powers of individual human reasoning to apprehend the true religion of Christ.[50] And there were warnings, just like Michelet's, from those Baden-dissenting ministers about the dangers of the confessional. Under Catholic dominion, women became "prostitutes for the servants of Rome," their husbands cuckolded by priests. The message was clear: "Those parents to whom the purity of their daughters is dear, are forced to forbid them to go to confession."[51]

Protestant secularism championed individual freedom even as it endorsed an asymmetrical division of labor between women and men. That apparent inequality was explained as the result of women's voluntary labor at home, their recognition that submission to a husband's authority was a consequence of the laws of nature and so in the best interests of domestic and social harmony. Alexis de Tocqueville, contrasting French aristocrats with American democrats, offered the observation that democracy in America was marked by women's "voluntary sacrifice of their will . . . freely accepting the yoke rather than seeking to avoid it."[52] Writes Modern about the thinking of nineteenth-century American evangelicals, "to become truly religious . . . was not to turn away from the world, but to cultivate a reasonable attitude within it and an attentive disposition toward it. To become truly religious, then, was to coordinate one's attitudes and behaviors with principles essential to the maintenance of civil society."[53]

Of course, and importantly, the association of Protestantism with ideals of individual freedom opened space for feminist claims for a more egalitarian vision of the relationship between women and men. Even within the terms of sentimental domestic ideology, the power of women's love could motivate certain forms of female public agency (authorship, as Dillon points out, but also antislavery, prohibition, and other morally driven movements), thus calling into question the reality of the idealized public/private distinction at the same time that it was invoked to justify unaccustomed political activity by women.[54] But those were minority efforts on the question of women's rights. The dominant vision of unequal gender complementarity remained in place, as did the idea that religious oppression was located elsewhere. To this day, anti-Muslim polemics underplay the Christian dimensions of secularism, which have nonetheless become part of the epistemic heritage not only of America but of "the West."

Colonial Exports; Postcolonial Imports

Historians of imperialism have documented the ways in which the "civilizing mission" involved the imposition of Victorian standards of domesticity, ideals of nuclear family households, and the separation of spheres on populations with very different forms of social organization. The role of Christian missionaries as agents of colonial domination is also well known. In the process of imperial expansion, European states negotiated protection for their religious emissaries with local rulers, developing theories of minority religious rights in the process. Saba Mahmood points to the development of a shared "sentiment of Christian fraternity," even as "the West came to understand itself as resolutely secular."[55] But it was in the area of what came to be known as "family law" that the association of women and religion was most clearly articulated in the colonies, and with lasting postcolonial effects. The process was a complicated one and it antedated the fall of the Ottoman Empire.

The modernization of the Ottoman Empire in the late nineteenth century was an effort by reformers to introduce capitalist development and bourgeois ideology, inspired by contacts with Western European countries and the study of Western law (the Napoleonic Code particularly). It involved, among other things, the transformation of shariʿa law—"a repertoire of precedents, cases, and general principles, along with a body of well-developed hermeneutical and paralogical techniques" into a standardized, modern code.[56] We might say, as Modern and Connolly do about American Protestantism, that in this way shariʿa was secularized. The new code established previously unknown distinctions between criminal, commercial, civil, and family law. Joseph Massad tells us that Egyptian jurists, looking to models in the West, standardized aspects of this family law.[57] In the process, notes Wael Hallaq, they eliminated the different schools of interpretation to which women had in the past applied for redress.[58] Muhammad Qadri Pasha was the first to designate family law as "personal status law" in 1893. Another Egyptian jurist, Abd al-Razzaq Ahmad al-Sanhuri expanded personal status law to include non-Muslims; his writings became the basis for civil codes in a number of Arab countries (including Egypt, Iraq, Syria, and Libya). Sanhuri's goal was to maintain shariʿa even as it was modernized. That was accomplished above all by introducing a sharp distinction between the sexes, identifying women with tradition, men with the forward movement of history.

Writes Massad: "What this project in fact intended was the new invention of Arab women (following European nationalist examples) as custodians of tradition and managers of the nation's moral life and that of its future generations."[59] This might involve equipping them with a modern education and with knowledge of home economics and hygiene, but it nonetheless "enforced asymmetry in duties and rights" for women and men.[60]

The distinctions established in these codes were retained, reinvented, or borrowed by imperial powers in Arab lands after the dissolution of the Ottoman Empire, and elsewhere. Law, writes Hallaq (about British rule in India), "was simply more financially rewarding than brute power. . . . The plan . . . rested on the assumption that local customs and norms could be incorporated into a British institutional structure of justice that was regulated by 'universal' (read: British) ideals of law."[61] Since personal status law seemed irrelevant to imperial conquest—"the construction of states *qua* states in the lands of Islam was not their aim"—it was initially left aside in the restructuring that took place.[62]

According to Janet Halley and Kerry Rittich and their collaborators, colonial expansion treated the spheres of the family and the market as separate juridical domains: family law and contract law.[63] Family law was theorized as an autonomous field by the nineteenth-century jurist, Friedrich Carl von Savigny, "and carried around the world as part of the influence of German legal thought."[64] It was an aspect of the rationalizing of legal practice. Contract law pertained to public market transactions and was defined as universally applicable; family or personal status law dealt with what was taken to be local custom (most often religious practice), as it addressed the private sphere: sexual relations, marriage, divorce, and children, but not property ownership, which was deemed a matter of contract law. Men were defined as the only legitimate property owners, even in situations (as in the India described by Indrani Chatterjee) where women had traditionally administered family wealth; regulation of all that involved women was left to family law (usually understood to be governed by religious belief and practice), now codified separately, distinct from all the other relationships with which it had once been entwined.[65] Mahmood writes that in the former Ottoman territories "colonial powers subjected pre-existing religious differences to a new grid of intelligibility. Under colonial rule, minority identity (bestowed by the state) became, paradoxically, sutured to a private attribute (religion) toward which the state claimed to be neutral."[66] In this way family law referred to (and in fact created) a domain distinct from men's public civic and market activities, "a privileged place in the regulation of the private sphere (to which the family, religion and sexuality [we]re relegated").[67] Following the discourse of secularism, religion, along with women, became the quintessential "other" of the secular (markets, property, contracts, politics, civic and criminal law).

The work of many scholars shows how this gesture to what was taken to be tradition in fact involved a rewriting of history—a new logic superimposed on older practices. The designation of family law as a separate realm did not leave "tradition" intact; rather, it involved transformation through processes of codification and standardization. What had once been an integrated set of social behaviors (family and property, for example, were inseparable), regulated according to local interpretation of specific circumstances, were now separated and subjected to different but formally defined legal jurisdictions. For example, Judith Surkis shows how the desire to free Arab-held lands for settler acquisition led the French in Algeria to circumscribe Muslim law to family matters, matters that, however, now excluded the previously intertwined realms of family, inheritance, and collectively owned property.[68] As Halley and Rittich put it: "The standard narrative—in which local powers entered into the colonial relationship holding their ancient, usually religious, Family Law as their most sacred ground—seems again and again to be a little skewed; so often, the coherence of tradition comes *later*."[69] If the narrative of tradition was established after the fact, the effect of the colonial designation of family law as the autonomous purview of local religious authorities was nonetheless enormous. Family law came to be identified with "tradition" (as the embodiment of the authentic cultural heritage of the colonized), and so with anti-imperialist nationalist aspirations. Those aspirations became synonymous with "customary" (timeless) practices of religion, sexuality, the family, and women—practices that, in fact, were most often the result of colonial interventions.

"The 'woman question' . . . became the fault line along which men and women negotiated ethnic boundaries, cultural identity, and social transformations," writes historian Beth Baron of debates between so-called secular modernizers and religious traditionalists in Egyptian nationalist movements.[70] Mahmood notes that in postcolonial Egypt, separate family laws imposed by the British have come to signify the political and cultural identities of different religious communities, as if they long antedated British intervention when, in fact, they are the product of it. This has meant that interreligious conflict (between minority Christian Copts and majority Muslims) "often erupts on the terrain of gender and sexuality."[71]

Massad describes the complicated relationship between modernity and tradition—conceived in terms of time and space—in the articulation of Jordan's postcolonial national identity this way:

> [W]omen, as residents of the private domestic sphere, and Bedouins, residents of the nonurban desert, signify, through their spatial locations, a temporal location, that of tradition, whereas men, considered as residents of the public sphere, and urbanites, through their spatial locations, signify the temporal location of modernity.[72]

In this division of labor, women (and Bedouins) are represented as embodying timeless tradition, while men represent the forward motion of history. More broadly, Halley and Rittich point to the ways in which family law

> played a role . . . in the ideological war waged between colonizer and colonized: stigmatizing the antagonist's *family* was one way to consolidate national legitimacy. . . . Thus Western legal minds have sometimes attached their universalizing ambitions to women's equality, affective marriage, and the nuclear family, and decried the subordination of women and the instrumentalisms of the patriarchal family that they saw in the populations they subjugated. . . . Nationalist, feminist, and cosmopolitan legal elites in the colonized world could find themselves in a bind: they now had Family Law in the form of tradition, and tradition as the marker of residual local legal authority; putting their nationalism, feminism, and/or cosmopolitanism into legal form—modernizing—would lay them open to charges that they were Westernizing.[73]

Reading Frantz Fanon on the question of veiling provides insight into the difficulties of articulating a position of modern anticolonial revolution—how to redeem the "Orient" without reproducing its Western signification? The French colonists had long figured their domination as an unveiling of Algeria's women, as "penetration" beyond the boundary established by the veil. During the Algerian war (1954–62), French women settlers staged unveiling ceremonies for Muslim women to identify their liberation with the French cause. At the same time the Algerian resistance used the veil to disguise its fighters, and it sent women dressed in Western clothing to bomb French sites. "In the beginning, the veil was a mechanism of resistance," Fanon wrote of the Algerian National Liberation Front, "but its value for the group remained strong. The veil was worn because tradition demanded a rigid separation of the sexes but also because the occupier was *bent on unveiling Algeria*."[74] Here the very identity of a liberated Algerian nation depends—literally and figuratively—on the treatment of its women as defined by religious precepts that had come to serve as a mark of its cultural particularity.

How remain true to some aspect of local religious heritage and at the same time create a modern nation-state? Retaining family law at once provided a solution—a way of dealing separately with majority and minority religions—but also presented a challenge to the sovereign authority of the newly created states. Even when religious law was adopted or deferred to, however, "tradition" was not untouched; rather, it was an adaptation of an already codified shariʿa to new circumstances. In country after country, modifications of family law established the supremacy of the husband in a nuclear family household and the equation of nationalism with masculinity. Massad indicates that in the Jordanian family law enacted after independence in 1947, revised in 1951, and again in 1976, "there is a discrepancy between the rights and duties of men and women not only toward the state but also toward each other as subjects of the state."[75] Hallaq cites a study of 1957 Moroccan family law that "convincingly argues that the so-called reforms in that country have indeed produced a consolidated patriarchal hold within a reinterpreted field of the

Shariʿa, while simultaneously undermining the intricate guarantees and multi-layered safety nets that the Shariʿa had provided in practice before the dawn of modernity and its nation-state."[76] Here it is the demands of modern state-making, and with it secularism's introduction of new classifications of separate spheres—not the hold of traditional Islam—that explains new forms of women's subordination, forms that (as we shall see in chapters 2 and 3) are not unlike those associated with the emergence of European nations. Both Hallaq and Massad note that gender inequality is not unique to postcolonial nations but a feature of modern nations, new and old, West and East.[77]

Attempting to disentangle the attribution of the subordination of women to the traditions of Islam and the association of feminism with Westernization, Kumari Jayawardena insists that it was the introduction of capitalism and certain bourgeois ideologies—the result of imperialist domination—and not opposition to Islam (or other Eastern religions) that led to the rise of indigenous feminisms in the Third World. Her 1986 study, *Feminism and Nationalism in the Third World*, calls attention to the ways in which "the creation and assertion of a cultural identity was itself dialectically related to the growth of imperialism."[78] In case after case (Turkey, Egypt, Iran, Afghanistan, India, Sri Lanka, Indonesia, the Philippines, China, Vietnam, Korea, Japan) she links feminist movements to national liberation struggles that were motivated by anticapitalism as well as by anti-imperialism (the two were linked), but that were also limited (as were their Western counterparts) by liberal notions of rights. "The women's movements in many countries of Asia achieved political and legal equality with men at the juridical level, but failed to make an impression on women's subordination within the patriarchal structures of family and society."[79] This subordination may find some of its justifications in religious teaching, she argues, but it is an effect of modernity, not of the stranglehold of tradition. Indeed, the position of women in family law is itself the product of secularizing influences.

And yet, all of this scholarship notwithstanding, women's subordination in postcolonial nations is regularly attributed to unchanging, "traditional" religious practice—these days Islam is the primary culprit. In this connection, Massad cites a 2003 report on "Arab Human Development" from the United Nations Development Program: "Most Arab personal status laws, with regard to Muslims and non-Muslims alike, are witness to legally sanctioned gender bias. This stems from the fact that personal status statutes are primarily derived from theological interpretations and judgments. The latter originate in the remote past when gender discrimination permeated society and they have acquired a sanctity and absoluteness in that confused area where the immutable tenets of religious creed interact with social history."[80] Or, as Joyce Carol Oates put it more simply, "the predominant religion of Egypt" was responsible for violence against women during the summer protests of 2013.[81] These refusals of history have to do, I think, with the persistence of the discourse of secularism—or, more specifically, with its contemporary reactivation. In that discourse, there is a powerful association between religion and women: they are religion's embodiments, its protagonists and its victims. For nineteenth-century Western secularists, it was "our" women who were thus represented; today it is those "others" in the (Middle) East. The "us" versus "them" contrast provides evidence for the triumph of Western freedom over the ever-lagging "Orient." But in the twenty-first century, as in the nineteenth, the identification of women with/as religion is not the product of timeless religious teaching; it is, rather, an effect of the way the discourse of secularism has organized our vision of the world.

CHAPTER TWO

Reproductive Futurism

IN THE DISCOURSE OF secularism, the existence of separate spheres for women and men was no longer attributed to God, it was taken as a natural fact. The insistence on nature's mandate was a distinctive aspect of nineteenth-century secularism. Human biology was the ultimate source of the unequal and distinctive roles for women and men. These roles designated women's bodies as the agents of reproduction—as guarantor of the future of the family and, by extension, the race and the nation—and men as embodied labor power, whether manual or intellectual. "When men fear work or fear righteous war," wrote Theodore Roosevelt, "when women fear motherhood, they tremble on the brink of doom; and well it is that they should vanish from earth, where they are fit subjects for the scorn of all men and women who are themselves strong and brave."[1] Even as the sexes were assigned to separate spheres, their most intimate relations came under public scrutiny. The public penetrated the private as a function of what Foucault calls "biopower," the designation of life "as a political object," indispensable to the development of capitalism and the state both for the "controlled insertion of bodies into the machinery of production and the adjustment of the phenomena of population to economic processes."[2] Sex, he tells us, was at the pivot of the two axes: the disciplining of bodies and the regulation of population.

In the discourse of secularism, the sexual division of labor was attributed to biology, but it also had an evolutionary dimension that linked the progress of civilization, and so of the white race, to specialized functions for each sex. Thus, the French sociologist Emile Durkheim thought that sexual and social differentiation evolved simultaneously. In the remote past, he noted, social relations were based on resemblance. The differences between men and women were hardly apparent. The sexes were of the same size and performed the same functions. Women, like certain female animals, actually took pride in their warlike aggressiveness. Sexual relations were casual ("mechanical"); there was no such thing as conjugal fidelity. The coming of rationality, expressed as the division of labor, changed all of this. Differentiation was a mark of civilization. Woman "retired from warfare and public affairs and consecrated her entire life to her family." As a result, "the two great functions of psychic life . . . [were] dissociated," women becoming specialized in "affective functions," men in "intellectual functions."[3] The British writer H. G. Wells echoed these themes, noting that "the trend of evolutionary forces through long centuries of human development has been on the whole towards differentiation. An adult white woman differs far more from a white man than a negress or pigmy woman from her equivalent male."[4] In 1908, Iwan Bloch declared that it was "obvious . . . that the whole of civilisation is the product of the physical and mental differentiation of the sexes."[5]

Historian Stefan Dudink notes the ambiguity of these widely held views: "Only advanced societies were supposed to have organised their social, political, moral and cultural life in accordance with true notions of sexual difference. Societies that did not abide by the rules of nature in this domain were, or would become, backward. So, to a certain extent, masculinity and femininity did become goals at a horizon of historical development. The concepts themselves, however, were firmly shielded from history."[6] Philosopher Cornelia Klinger points out that Hegel placed women's role within the family and characterized women as an eternal presence. Even the experience of time was said to differ according to sex: women's was the cyclical time of nature, men's the linear time of history. Georg Simmel saw woman as the guarantor of an otherwise threatened wholeness. "The woman represents such a unity in contrast to the man, who is bound up with the dispersed multiplicity of inestimable life."[7] The notion of a division of labor implied complementarity—the different sexes performed different but necessary functions in "a harmony of corresponding inequalities" based on historically evolved natural differences between the sexes.[8]

At least since the 1520s, doctors had insisted that the bodies, and so the natures, of men and women were totally different.[9] But from the eighteenth century on, the argument took on a new and more powerful form: the nervous body was the key to the change. Early sensationalist psychology made no distinction between women and men. Bernard Mandeville, for example, in *The Fable of the Bees* (1714), insisted that gender differences were the result of differences in education and custom: "There is no labour of the Brain, which Women are not as capable of performing, at least as well as Men."[10] But by the later eighteenth century, it was generally held that women had a finer nervous system and so a greater sensibility than men. In England, Barker-Benfield writes, this view "became a central convention of eighteenth-century literature."[11] To be sure, there were critics of the notion that women had a different nervous structure (Mary Wollstonecraft was among them), but the view was popularized in England, Barker-Benfield suggests, by its wide incorporation in the novels of the day.[12] In France, there was a similar recourse to neural physiology. The French historian Jules Michelet's comment was effusive, and widely shared: "She is nothing like us. She thinks, talks, and acts otherwise. Her tastes are different from our tastes. Her blood does not flow like ours; sometimes it rushes, like a storm's downpour. She doesn't breathe like us. . . . She doesn't eat like us. . . . Women have a different language."[13] This led Michelet to argue for women's necessary dependence on men, on their need for the care and tutelage of their husbands. As women provided affective sustenance, men must provide direction and leadership. His conclusions echoed more than a century of learned opinion on the implications of differences of sex. The comments of Dr. J. J. Sachs, writing in 1830, were typical: "Sexual differences are not restricted to the organs of reproduction, but penetrate the entire organism. The entire life takes on a feminine or masculine character."[14] The Scottish biologist Patrick Geddes distinguished male and female temperaments this way: The male exerted "greater power of maximum effort, of scientific insight or cerebral experiment," while the female had "greater patience, more open-mindedness, greater appreciation of subtle details and consequently what we would call more rapid intuition."[15]

For some nineteenth-century scientists and social scientists the difference of sex was about the physics of energy: males were thought to expend energy in acts of intellectual creativity, while women stored it "to meet the cost of [physical] reproduction."[16] The American, Dr. Edward Clarke, argued in his *Sex and Education* (1873) that sustained intellectual activity would diminish the energy women needed for reproduction. Too much study, he warned, would compromise their child-bearing organs, endangering not only themselves but the future of the race. English writers sounded a similar theme: Women might be granted education and even a voice in domestic affairs, wrote G. Allen in 1889, "But what we must absolutely insist upon is full and free recognition of that fact that, in spite of everything, the race and the nation must go on reproducing themselves."[17]

Anatomical renderings of human skeletons since the eighteenth century had emphasized (indeed exaggerated) the greater size of the female pelvis and the superior size of the male skull.[18] The low/high comparison was implicit: the nether regions of women corresponded to their exclusive reproductive function; the exalted height of men's skulls contained their larger brains, the source of rationality and creativity. Men's brains were considered the seat of their presumed superior reasoning power. (This despite many questions raised by scientists and phrenologists alike about the brain's integrity as a singular organ.) The brain was at once the concrete embodiment and the elusive site of men's conscious rationality, the locus for their self-mastery. An eighteenth-century German writer, Georg Sarganeck, found that "from anatomy it is common knowledge and undeniable that the fabrication of the testes is extremely close to the structure of the brain."[19] Historian Isabel Hull explains that for Sarganeck "semen was . . . the metaphoric link between brain and nerves, whence arose male creativity, that is intelligent, innovative action upon the world."[20] The testes/brain connection was an ancient one, to be sure. But Hull notes that "the important point is that in the eighteenth century as creativity came to be reinterpreted as overwhelmingly rational-intellectual, as occurring in science, institution-building, and manufacturing, it could be ascribed exclusively to males with the help of a model that had long since associated brainpower, life force, and male sexual apparatus."[21]

Brain size was an important manifestation of male superiority for eighteenth- and nineteenth-century commentators. It was an aspect of scientific racism as well as of gender differentiation. As a racial characteristic, it distinguished civilized men from barbarians; in regard to gender, a disparity in brain size between the sexes marked the advance of civilized societies. In this representation the racial contrast established the superiority of a nation; the gendered contrast, in turn, ratified the racial difference and secured the dominance of white men. Durkheim, citing the crowd psychologist Gustave Le Bon, articulated the fantasy when he reported that "with the progress of civilization the brain of the two sexes differentiates itself more and more. According to . . . [Le Bon] this progressive chart would be due both to the considerable development of masculine crania and to a stationary or even regressive state of female crania. 'Thus,' he says, 'though the average cranium of Parisian men ranks among the greatest known crania, the average of Parisian women ranks among the smallest observed, even below the crania of the Chinese, and hardly above those of the women of New Caledonia.' "[22]

In this comment the question of "whose was bigger" was racialized as well as gendered. Brain size functioned as a proxy for the phallus and the power it represented, the power of European white men over white women and people of color.[23] If the German Sarganeck made the brain/phallus link explicit by associating semen with superior functioning of the cerebral organ, the French Le Bon made white males' superiority a matter of that organ's size; it was the natural proof that they were destined to rule. As for women, they were destined to breed. An article in the *Encyclopédie* on "The Skeleton" in 1765 compared differences in all aspects of bodily structure and concluded that "the destiny of woman is to have children and to nourish them."[24] More than a century later, an English gynecologist pointed to the "gigantic power and influence of the ovaries over the whole animal economy of woman."[25] Queen Victoria was often referred to this way: "She is a Queen—a real Queen—but she is a real Mother, and true Wife."[26] Likewise, the American Dr. Horatio Storer insisted that "woman was what she is in health, in character, in her charms, alike of body, mind and soul because of her womb alone."[27] And in France, Michelet, upon seeing drawings of the female reproductive system, concluded: "Man is the brain, woman the uterus."[28] To her, the actual reproductive function (with all its messy, unpredictable fluidity), to him the rational management of her, and so of the source of life itself. The difference of sex was conceived in terms of an unequal complementarity: women were the instruments through which men controlled the direction of life.

"Disenchantment"

For secularists the periodization of traditional and modern rested on a sharp contrast between religion and science. Biology especially was mobilized to provide certainty where the presumed loss of religious guarantees had introduced uncertainty. In place of (or alongside) church doctrines, secularists offered medical treatises and legislative enactments based upon them. Instead of the biblical account of Genesis, they turned, in the nineteenth century, to gynecology: life as a spontaneous, autonomous product of women's reproductive cycle.

Woman as Nature, Nature as Woman—there was no outside source for life. Nor for thought. That came from science, from man's ability to abstract and divide, to rationalize life by identifying its divisions of labor. Science was, after all, the subordination of Nature to man's will, to the calculations and techniques that were the source of their own authority.

Even as they hailed the progress of science and deemed religion a matter of (at best) private concern, secular theorists worried about the public impact of the substitution of science for religion. How would it affect ethics, morality, and the very meaning of life? If religion belonged only to the realm of the irrational, Max Weber pointed out, there would be a real loss for human sensibility—as his use of the word "disenchantment" implied. "The fate of our times is characterized by rationalization and intellectualization and, above all, by the 'disenchantment of the world,'" he wrote. "Precisely the ultimate and most sublime values have retreated from public life either into the transcendental realm of mystic life or into the brotherliness of direct and personal human relations."[29] The very word "disenchantment" suggested the loss not only of shared illusion and its accompanying delights but also of "the ultimate and most sublime values"—distinctive and universal qualities that nurtured human life. According to Weber, the "disenchantment of the world" did not destroy these values but privatized them, removing them as direct inspiration for public activity. In their place "technical means and calculations" provided a sense of human mastery, ending the need for appeals to the mysterious powers of spirits or gods. But, Weber cautioned, "intellectualization and rationalization are not increases in knowledge"; they are another way of seeking mastery. In the absence of external causes, they are attempts by humans to be agents of their own lives.[30] Weber associated this agency not with all men, but with what he termed "manliness"—the ability to master the "technical means and calculations" with which to face the world without illusion or the comforts of religion.

Technical agency was, however, acquired at a cost. The emphasis on the superiority of rational calculation, the insistence that reason was the practical guide for men's lives, meant the denigration of all that was deemed unreasonable, its assignment to another realm. From this followed the notion of separate spheres: public and private, reason and passion, objective and subjective. Weber, as many of his contemporaries, thought that the private spheres (he considered that there were more than one) offered compensation for the alienating effects of bureaucratic rationality in public life; they were a kind of residue, necessary but insufficient for the evolution of modernity. Weber contributed to the idealization of the public/private distinction, even as he wrote critically of its impact. His notion of disenchantment has become (to this day) one of the organizing principles of the secularism discourse.

Weber's notion of spheres was about exterior and interior states of being. He conceived of tensions within individuals who, in the external, highly rationalized realms of economics and politics, yearned "inwardly" for less material forms of fulfillment. If the public sphere was about technical proficiency, the private spheres were the locus of affect, passion, and the irrational. "The general result of modern forms of thoroughly rationalizing the conception of the world and of the way of life, theoretically and practically, in a purposive manner, has been that religion has been shifted into the realm of the irrational."[31] Not only religion but various forms of artistic and erotic activity as well. "Art is salvation from routines of everyday life and especially from increasing pressures of theoretical and practical rationalism."[32] As for sexual love, "the boundless giving of oneself is as radical as possible in its opposition to all functionality, rationality, and generality. It is displayed here as the unique meaning which one creature in his irrationality has for another, and only for this specific other. . . . The lover realizes himself to be rooted in the kernel of the truly living, which is eternally inaccessible to any rational endeavor."[33]

Disenchantment meant the privatizing of religion, emotion, and sex; they became dimensions of interior experience, according to Weber, but also feminized attributes in the eyes of his contemporaries—philosophers and politicians alike.[34] In their view there was a geography implicit in the notion of separate spheres: the public political marketplace was the scene of masculine competitive rationality, the private domestic hearth provided a refuge from that harsh world, consolation in the form of women's affective sensibilities. There was also a notion of temporality attached to the idea of separate spheres. While modernity, embodied in markets and political institutions, was associated with the forward march of history, the private sphere held all that was immutable; it was the repository of tradition, untouched by the movement of time. Klinger puts it this way: "In the face of the dark aspects of the process of rationalization, a bright light is cast on the realm it touches the least: in the special ever more isolated sphere of the family, and in woman at its center, what had otherwise been lost is found again."[35]

Yearning for Eternity

The loss of religion haunted the theorists of the new science, raising doubts about the ability of the secular to account for all aspects of life. "Viewed from a purely ethical point of view," Weber wrote, "the world has to appear fragmentary and devalued in all those instances when judged in the light of the religious postulate of a divine 'meaning' of existence."[36] Weber's discussion of modernity rested on an idealized vision of an enchanted, more spiritually fulfilling past. It expressed secularism's account of itself as a clean break with the past, as a new stage in the unfolding of the progress of history.

But, as Weber knew, secularization was not an entirely triumphalist process. It could no longer guarantee immortality, or some kind of spiritual life after physical death, nor was it possible to imagine death as continuous with life; instead, death became a break, an unwelcome "rupture."[37] Weber notes that rational inquiry was inadequate for the job: "Science has created this cosmos of natural causality" but "has seemed unable to answer with certainty the question of its own ultimate presuppositions." The lack of certainty was displaced onto a search for "inner-worldly perfection" in terms of "culture," but the endless pursuit of new entertainments attested not only to the "meaninglessness of death" but also to the "senselessness of life itself." "[C]ulture's every step forward seems condemned to lead to an ever more devastating senselessness."[38]

Despite heated debates from the eighteenth century on spontaneous generation, scientific dissection of ova and embryos, detailed analyses of the workings of female reproductive organs, and investigations into disease and its etiology, science could provide no ultimate accounting for death.[39] Or perhaps it's better to say that death eluded reason's calculating controls. Foucault put it this way: "[D]eath is power's limit, the moment that escapes it. Death becomes the most secret aspect of existence, the most 'private.'"[40] Philippe Ariès elaborated the point: "In the modern period," he wrote, "death, despite the apparent continuity [with earlier times] of themes and ritual, became challenged and was furtively pushed out of the world of familiar things."[41] A 1910 court ruling in the state of Washington provides a good example of the thinking behind the privatization of death. The judges maintained that a funeral parlor should not be located in a residential neighborhood:

> [I]t may be accepted as within the common knowledge of man, that the immediate presence of those mute reminders of mortality, the hearse, the chapel, the taking in and carrying out of bodies, the knowledge that within a few feet of the windows of one's dwelling house where the family sleep and eat and spend their leisure hours, autopsies are going on, that the dead are there, cannot help but have a depressing effect upon the mind of the average person, weakening . . . his physical resistance and rendering him more susceptible to contagion and disease.[42]

Here the mere acknowledgment of death is potentially fatal. Death's furtive banishment, its confinement to a secret, "private" existence is the only possible way to stay alive.[43] Ariès notes that there was a change in the conceptualization of the relation between sex and death from the seventeenth century on: "Like the sexual act, death was henceforth increasingly thought of as a transgression which tears man from his daily life, from rational society, from his monotonous work, in order to make him undergo a paroxysm, plunging him into an irrational, violent, and beautiful world."[44]

Weber comments this way on the loss of religious explanations for death: "[T]he stronger the more systematic the thinking about the 'meaning' of the universe becomes, the more the external organization of the world is rationalized, and the more the conscious experience of the world's irrational content is sublimated."[45] In the absence of consolation, then, sublimation. Sublimation in the classic Freudian sense: the turning of unappeasable anxiety to socially constructive ventures. A. K. Kordela describes it as the "administration and management of the subject's relation to mortality and immortality, as compensation for the loss of eternity."[46] The guarantee of immortality comes with biological reproduction as the sole legitimate aim of sexual intercourse—securing life's meaning by deferring its realization to succeeding generations. Lee Edelman names it "reproductive futurism" and characterizes it this way: "Children secure our existence through the fantasy that we survive in them."[47] André-Jean Arnaud's close reading of the Napoleonic Code (1804) also sees it in these terms: "The child . . . remains practically—in the code's conception—a property of the father until his death. In a sense, the code responds here to the *anxiety* about death by providing a 'means of survival.' "[48] Robert Nye adds that the code gives a father the same dominion over his children—his biological capital—and his material assets. Both are "aspects of the same process of self-perpetuation."[49]

Jacques Lacan offered an explanation in terms of the unconscious for the way the connection between love and death was conceived. In Lacan's rereading, Freud's positing of an opposition between destructive and life-affirming drives is rendered instead as a paradox of modern subjectivity. According to Lacan, the quest for love (which takes the form of a search for a sexual relationship) is ultimately driven by an unconscious desire to recapture one's imagined, lost wholeness—the time before the individuation effected by castration. The fulfillment of that (impossible) desire, however, remerging with the mother, would result in the death of the subject, his or her obliteration as an independent being. The sublimation of this dilemma—of what Lacan deems a longing for pre-oedipal fusion and Kordela calls "a yearning for eternity"—comes in the form of Edelman's reproductive futurism. Sex becomes the alternative to death in the age of disenchantment only when it is endowed with rational (reproductive) purpose. In Weber's words, "The knowing love of the mature man . . . reaffirms the natural quality of the sexual sphere, but it does so consciously, as an embodied creative power."[50] The conscious imposition of reproductive meaning not only seeks to tame the unruly sex drive, but brings women ("the sex") under control. Sex is separated from death when men direct women exclusively to life-bearing activity. Here is secularism's answer to the uncertainty of life without God.

For the secular Western imaginary, reproduction was understood to be a mandate of nature as revealed by scientific inquiry. In this regard, Kordela notes a contrast in the modern representations of aristocratic in contrast to bourgeois regimes of reproduction. From the modern perspective, aristocratic currency was said to lie in genealogy, in ties to ancestors and to antiquity. It was described as backward looking, based on the purity of bloodlines anchored in the past as legitimation for present social standing. Reproduction assured that the future would secure the past. Bourgeois currency (modernizing, secularizing), in contrast, had to do with producing progeny for the future, projecting the present forward. Of course, heredity mattered (and nineteenth-century medical science was obsessed with what we now think of as genetic transmission). But this was an outlook focused on the indefinite extension of life, the peopling of the future as the way of guaranteeing the perpetuation of the present, a way of conquering death. In the retrospective periodizing of modernity, aristocratic regimes were associated with death, bourgeois regimes with life. Modern generational continuity ensured not only family posterity but the ongoing life—and the racial purity—of the nation. Indeed, the health of nations was early taken to be synonymous with the growth of their populations and their economies. It was no accident that the science of demography accompanied the consolidation of nation-states, and that fears of depopulation led to the monitoring of all manner of activities taking place in the so-called private sphere. At the same time, Malthus and his followers spoke of the need to control unlimited explosions of population that could undermine healthy national growth. If the degrading effects of poverty were to be avoided, there needed to be rational management of the reproductive force of the nation. "The old power of death that symbolized sovereign power," Foucault wrote, "was now carefully supplanted by the administration of bodies and the calculated management of life."[51]

The Conjugal Couple

The secular focus on reproduction put extraordinary emphasis on marriage and on the conjugal family as a primary unit. It was the institution that mediated private desire and public interest, and that provided the immortality once promised by religion. Marriage was defined as the locus not only of reproduction (this had also been the case for aristocrats, who pursued amorous "dangerous liaisons" extramaritally) but also as the only site for love. The affective nuclear family was everywhere sentimentalized, imagined as the repository of emotional gratification. Writing about the United States in the nineteenth century, Brian Connolly astutely captures the mission of the sentimental nuclear family:

> Whether in marriage or the affectionate relations between parents and children, the family ordered the democratic republic, supplying its necessary virtues, serving metaphorically to pacify violent conflict, and functioning as a training ground for the regulation of desire and passion through reason and benevolence. . . . Private, virtuous, sentimental, affectionate, egalitarian, the nuclear family was the liberal democratic republic's last best hope, a bulwark against the easy slippage from liberty to licentiousness, democracy to

> anarchy. Moreover, it was the disciplinary institution in antebellum America.[52]

In the family, private desire was disciplined, endowed with rationally useful purpose. Anxiety about death was displaced onto scientific preoccupation with women as the perpetrators of life and with men as their legal and economic guardians. I argued in chapter 1 that in the discourses of secularism women and religion were identified with each other, each described as belonging to the domain of the private, each defined as at once a consolation for and a potential danger to the rationalizing forces of the market and the polis. If their alliance was said to be inevitable—a feature of women's innate sensibility and greater proximity to life and death—it was also troubling since, if left unchecked, it could undermine the rational purpose that necessarily organized state power. The danger each represented required intervention, regulation in the name of securing the future of the emerging nation-state. Here the instability of the public/private divide was clearly revealed: the spheres were not autonomous but hierarchically interdependent. The terms of regulation varied by state when it came to religion. In contrast, the terms of regulation pertaining to women and family were remarkably similar across nations, focusing on the conjugal couple and, within it, the primary role of reproduction and thus of mothers.

The institution of marriage was depicted as the fruit of civilization, the realization of nature's mandate. Any number of commentators studied it in the nineteenth century: Engels, Bachofen, Darwin, Westermarck, Durkheim, John Ferguson McLennan, and Lewis Henry Morgan among them.[53] Morgan offered a universal evolutionary model:

> As now constituted, the family is founded upon marriage between one man and one woman. A certain parentage was substituted for a doubtful one; and the family became

> organized and individualized by property rights and privileges. . . . Upon this family, as now constituted, modern civilized society is organized and reposes. The whole previous experience and progress of mankind culminated and crystallized in this one great institution.[54]

In this vein, the American jurist Joseph Story commented that "marriage is treated by all civilized nations as a peculiar and favored contract. It is in its origin a contract of natural law." It was, he went on, "the parent, not the child of society."[55] In Germany Johann Gottlieb Fichte offered the opinion that "[t]he marriage relation is the true mode of existence of grown persons of both sexes, required even by nature."[56] Fichte equated civilization with adulthood; the maturation process of societies, like that of individuals, was a "natural" one. The minister of cults under Napoleon, Jean-Étienne-Marie Portalis, thought that marriage was "neither a civil nor a religious act, but a natural act which has drawn the attention of legislators and which religion has sanctified."[57] The French sociologist, Frédéric Le Play, maintained that "private life stamps public life with its character. The family is the foundation of the state."[58]

The impact of Western models—whether legally imposed by colonizers or imported by colonial elites—is striking in this regard. Although there were clearly differences of culture and politics in the non-West, the importance of marriage as key to the logic of modern state formation incorporated Western policies. In nineteenth-century Iran, studied by Afsaneh Najmabadi, the influences of the West led rulers to stigmatize homoerotic practices, insisting instead that love and reproduction be located only in the married heterosexual couple.[59] Hanan Kholoussy notes that in Egypt "motherhood was fundamental to the constitution of national identity and entailed the formation of a series of discursive practices that demarcated women as both a locus of Egyptian 'backwardness' and a sphere of transformation to be modernized."[60] During the Hashemite monarchy in Iraq (1921–58), according to the research of Sara Pursley, modernizers studying Western institutions sought to outlaw Shiite temporary marriages (those concluded for the immediate purposes of sexual pleasure), insisting that permanent unions for the purposes of reproduction were the only form of marriage the state would sanction.[61] There politicians passed a series of laws in 1958 and 1959 (among them land reform, labor laws, and a law for the protection of children) that aimed at stabilizing the institution of the family—the state's reproductive agent. Modern mothers were depicted as liberated from "messy, localized traditions" and as able to devote themselves instead to a "hygienic, orderly, rational, safe" domesticity, aimed at securing the nation in perpetuity. "Having been finally freed from the past," Pursley remarks, "the nation's women were henceforth to be trapped in its future."[62] Put another way, women were the instruments by which men were able to secure their visions of the future as a continuation of the present. Marriage ensured not only the protection of family property but guaranteed the (racial, ethnic) homogeneity of the "people," who were imagined to be the nation's constituents. It also offered, in a secular context, a promise of the immortality once found in religion.

Gender asymmetry was at the heart of these definitions of marriage. An anonymous German put it succinctly: "Never must equality extend to the qualities of the sexes." Herder put it more poetically: "There must be consonant tones to produce the melody of life and of pleasure, not unison."[63] Liberal theologians in Baden echoed these views, attributing to "Nature" the necessary inequality between the sexes.[64] The Dutch Liberal minister of justice noted in 1900, "the character of marriage is . . . in my view, incompatible with a principled equality between man and woman."[65] The French Portalis warned that "conjugal society could not exist if one of the spouses wasn't subordinated to the other."[66] Laws that regulated nationality gave priority to paternity; in cases where a mother came from another land, the father's nationality prevailed.[67]

The linking of sex to marriage and reproduction was not new, but its modern form in the West stems from the Protestant Reformation, the origin for Weber and many others of individualism and the privatizing of religion that set in motion the processes of secularization. Weber speculates that the disciplining of sex by marriage was an aspect of early religious teaching, initially a priestly attempt to tame the wild eroticism of orgiastic sects, but later a feature of Protestantism. Durkheim thought that marriage directed women's sexual desire (more "instinctual" than men's) to socially desirable moral purposes.[68] Janet Jakobsen links Protestant notions of freedom to the regulation of sexuality by marriage. For Luther, she says, "Protestant freedom is an incitement to sexuality over against the celibacy of priestly and monastic life, and it is an incitement specifically to matrimonial and reproductive sexuality."[69] Her more general point, following Weber, is that secular notions of individual freedom (and so, too, of morality) depended on channeling sexuality within marital bonds and devoting it to the production of children. Indeed, the very conception of childhood as a separate stage of life is an aspect of modernity. Ariès has shown that the sciences of childhood (pediatrics, age-based pedagogy, the identification of adolescence as a developmental stage, specialized clothing), as well as visual representations that portray children as children and not as small adults, date from the late seventeenth century.[70] From the eighteenth century on, Jacques Donzelot tells us, doctors and administrators produced "abundant literature on the theme of the conservation of children." Of particular concern was the high mortality of infants confined to wet nurses and of children in orphanages.[71] The need to save children was tied to the realization of the promise of an imagined future, endlessly deferred, wherein the meaning of life would somehow be revealed.[72] Edelman notes that it is not so much real children as an iconic Child who embodies this promise, "the promise of a natural transcendence of the limits of nature itself."[73] The iconic Child, from one perspective a substitute for Christ the redeemer, eludes death, but it is not heavenly resurrection he promises. Instead, this Child offers the "guarantee that the social world in which we take our place will survive when we do not."[74]

Pursley develops this point by suggesting that the temporality of modernity is, paradoxically, static. The nation-state and the family, she says, are the two institutions that produce modern forms of timelessness. She notes that the "clock time and calendar time that measure modern homogeneous linear time, and which emerge with the rise of the modern nation-state, are predicated on uniform duration and endless repetition."[75] Anne Martin-Fugier offers a similar observation: "The family embodied two contradictory qualities. It was regular owing to the repetition of periodic family rituals. Yet this regular and cyclical time, smooth and uninterrupted—a time that was not oppressive to individuals but that flowed through them, as it were, in a biological continuum—was meant to establish a kind of eternity."[76] The predictable, natural fact of the difference of sex provided enduring stability both for the family and the nation. The stability was at once outside of time—the sexual division of labor and the marriage that institutionalized it were said to be "natural" phenomena—and in time, it guaranteed that the present would usher in the future, thus dispensing with death and the need for the comforts of religion in the face of mortality.

The Policing of Families

As gender difference assumed a new and foundational role for the discourse of secularism as the guarantee of the perpetuation of the nation, the conjugal family became a matter of increasing public concern. Husbands, wives, women, sexual behavior, children—all aspects of the private domestic sphere—were necessarily objects of state regulation. Responsibility for keeping records on marriage, birth, and death moved from religious institutions to state bureaucracies. Laws on marriage (age of the partners, adoption, inheritance, criminalization of adultery, determination of the legitimacy of children, the rights of illegitimate children, the limits of parental power, and grounds, if any, for divorce) proliferated (many of them based on the Napoleonic Code of 1804); philanthropic societies promoted marriage among the indigent and the working poor.

The "policing of families," in one historian's description of nineteenth-century France, involved regular intervention by state agents, as well as the creation of state-run institutions, to address such issues as hygiene, education, housing, and moral conduct.[77] These typically involved the monitoring of any sexual behavior not devoted to reproduction. Nineteenth- and early twentieth-century doctors attacked contraception and abortion as (in the words of one American practitioner) "a direct war against human society." If not stopped, these practices would lead, he predicted, to "the rapid extinction of the American people."[78] And everywhere in the West female midwives were displaced by male gynecologists who were thought better able to manage women's procreative powers in the name of national hygiene. Doctors, legislators, and moralists were obsessed with combating masturbation, defined as a solitary, wasteful, and objectless sex act. They were also determined to root out infanticide as a crime not only against nature but against the populationist mandates of the state. Hence, campaigns against prostitution and venereal disease, as well as the association of homosexuality with perversion. Hence, attention to monitoring crowded working-class housing, conceived as a hotbed of incest and contagion.[79] These policies consolidated a class and racialized vision of national homogeneity, even as the stated goal was integration or assimilation. The white middle-class family became the standard for measuring the acceptability (or not) of "other" groups for full membership in the community of the nation. In the discourse of secularism, human standards replaced those once attributed to God.

In the colonies, many legislators and others worked hard to ensure that interracial marriage be avoided. A variety of opinions were expressed on the subject, some warning that miscegenation would dilute the strength of the "superior races." Others indicated tolerance for amorous indulgences with natives that did not result in marriage or children; still others (a distinct minority) wondered if such alliances and their offspring might be a way of confirming the conquerors' domination. There was little question that "savage" sexual practices were contrary to imperial goals. German writers, for example, portrayed African women as "depraved, prey to uncontrolled and insatiable sexual appetite."[80] France distinguished between its own civil codes for marriage and the personal status law of native populations, which granted to local religious authorities regulation of marriage, sexual practices, and family organization (allowing polygamy to continue, for example, even as it was outlawed in the metropole).[81] In this way a clear contrast around what counted as marriage was established between higher and lower forms of civilization; the lower forms of civilization were depicted as infested with superstitious, primitive religious beliefs.

In Britain and France, philanthropists, feminists, and legislators organized societies to encourage female emigration to the colonies for a number of reasons: to find employment for an excess of single women, to provide educators for native populations, and in order to provide eligible women ("decent" middle-class women) as wives to male settlers who needed white partners if they were to "people the colonies" and so guarantee a permanent presence for the settlers. There was some worry expressed about whether these societies were only for the purpose of "matrimonial colonization," and even the most forceful advocates of exactly that aim tried to avoid stating it outright.[82] For example, M. J. Chailley-Bert, after many pages of listing all the other reasons for encouraging the emigration of single women to the French colonies, argued in 1897 that there was an available "stock—if I will be allowed this commercial expression . . . of young girls, unemployed and without a future" who were good candidates as marriage partners for male settlers.[83] He added that the colonies were a more fertile place for the future of the French race. If natality was diminishing in the metropole as a result of the bad influences of industry and urban growth, in the colonies "the natural fecundity of the [French] race would be reestablished" by such marriages in the lush agricultural environment of the East.[84]

These marriages were conceived in terms of nuclear family households, and they served not only to normalize family practices but also to impose a single standard of property ownership in the hands of the male head of the household. In the United States, Native American Indians' communally based landholding was considered irrational, contrary to the requirements of contract law. A multiple strategy was developed to change this. A system of education that enrolled Indian children in boarding schools aimed at weaning students from tribal kinship alliances by teaching the virtues of (white) "civilized home life."[85] The commissioner of Indian Affairs from 1887 to 1892, Thomas J. Morgan, referred to Indian children as "homeless" and "ignorant of those simplest arts that make home possible."[86] The aim was to inculcate models of family as individual domestic units in which men treated women "with the same gallantry and respect which is accorded to their more favored white sisters."[87] The school policy, writes Mark Rifkin, reinforced a federal program (the General Allotment Act of 1887) that removed land from tribal control by requiring individual ownership. "One of the chief mechanisms for doing so was the institutional erasure of native forms of kinship and the collective geographies established and maintained through these webs of attachment/obligation. Not only were allotments parceled out to each 'head of family,' thereby soldering occupancy to a particular vision of what constitutes a family unit, but the act mandated that 'the law of descent and partition in force in the State or Territory where such lands are situated shall apply thereto,' creating a barrier to native efforts to merge land claims through extended chains of familial belonging or to maintain ties of tribal indentification through the transfer of land along alternate lines of descent/affiliation."[88]

In Germany, conservative governments and social scientists fixed on the nuclear family household as an alternative to what they perceived to be the chaos and potentially subversive politics of urban, working-class life. According to historian Andrew Zimmerman, sociologists (among them Max Weber) studied sharecropping arrangements in the post–Civil War American South. They hoped that state support of single-family farms might provide a bulwark against social democracy in the Prussian East and later in their colonies in Africa. They imagined farmers grouped in small households as "bastions of paternalist hierarchy," which would secure "the entire well-being of the nation," the "political constitution and more."[89] Pursley describes a failed development project in Iraq in the 1940s and '50s (the Dujaila Land Settlement Project) in similar terms. The goal was to establish independent rural households, centered on a wife trained in home economics, not in order "to foster the capitalist development of agriculture. . . . Rather it was to contain the sociopolitical disorder effected by already-existing capitalist development. The function of state-promoted land settlements based on the model of small 'family' or 'independent' farmers was to absorb a 'relative surplus population' in the countryside, making it responsible for its own subsistence and keep it away from the cities."[90] Here is an example of a policy aimed not explicitly at women but at addressing "sociopolitical disorder" in the wake of capitalist development. As the family became the unit for imposing order, the place of women in it was explained in terms of the domestic role they "naturally" occupied in the secularism discourse. In these families, Pursley adds, it was not only individual title to land that secured the independence of farmers but their "legally consolidated patriarchal control over a woman and children in a newly defined 'family.' "[91] This model of the nuclear family farm as the foundation of the health of the nation endured, she concludes, long after the failure of the Dujaila Project. It became a part of the platform of the revolutionaries who overturned the monarchy in 1958.

Political Economy

The nuclear family was centrally important for capitalist development. In the discourse of secularism, it was depicted as not only the incubator of nations but also the incubator of labor power, the value-producing energy associated with male bodies. For the theorists of political economy, men's superior strength and skill made women "imperfect" workers but also cheaper to employ for certain routine, unskilled tasks. The writings of these eighteenth- and nineteenth-century theorists identified gender difference as a structural aspect of the capitalist economy. Men must earn a "family wage" to sustain their wives and children, Adam Smith wrote, otherwise "the race of such workmen could not last beyond the first generation." In contrast, women's wages were defined as supplemental, "on account of her necessary attendance on children . . . [these wages are] supposed no more than sufficient to provide for herself."[92] According to the French economist Jean-Baptiste Say, women's childbearing and household labor did not produce value; it was instead the raw material upon which men's wages acted to ensure the production of a new generation of workers. Eugène Buret wrote in 1840, "From the point of view of industry, woman is an imperfect worker."[93]

Eli Zaretsky pointed out in his 1976 book, *Capitalism, the Family, and Personal Life*, that these views served the needs of the capitalist economy: "The wage labour system [that] socialized production under capitalism is sustained by the socially necessary but private labour of housewives and mothers. . . . In this sense the family is an integral part of the economy under capitalism."[94] The designation of the domestic sphere as "private," however, denied its economic function. In this way, as Elizabeth Maddock Dillon suggests, the economic value of women's domestic labor was occluded by its representation as voluntary activity, motivated by love. This served not only to offer men consolation for the predations of the factory and the market, but also to suggest a private space of freedom for the development of the liberal subject "through affective abundance and nonutilitarianism."[95] The "ideological payoff" of sentimentalized domesticity "is intimately related to the symbolics of freedom," she writes.[96] Moreover, the private sphere is understood as a space of empathetic identification with others, the kind of identification that Adam Smith saw as the basis for any individual's sense of self and that Marx considered a prerequisite for exchange. Writes Dillon, "one has value within this system only insofar as one corresponds to the desire of the other; the desire of the other constitutes the self."[97] For her, the private/public, domestic/market, woman/man division of labor adds the political dimension of liberal freedom to capitalist relations of production and definitions of economic value.

The gendered representation of work was widespread. Labor leaders echoed the discourse of political economy as they campaigned for a family wage for men. For example, Henry Broadhurst told the British Trades Union Congress in 1877 that union members had a duty "as men and husbands to use their utmost efforts to bring about a condition of things, where their wives should be in their proper sphere at home, instead of being dragged into competition for livelihood against the great and strong men of the world."[98] Of course, the male unionists also worried that the employment of women would depress their wages, and they were invested, as well, in protecting the masculine identity of their trades. But they operated within a discourse that, far more stringently than in the past, envisioned the labor market in gendered terms that promoted as ideal the maternal and domestic, non-wage-earning role of women. Donzelot writes that "the woman at home, the attentive mother is the man's security, the privileged instrument for the civilization of the working class."[99] The title of an 1861 book by Jules Simon, *L'ouvrière, mot impie, sordide*, echoed across the classes, equating women's work for pay (an existing and, indeed, increasingly apparent social reality), not only with their own degradation and early death but also with increased infant mortality, and thus the loss of the workforce of the future. When Simon argued in 1890 for maternity leave for working women, he did so "in the name of the evident and superior interest of the human race." Protection was due to those persons, he said, "whose health and safety can only be safeguarded by the state."[100]

Of course, there was resistance to these ideas across the political spectrum. Liberals, socialists, and feminists suggested that reproduction, like production, should be organized collectively, and that women should be given equal access to education, jobs, and citizenship, despite the fact that it was they who bore children. Mary Wollstonecraft's *Vindication of the Rights of Woman* (1792) railed at the unjust laws and practices that denied women education and political rights. In the next century, John Stuart Mill, in the *Subjection of Women* (1869), denounced and repudiated the idea that there were natural differences that justified inequality between the sexes. Alternative visions of sexual alliances and family arrangements were central to so-called utopian socialist experiments in Europe and the United States in the nineteenth and twentieth centuries, and these included creating communal households and attributing economic value to women's unpaid domestic labor. Writes Zimmerman, "Just as sexuality, kinship, and the household were fundamental to policies of racial and national domination, of opposition to social democracy and of the control of free labor developed by the Prussian state and the Verein für Sozialpolitik, so too were they central to the critique of these policies by the Social Democrats."[101] These critiques only underline the fact that the politics of modern nation-states included—crucially—the management and control of the supposedly private lives of their populations; sharpened lines of gender difference were integral to the dominant vision that emerged.

The Matrix of Sexual Difference

In secularism's version of history, the decline of religion was replaced by the rise of science; Nature took the place of God, immortality was achieved through human reproduction, and the complementary roles of the sexes secured the present and the future. Men's public alienation was redeemed by women's private affection, and the fragmenting activities of markets and politics were made whole again in the bosom of the domestic hearth; the unity and immortality—of the race and the nation—were now secured by the nuclear family household, the only legitimate site for sexual intercourse as "embodied creative power," sex restricted to a reproductive mandate, issued not in the name of God but of national salvation. With this "reproductive futurism," the quest for wholeness and the ultimate meaning of existence was displaced onto the production of children, in Edelman's terms the iconic Child, who promised to confirm the fantasy that there was an ultimate meaning for life that could be known and realized.

The focus on reproduction substituted scientific assurance for religious consolation; it displaced anxiety about death onto a political program devoted to the perpetuation not only of life but also of the nation. With it, a gendered division of labor became foundational to (inseparable from) the Enlightenment vision of representative government and the imagined wholeness and racial purity of nations. It was a gendered division of labor that defined secularism and was deployed in its name. Attributed to an incontestable Nature, the differences between women and men were, by definition, by analogy, and by metaphoric association, a matrix for the entire social and political order.[102]

CHAPTER THREE

Political Emancipation

THE DEMOCRATIC REVOLUTIONS of the eighteenth century are often cited as the dawn of the secular age, or at least of the opening of the possibility for gender equality, even though neither the American (1776) nor the French (1789) Revolutions extended the right to vote to women. Once the individual (shorn of its social markers) became the unit of political identification, it is said, it was only a matter of time before citizenship was extended to the female sex. Moreover, this line of argument continues, the promise of equality for all became the ground on which women could aspire to inclusion, claiming the irrelevance of their sex for the exercise of civil and political rights.

Certainly, the ideal of equality inspired women's movements in the wake of those revolutions, but winning the vote took more than a century of struggle. And even when the vote was won, the question of women's suitability for politics remained; sex never became irrelevant for the exercise of citizenship. The sexual division of labor at the heart of the secularism discourse framed the arguments pro and con. Although

Abigail Adams urged her husband, John, one of the architects of the American Constitution, to "remember the ladies," it wasn't until 1919 that the Constitution was amended to enfranchise those ladies. Adams's reply to his wife sums up the determination of the Founding Fathers: "Depend upon it," he wrote, "we know better than to repeal our Masculine systems."[1] In France, despite Olympe de Gouges's 1791 Declaration of the Rights of Woman and of the [Female] Citizen, which, in the name of "the sex superior in beauty as in courage during childbirth," proclaimed "the following rights of woman and citizen," French women voted for the first time only in 1945.[2] Historian Eliane Viennot notes a long history of determined exclusion: "Whatever the regime or the electoral system," men in positions of power from the eighteenth to the twentieth century "were massively opposed to equality of the sexes and they worked hard to be sure that inequality endured."[3] Revolutionary ideology and democratic practice were disseminated widely in Western Europe (especially in the countries brought under Napoleonic influence or control), and as a consequence nowhere did women vote in national elections until the twentieth century.[4] (Switzerland was the last democratic nation to extend the vote to women—in 1971.)

The resistance to women's citizenship had less to do with the necessarily slow but inevitable progress of liberal democratic ideas than it did with a contradiction at the very heart of the political thinking that articulated them—a political thinking integral to the discourse of secularism. Liberal political theory postulated the sameness of all individuals as the key to their formal equality—abstracted from their circumstances there was no discernable difference among them, they stood as equals before the law. At the same time there were differences that were thought to refuse abstraction—people in a state of dependency (propertyless peasants, wage laborers, women, children, slaves) could not be counted as autonomous individuals—autonomy, after all, was at the heart of the very definition of individuality. There was, however, an additional reason for the exclusion of women, and that had to do with the presumed natural difference of their sex. Was the sameness of individuals an effect of the law's abstraction or a prerequisite for it? Could the law's abstraction override the dictates of nature? These questions troubled political theorists as they constructed the rules of secular government; over and over we find them assuring their publics that (in the words of a French minister of education in 1880) "equality is not identity." Granting women access to education, Paul Bert argued, would not make men and women the same.[5] But when it came to politics, the lack of the sameness of women with men ruled out equal access to the rights of citizens.

On the question of race, for reasons both principled and political, the French enfranchised slaves in 1794 and granted men of color the status of citizen. (Free men of color had been enfranchised in 1792. Napoleon reinstituted slavery in the colonies in 1802 and then abolished the slave trade—but not slavery—in 1815. Slavery was finally abolished in 1848.) But women were a different story. If a small minority of representatives argued for extending the vote to them, the majority thought they didn't belong in the political sphere. The Jacobin leaders put it starkly in 1793 when they outlawed women's political clubs. Invoking the biological difference of sex, upon which secularism's discourse rested, André Amar, a member of the Committee on General Security, explained why women should not be allowed "to exercise political rights and meddle in the affairs of government":

> Because they would be obliged to sacrifice the more important cares to which nature calls them. The private functions

> for which women are destined by their very nature are related to the general order of society; this social order results from the differences between man and woman. Each sex is called to the kind of occupation which is fitting for it; its action is circumscribed within this circle which it cannot break through, because nature, which has imposed these limits on man, commands imperiously and receives no law.[6]

Thomas Jefferson, whose views on the inferiority (in "beauty and intelligence") of blacks justified their enslavement, thought white women too sensitive for politics. He lauded American women "who have the good sense to value domestic happiness above all other. . . . Our good ladies, I trust, have been too wise to wrinkle their foreheads with politics. They are contented to soothe and calm the minds of their husbands returning from political debate."[7] In the early American republic, women were defined as Republican Mothers, charged with preparing their sons to be citizens of the future. If this meant encouraging women's education and granting them certain prerogatives in relation to the care of their children, it did not mean recognizing them as public figures with a right to vote.[8]

The disqualification of women from politics antedated the democratic revolutions; it was embedded in the political theory upon which those revolutions were based. In a 1988 book, the political theorist Wendy Brown tracked the association of manhood and politics from the Greeks to the twentieth century. In different variations, the theme is the same: men's ability to reason and contemplate distinguishes them from women, whose bodies interfere with access to higher thought.[9] "The internal influence continually recalls women to their sex," wrote a French scientist echoing Jean-Jacques Rousseau, "the male is male only at certain moments, but the female is female throughout her life."[10] Woman, in other words, was synonymous with her body, and since, as Brown writes, "political freedom was freedom from bodily necessity," women were, by definition, politically (and irremediably) unfree.[11]

Historians have suggested that despite its long history, this distinction between the sexes intensified with the advent of secular modernity. Isabel Hull's monumental work on late eighteenth-century Germany documents the increasing emphasis on the distinction between the sexes as secularization redefined the public sphere. "It was in the context of civil and criminal codes that the central bureaucratic reformers discussed how sexual behavior fit into the new world they were creating."[12] This thinking relegated marriage and family—and men's control of both—to a private sphere in which the father/husband's power was exercised outside the purview of state intervention. State law placed the family beyond public scrutiny, while civil codes ensured men's right to rule in that domain. Writes Hull of the relation between husband and wife, "her unfreedom created his freedom, his position as private dominator qualified him to participate in the wider public sphere of equals. . . . The key relation that qualified a citizen was therefore a sexual relation of domination, for . . . the family was the product of a publicly defined and privately consummated sexual relation. The civil and the sexual mutually constituted each other."[13] This mutual constitution became "archetypical," she concludes. "To the end of the nineteenth century and beyond [it] continued to permeate official and unofficial institutions and ideologies (liberal, conservative, even socialist and national-socialist), as well as the everyday expectations of the people who inhabited the new order."[14]

The American and French Revolutions clarified these changes—in Europe often through the Napoleonic Code, which remained in force for decades and was widely disseminated. A "consequence of revolution," Geneviève Fraisse and Michelle

Perrot concluded, "was that the separation between public and private space became more pronounced: a careful distinction was drawn between private life and public life, between civil society and political society. Ultimately, it was through this distinction that women were kept out of politics and reduced to dependence in civil society."[15]

Writing in 1988, the feminist political theorist Carole Pateman maintained that the social contract, understood to be the ground on which the new republics were founded, was, in fact, a sexual contract. "Civil individuals form a fraternity because they are bound together by a bond as men. They share a common interest in upholding the original contract which legitimizes masculine right and allows them to gain material and psychological benefit from women's subjection. . . . The civil sphere gains its universal meaning in opposition to the private sphere of natural subjection and womanly capacities. The 'civil individual' is constituted within the sexual division of social life created through the original contract."[16] Pateman notes the exceptional quality of the sexual contract in the general world of contracts; it is understood not to be the result of equal parties agreeing to cooperate, but instead this contract is the confirmation of a relationship of unequals. Women, following the order of nature, *consent* to their subordination. "A woman agrees to obey her husband when she becomes a wife; what better way of giving public affirmation that men are sexual masters, exercising the law of male sex-right, in their private lives?"[17]

In his account of his travels in America, Alexis de Tocqueville referred to this supposedly natural subordination in a chapter called "How the Americans Understand the Equality of Man and Woman." In it he provided an example of the way in which the contrast between a claim for the equality of the sexes, on the one hand, and the hierarchical and unequal divisions of labor between them, on the other, were resolved by the liberal notion of individual consent. The division of labor, he said, followed "the great principle of political economy that dominates today's industry."[18] "Democratic equality" between men and women required adherence to "natural" divisions of labor between them. American women's "superiority," he suggested, was based on their willing and wise subordination to a husband's authority. An asymmetrical complementarity was the rule. "They believed that every association needs a leader in order to be effective and that the natural leader of the conjugal association was the man. Hence they did not deny him the right to direct his helpmate, and they believed that in the small society consisting of husband and wife, as in the larger political society, the purpose of democracy is to regulate and legitimate necessary powers and not to destroy all power."[19]

As in Tocqueville's comment, in the discourse and practice of modern Western secular nations, the justification for denying women citizenship rested on the marriage relationship, the ultimate embodiment of the private/public distinction, which in turn rested on, and confirmed, the naturalness of the difference of sex. Since the destiny of all women was thought to be marriage, no distinction was made between women who might by choice or circumstance remain single and those who became wives. The elimination of religion as the ground for politics required a new institutional foundation. Wrote one commentator, "the citizen is tied by marriage to the state, as the clergyman is by celibacy to the church."[20] Marriage provided for the state the children upon whom the future depended, and it confirmed the maleness required for the exercise of political power. It also embodied a natural hierarchy upon which other social distinctions could be based. "The family image came to figure hierarchy within unity," Anne McClintock writes. "Because the subordination of woman to man and child to adult were deemed natural facts, other forms of social hierarchy could be depicted in familial terms to guarantee social difference as a category of nature."[21] This was often the case in slaveholding and colonial discourses where "slaves" or "natives" were represented as childlike subjects at once dependent upon and in need of the rule provided by their masters.

Origin Stories

The relationship of marriage to the state was central for rethinking the bases of secular political rule. For Locke, Rousseau, and others, the alternative to absolutism rested on the consent of those who were subjected to patriarchal rule, sons to fathers, wives to husbands. Locke imagined that "twas easie, and almost natural for Children by a tacit and scarce avoidable consent to make way for the *Father's Authority and Government*."[22] Rousseau took the family to be the initial step out of the state of nature: "the first difference was established in the ways of life of the two Sexes, which until then had had but one."[23] The origin of secular politics, its very possibility, rested on monogamy. In Pateman's terms, the sexual contract made possible the social contract.

In *Totem and Taboo*, Freud offered a theory to account for these origin stories from a psychoanalytic perspective. In his interpretation (which I find most helpful for thinking about these questions of gender and politics), the primal father's power lay in his monopoly of all pleasure; lesser men eventually kill (and in Freud's version eat) him in order to gain the access that they have been consistently denied. By devouring the father figure, the men retrospectively become brothers. Freud says that in this way they "accomplished their identification with him, and each of them acquired a portion of his strength."[24] Coming into their own as adults required the sexual initiation that the father had forbidden them: an appropriate woman of their own. The brothers instituted a prohibition of incest to ensure that this woman would not be a mother or sister, all of whom had been game for the primal father's seductions. The rule of the sons then replaced the absolutism of the father, some form of fraternity overthrew the reign of the king, and modernity was born. In Freud's terms an "ideal father" replaced the primal father; it is he (or they—the sons acting collectively to achieve this ideal) whose actions must protect society from a return of excess. "In thus guaranteeing one another's lives, the brothers were declaring that no one of them must be treated by another as their father was treated by them all. They were precluding the possibility of a repetition of their father's fate."[25] There were nonetheless continuing rivalries among the brothers, and these were managed by assigning to each a smaller, tamer version of what they rebelled against: "The family was a restoration of the former primal horde and it gave back to fathers a large portion of their former rights. There were once more fathers, but the social achievements of the fraternal clan had not been abandoned."[26] The new regime stands for (in Joan Copjec's words) "the evacuation, or drying up, of excess enjoyment and thus for the possibility of pleasure's even apportionment."[27] The laws of marriage, in this vision, guarantee "pleasure's even apportionment," ensuring that each brother has his own woman and that no brother has more than one. In the realm of the psyche, shared political power depends on the disciplining of sexuality by marriage, the containment of desire within a socially beneficial familial unit. In the political realm, the idea of abstract individualism rests on a presumed sameness, whatever the social differences among men (and not all men, only those—usually white—whose higher rationality defined them as autonomous individuals). We might characterize this with the formula: one man, one woman; one man, one vote.

Whose sexuality is at issue in the wake of the parricide? There are two possibilities and they are related. The first, suggested by the work of French psychoanalyst Jacques Lacan, is that the danger of excess lies with the brothers, who compete among themselves in order that one of them will be able to exercise the slain father's power. Freud noted that the rivalry among the brothers continued after the father's death. "Each of them would have wished, like his father, to have all the women to himself."[28] This fantasy, the notion that his likeness to the father exempts one of the brothers from castration and so gives him access to all the women—Lacan calls it the "phallic exception"—is ever-present. The apparent claim to an individual man's uniqueness is actually a collective male fantasy—and therein, of course, lies the trouble. Since there is no single body that can act as the concrete referent for power—as the king's did when he was considered the divinely ordained occupant of the throne—the question of how to discern possession is an open and anxious one.[29] The emphasis on reason and (some) men's brains as the sign of this power, I suggest, is a displacement of that anxious question to the lofty heights of abstraction, a recognition that the penis is a poor substitute, though it remains the distinguishing feature of masculinity.[30] Indeed, masculinity (referring concretely to the sex of the primal father and symbolically to the phallus he wielded) remained the criterion that the founding brothers insisted upon. The French socialist-feminist Jeanne Deroin, who was prevented on the grounds of her sex from running for office during the Revolution of 1848, exposed the dilemma that men faced as they at once avowed and denied their bodies as justification for their exclusive power. Responding to Pierre-Joseph Proudhon's comment that women legislators made as much sense as male wet nurses, she asked, "and what organs are necessary for becoming a legislator?" Proudhon offered no response to her exposure of the phallic underpinnings of politics.[31]

The other possibility, the one seized on by early political theorists, is that women represent the danger of excess that the brothers now have to guard against. In this scenario, the appetites of the primal father are, in effect, attributed to women's provocation. She is Eve, the seductress, the initiator of the Fall. It is women who threaten to subvert men's rationality, to lure them off course. Rousseau warned in *Emile* that, unlike men, women could not control their "unlimited desires." It was only the imposition of modesty that prevented "the ruin of both [sexes]," otherwise women's lust would lead mankind to "perish by the means established for preserving it."[32] Hegel thought that women were driven by intrigue and particular interests, unfit for the universal mission of government. He warned that if "women hold the helm of government, the state is at once in jeopardy."[33] Marriage, for these authors, is not only the channeling by modesty of women's sexuality into restrained displays of affection but the institutionalization of the separation of spheres—the literal containment of women's unruly desire within the walls of the home.

The two possibilities are, of course, linked. Lacan points out that, in the realm of the unconscious, women's desire serves to confirm men's fantasy of possession of the phallus, both personally and politically. Without her, there is no proof of his potency. But the proof must remain indirect, at least at the level of public representation, where men's claim to equality rests on abstraction (on the presumed sameness of the brothers) and all sexuality is located concretely in women's bodies. Women's desire confirms men's possession of the phallus; that so-called private relation of familial sexual intimacy, in turn, establishes men's potency and so their right to political power.[34]

Judith Surkis shows how these ideas were implemented during France's July Monarchy (1830–48). In that moment of constitutional limits on the king, the new rulers wrestled with questions about how to ground the abstractions of law and sovereignty. For them, men's actual bodies represented "an obstacle to their accession to universality," as can be seen in political caricature and police enforcement of public "decency." While "administrative regulation of female prostitution [was] increasingly streamlined and rationalized in the 1830s," similar male behavior was deemed more "obscene." It was taken to violate a norm of discretion, applicable solely to the public display of male bodies. "In a simultaneously symbolic and practical sense, men's bodies were not supposed to be seen. In order to accede to the privileges of citizenship on the eve of the Revolution of 1848, men's bodies needed to become publicly invisible and in a sense, private."[35] At the same time, women's bodies were on public display, their explicit sexuality evidence of their incapacity for exercising the rights of citizens, and so for the need to keep them at home. Man's public legitimacy rested on the confinement of sexuality to the marital bed, where the desire of a woman awaited him. That desire, publicly understood to be femininity's defining trait and psychically the confirmation of men's unique possession of the phallus, disqualified her from membership in the body politic.

Indeterminacy

For many philosophers and political theorists, the translation of these psychic processes identified by Freud and Lacan took modern marriage to be a relationship of "ethical responsibility," not only between husband and wife but among men. It signaled a bounded relationship, legally protected from trespass: one man/one wife was a golden, unbreakable rule. Coveting a neighbor's wife was taboo. Divorce was rarely permitted (and if it was, the terms of the settlement gave greater advantage to men than to women); infidelity was both a moral and a legal crime. These were not mere remnants of religious teachings (as some of the language implies), but doctrines central to the conceptualization of the modern secular state and to which discourses of secularism implicitly and explicitly referred.

These doctrines addressed the transformation that "disenchantment" brought to the legitimation for political power. The loss of preeminent religious authority meant the loss of a transcendent affirmation for this power. Possession of the phallus, the symbol of the ruler's power, was no longer the prerogative of God's representative on earth. And, as the reign of kings (and the occasional queen) gave way to representative systems of government (parliaments, constitutional monarchies, republics, democracies), the physical body of the ruler as the incarnation of sovereignty was replaced by a set of disembodied abstractions: state, nation, citizen, representative, individual. Claude Lefort puts it this way: "the locus of power becomes an empty place . . . it is such that no individual and no group can be consubstantial with it—and it cannot be represented."[36] The impossibility of representation, he continues, leads to a permanent state of uncertainty: "The important point is that democracy is instituted and sustained by the dissolution of the markers of certainty. It inaugurates a history in which people experience a fundamental indeterminacy as to the basis of power, law and knowledge and as to the relations between *self* and *other* at every level of social life."[37]

The exercise of power, shorn of its external authorization, became self-legitimating. In Weber's terms, "Bureaucratic rule was not and is not the only variety of legal authority, but it is the purest . . . [T]he 'jurisdictional competency' . . . is fixed by *rationally established* norms, by enactments and decrees, and regulations, in such a manner that the legitimacy of the authority becomes the legality of the general rule, which is purposely thought out, enacted, and announced with formal correctness."[38] (This abstract, calculating force is what I take Foucault to mean by power.) There is, then, no outside affirmation of the laws men create. The circularity of the system is apparent: "modern power is immanent in the very relations that structure the social order."[39] Or, as Lefort puts it, "only the mechanisms of the exercise of power are visible, or only the men, the mere mortals, who hold political authority."[40] In the abstract, the impossibility of power's representation is clear. But for those who implemented the system, the question of *who* was charged with articulating and enforcing the decrees remained. For them, the very impossibility of representation called for decisive resolution.

The resolution chosen—an appeal to a natural sexual division of labor—rested on another uncertainty, that of the ultimate meaning of the difference of sex. Psychoanalytic theory has taught us that the conundrum of gendered identity revolves around the difference of sex. There is no clear fit between cultural explanations and phantasmatic theories of this difference, even in the face of normative regulation; no neat correlation in the course of a lifetime between individual perceptions and social laws. The meanings of our bodies and our desires cannot be restrained or pinned down, even as they are submitted to various forms of discipline and social regulation. Gender—the attribution of meaning to sexed bodies—is the implementation of the always imperfect attempt at discipline; it is the way cultures seek to bridge the relationship between the psychic and the social. Gender consists of historically specific articulations defining the male and female that aim to settle the indeterminacy associated with sexual difference by directing fantasy to some political or social end.[41] The more challenges there were to these articulations, the more adamant was the insistence on their immutability.

The emergence of modern nations brought with it a new insistence on the immutability of gender roles and the policing of sexual activity to keep them in place. On the one hand, the natural difference of sex was the referent that provided legitimation for men's political authority; on the other, men's political authority was evidence for nature's mandate. The difference of sex, in other words, is the key to the seeming resolution of the impossibility of representation that Lefort theorizes; without it, the illusion of certainty cannot be sustained. But it is not a definitive resolution since there is no stable meaning for the difference of sex—hence the repeated expressions of anxiety about whether the extension to women of education and various civil rights (divorce, inheritance of property, guardianship of children) would obliterate the lines of sexual difference and make women and men "the same."

This confusion of the sexes, according to one medical commentator, posed to the nation the terrifying danger of "moral anarchy."[42] In the wake of World War I, historian Mary Louise Roberts writes, "the blurring of the boundary between 'male' and 'female'—a civilization without sexes—served as a primary referent for the ruin of civilization itself."[43]

Suffrage: For and Against

In the struggles over the right to vote, the discursive frame of the separation of spheres operated to limit the kinds of arguments that were possible. Since the vote was at once a recognition and a confirmation of male public authority, women's suffrage movements were seen as particularly threatening. They were taken to deny women's childbearing function, the guarantee of the future of the family, the race, and the nation. But above all, they seemed to call into question men's dominant position in the family, as well as the very qualities that defined masculinity, especially those that equated access to political power with possession of the phallus. The French revolutionary Condorcet had, as early as 1791, refuted the logic that denied women the vote on the grounds of their maternity. "Why should individuals exposed to pregnancies and other passing indispositions be unable to exercise rights which no one has dreamed of withholding from persons who have the gout all winter or catch cold quickly?" he asked.[44] Condorcet saw no problem in extending formal equality to women—it would not affect either their physical or social roles, he thought. But his arguments went unheeded. The power of the secularist discourse prevailed; citizenship and femininity were taken to be antithetical, a violation not only of the gendered division of labor but also of the necessary identification of masculinity with power.

In France one could hear these arguments throughout the late eighteenth and nineteenth centuries. Olympe de Gouges was guillotined by the revolutionaries in 1793 "for having forgotten the virtues that belong to her sex."[45] When the Society of Revolutionary Republican Women was outlawed in 1793, they were deemed "impudent women who want to become men."[46] "To summon women concurrently with men in the virile functions would be only to annihilate feminine genius. . . . They must do things that men don't do," opined Ernest Legouvé in 1849, an advocate of women's education, but not of granting them the vote.[47] Another commentator in this period warned of the "hermaphrodism" that would result when women left the home for the public forum. Tocqueville granted that democracy meant equality for all people, but insisted that it did not require sameness: "There are people in Europe who, confounding together the different characteristics of the sexes, would make man and woman into beings not only equal but alike."[48] Labor leaders predicted that women who engaged in men's work (in the printing trades in this instance) "will be deformed by taking on the look, the voice, and the gross mannerisms of the men she associates with in the shop."[49] And confronted by two feminists who entered a polling place on election day in 1908 intending to vote, an official reported to the court that the scene produced in him an awful stillness, as if he had seen the Medusa—in a Freudian reading, an expression of the fear of castration. In this scenario, sharing the right to vote with women is taken as the loss of a defining characteristic of masculinity. A journalist commenting on the invasion of the voting place by Hubertine Auclert, one of the feminists, asked, "Is it our resignation as men that dame Hubertine asks of us? Let her say it frankly."[50]

In Belgium, political parties tended to agree on the woman question, even as they fought over the enfranchisement of workers in the nineteenth and early twentieth centuries. Eliane Gubin and her colleagues write of the debates about who should vote: "The conquest of political power symbolized, in the mentality of working class as in the bourgeois mentality, the appropriation of a virile space which would certainly have lost its prestige if citizenship had been shared with women."[51] (In Belgium, women were admitted to vote in local elections in 1920, but did not vote on the national level until 1948.)

In the United States John Adams confided to a male correspondent in 1776 that he thought women lacked the capacity for politics, saying, "their delicacy renders them unfit for practice and experience in the great businesses of life."[52] Faced with a renewed campaign for women's suffrage in the early twentieth century, former president Grover Cleveland said that female voting would overturn "a natural equilibrium so nicely adjusted to the attributes and limitations of both [women and men] that it cannot be disturbed without social confusion and peril."[53] Antisuffragists in 1918 charged feminists with advocating "non-motherhood, free love, easy divorce, economic independence for all women, and other demoralizing and destructive theories."[54]

In England, Tories and Liberals were of the same mind in reaction to John Stuart Mill's unsuccessful call for women's enfranchisement in 1867. The natural difference of the sexes "made men more capable of direct government and women more fitted for private influence," said one.[55] "The physical dependence of women on men, combined with their difference of organization is the justification of government by men," proclaimed another.[56] Allowing women to vote would result in their becoming more masculine, these opponents of suffrage insisted, thus blurring the natural boundaries between the sexes. In 1884, William Gladstone, then prime minister, urged the House of Commons not to endorse a bill extending suffrage to women on the grounds that "a permanent and vast difference of type has been impressed upon women and men respectively by the Maker of both. . . . I am not without the fear lest beginning with the State, we should eventually be found to have intruded into what is yet more fundamental and more sacred, the precinct of the family, and should dislocate, or injuriously modify, the relations of domestic life."[57] Others warned that a "sex war" would follow passage of such a bill, introducing "hysterical and spasmodic features," more characteristic of French and American politics than of the English parliamentary system. Scottish biologist Patrick Geddes summed up these objections when he argued in 1889 against extending voting rights to women by pointing to the different economies of cell metabolism: "the hungry, active cell becomes flagellate sperm, while the quiescent, well-fed one becomes an ovum."[58] It followed that women belonged in the private/

domestic sphere, men in the public/political realm: "what was decided among the prehistoric *Protoza* can not be annulled by act of parliament."[59]

Suffragists replied to these objections in a variety of ways, but (as I have shown elsewhere) had difficulty separating the demand for equality from the matter of the difference of sex.[60] Equality was a human right, some argued, and women were as human as men. But if equality either required or created sameness, then how could women qualify as citizens? How could they at once acknowledge the difference of their sex and yet refuse the idea that it mattered for their deportment and for their ability to engage in politics?[61]

Some insisted that the requirements for voting and engaging in politics had nothing to do with their bodies. Invoking Descartes's mind/body distinction, they claimed that there was "no sex in mind."[62] Others welcomed the masculine label, seeing it as merely a label and not in any way a danger to physical differences between women and men: "if to have a warm interest in great national and public concerns, and to wish to help in them with our own best work, is to be masculine, then let us be masculine, and be proud of being so. No virtue ought to be monopolised by either sex."[63] (Here "either sex" suggests that anatomical difference is not abolished, but that it is irrelevant for participation in politics.) Still others invoked the need for women's specific interests (children, family, health) to have national representation. In England, Millicent Fawcett replied to opponents of suffrage, "We do not want women to be bad imitations of men; we neither deny nor minimize the differences between men and women. The claim of women to representation depends to a large extent on those differences. Women bring something to the service of the state different from that which can be brought by men. Let this fact be frankly recognised and let due weight be given to it in the representative system of the country."[64] In the United States some suffragists distinguished themselves from the "perverse theories" of feminists (who began to organize as such early in the twentieth century). "The right to vote is not based on contrasts between the sexes nor on animosity of one sex against the other." Unlike feminists, these suffragists did not "wish to force womanly attributes on the man." Rather they sought "willing cooperation on the common ground—the Public Welfare."[65]

Some feminists took the notion of the complementarity of the sexes further, modeling their notion of the government of the state on the domestic household. The French socialist Jeanne Deroin thought women could bring a sense of order to "this large, badly administered household called the State."[66] She, and Hubertine Auclert a generation later, equated the "social" (family, children, welfare, hygiene) with women's interests—their experience qualified them to speak and act on these matters—matters for which men were considered to have little expertise and even less interest in pursuing. The problem was that the invocation of the social, even as it expanded the possibilities for women's action, reinscribed the notion of separate and unequal—masculine and feminine—spheres.

The emergence of the idea of the "social" in the nineteenth century provided, writes Denise Riley, "an arena for domesticated intervention."[67] It was "a blurred ground between the old public and private, voiced as a field for intervention, love, and reform" by people of all political stripes, but particularly by women. It opened the way for "some women to enter upon the work of restoring other, more damaged women, to a newly conceived sphere of grace."[68] These middle- and upper-class women became social workers, factory inspectors, philanthropists, and reformers engaged in the moral and physical uplift of the women of the working class and their families; some took up the cause of reform in the colonies as well. The social was a feminized sphere, distinctly separate from the political. As one opponent of the vote for women argued, representing the social in Parliament would compromise the "broader" view of politics that men must attend to. "The character of the legislation of a woman-chosen Parliament would be the increased importance which would be given to questions of a quasi social or philanthropic character (viewed with regard to the supposed interests, or the partisan bias of special classes, rather than to broader considerations of the public weal) in excess of the great constitutional and international issues which the legislature was empanelled to try."[69] Women would reduce the universal reach of politics, introducing disparate and divisive particularities that didn't represent the general interest.

This view of the social cordoned off women from the masculine worlds of politics and assumed further that public attention to welfare issues drew upon a natural inclination or sensibility of women. The difference of sex, still understood as an asymmetric relationship based upon inherent natural differences—men on top, women subordinate in some way to them—and necessarily organized in separate spheres remained, well into the twentieth century, the dominant model for representing gender in modern Western nation-states.

After the Vote

Despite suffragists' hopes that equality in all realms would follow from the extension of the franchise, this was not the case. In most countries, women were admitted to citizenship not as individuals but as a collective social category. Abstraction from that category meant it might be irrelevant for purposes of voting—but the category itself remained a feature of civil society and social life. Although women were now entitled to vote, the perception of them as what Simone de Beauvoir called "the second sex" did not disappear. Indeed, it is significant that de Beauvoir wrote her book in 1949, some five years after women in France had won the political rights of citizens. "[A]bstract rights . . . have never sufficed to assure to woman a definite hold on the world," she wrote, "true equality between the two sexes does not exist even today."[70] Instead, the granting of citizenship to women confirmed their status as a distinctive and definable natural social category. Women, de Beauvoir argued, even if they gained a measure of economic independence, could never achieve the status of fully autonomous individuals as long they as they continued to serve as "others" to men. While men could conceive of themselves as self-created individuals, women were doomed to a life of "immanence," to the endless repetition of feminine functions—maternity, certainly, but the chief of which was the confirmation of men's masculinity and with it their sovereignty. (Here we find a philosopher's version of Freud and Lacan's psychoanalytic insight.)

> The advantage man enjoys . . . is that his vocation as a human being in no way runs counter to his destiny as a male. Through the identification of the phallus and transcendence, it turns out that his social and spiritual successes endow him with a virile presence. He is not divided. Whereas it is required of woman that in order to realize her femininity she must make herself object and prey, which is to say that she must renounce her claim as a sovereign subject.[71]

Even as they gained the right to vote, women were marginalized in political processes; for example, political parties rarely nominated women for elective office except in districts where they knew they would lose. In the United States a bitter editorial in the *Woman Citizen* in 1922 noted the lack of change since passage of the Nineteenth Amendment to the

Constitution: "It is clear that the barriers in the way of women being elected to any political office are almost insurmountable. The dominant political parties do not nominate women for political office if there is any real chance for winning. Political offices are the assets of the political machine. In general, they are too valuable to be given to women."[72] As late as 2000, even after passage of the French law on parity—which sought to ensure equal access for women and men to political office—the same kinds of subterfuge existed. The major parties paid fines rather than propose women for seats in winnable districts; they refused to put women at the head of lists in contests based on proportional representation; leaders professed not to be able to find suitable women candidates and suggested that although women might know something about local matters, they were not qualified to address the larger issues of national politics. If anything, the law—designed to eliminate sex as a serious consideration—made the issue all the more visible. One woman candidate for a seat in the National Assembly noted that she had been advised to run as a woman. Yet, she concluded, "if one has to be a woman, it's at the risk of not being political."[73]

The question of whether invoking womanhood or femininity was a disabling factor for politics haunted women's advocates in the wake of successful suffrage campaigns. Denise Riley notes that there are always risks involved in calling attention to the situation of women: "the very iteration of the afflicted category serves, maliciously, not to undo it but to underwrite it."[74] Nancy Cott has provided detailed evidence for the extreme difficulty—if not the impossibility—of avoiding this risk in the United States in the 1920s and '30s. (Her insights apply more generally across the nations of Europe, albeit with different timing and in different specific articulations.) Was there a woman's vote to appeal to? Some argued it was unavoidable, others that it was a trap. Male politicians deemed such an appeal the onset of a sex war. Feminists on one side of the debate pointed out that divisions of class and race made any notion of a singular appeal to "women" both illusory and impractical; on the other side, some argued that a universal experience of womanhood (based on maternity) overrode other differences and gave women a common interest not only in children and health but in matters of war and peace.

On the issue of protective legislation, there was similar discord among feminists, some insisting that women's vulnerability required legal protection from employers who would abuse it, others claiming that such legislation would simply reaffirm sex-segregated labor markets and the inequality they enshrined. The 1930s saw the rise of ideas of companionate marriage among sociologists and psychologists: women and men were depicted as (among other things) enjoying the same rights to sexual fulfillment (but always contained within heterosexual marriages—lesbianism was considered abnormal and unfeminine). Yet, Cott points out, whereas feminists had viewed sexual liberation as a triumph over the old unequal divisions of labor (in families, but also in sexual partnerships more generally), it was not the vision offered in the postsuffrage era. Rather, women continued to be assigned the burden of child-rearing and household management, even if they also earned wages outside the home. The courts ratified this view: even if working wives were legally on a par with single women, judges nonetheless continued to grant husbands "the common law right to his wife's services in the home" well into the twentieth century.[75] And it wasn't until 1975 that the US Supreme Court struck down state laws that either exempted women from jury service entirely or required special training for them.

There were new branches of science and pedagogy that gave women new professional opportunities—home economics, maternal and child welfare—even as they reproduced stereotypical representations of separate spheres for women and men. If some of those spheres were now also public, they nonetheless were understood to follow from the inherent nature of womanhood. Maternalism could expand women's sphere, but only within certain limits, as Seth Koven and Sonya Michel have shown. "Maternalist women put an unmistakable stamp on emerging welfare administrations," they conclude in a survey of the United States, France, Germany, and Great Britain. "[B]y identifying and insisting on issues of gender-based needs, women challenged the male monopoly on public discourse and opened it up to discussions of private values and well-being."[76] Nevertheless, they conclude, "for female activists and clients alike, the political process that culminated in the passage of protective and welfare legislation for women and children functioned, in an exaggerated fashion, as a Weberian 'iron cage': they found dissonance between means and ends, their own motives and ultimate policy outcomes."[77] This led some feminists to condemn maternalism as a strategy for achieving equality. The French psychiatrist Madeleine Pelletier warned against celebrating maternity as a feminist strategy: "Never will childbirth give women a title of social importance. Future societies may build temples to maternity, but they will do so only to keep women locked inside."[78]

In new depictions of the gendered division of labor, men were portrayed as producers, women as consumers. In the area of professional employment, the 1920s saw a brief increase and then a marked decline. "By the 1930s," Cott notes, "professionally employed women were a declining proportion of all employed women, as well as a declining proportion of all professional workers."[79] This was, only in part, a result of the Great Depression; other factors included the employer practice of dismissing women who married or became pregnant, thus making the "home versus work" conflict particularly acute for white-collar and professional women.

Overall, Cott concludes that the suffragist and feminist dream of some kind of perfect equality—at work, at home, in politics—was unrealized in the course of the 1920s. "Advertising collapsed the emphasis on women's range and choice to individual consumerism; the social-psychological professions domesticated Feminism's assertion of sexual entitlement to the arena of marriage. Feminist defiance of the sexual division of labor was swept under the rug. Establishing new formalisms, these adaptations disarmed Feminism's challenges in the guise of enacting them."[80] Hester Eisenstein's work on the United States adds another dimension to this history. She suggests that in the 1960s women were often hired in some jobs (redefined as women's jobs) in an effort to undercut white male unionizing efforts. They became an alternative, cheaper labor supply when men demanded higher wages. Here the motivation was not a liberal secular commitment to women's rights but an attempt to defeat the labor movement and exploit women.[81]

Writing about Europe in the period 1945 to 1975, the French sociologist Rose-Marie Lagrave echoes Cott's and Eisenstein's conclusions. Even as the number of women professionals and wage earners increased, she points out, so did the sexual division of labor in the workplace. "The economic theory of the dual labor market (primary and secondary) legitimated the sexual division of labor by portraying it as a natural part of the economy."[82] Despite the fact that women gained access to education and jobs, and are protected by law, she concludes, they are "deceived by their own triumph[;] they rarely protest the hidden forms of inequality and the rampant sexism they face. The status quo has the appearance of legitimacy, all the more so in that its reality is covered by a cloak of rhetoric proclaiming equality between the sexes."[83]

A Repeating Pattern

The persistence of gender asymmetry in the face of political transformation (revolution, constitutional amendments, laws enfranchising women) is a striking feature of modern nation-states—and not only in the West. As new nations embraced modernity in the wake of the dissolution of the Ottoman Empire, similar patterns emerged to those I have been describing, even in places where Western Protestant notions of religion as a matter of private individual conscience did not exist. In Turkey, the Kemalist revolution in the 1920s insisted on the visibility of women in public space. They were urged to shed their veils, recruited as teachers and public servants in the early years of the republic, and granted the right to vote in 1934. Modeled on the *laïcité* of the French republic, the Turkish nation imported civil and criminal codes from Italy and Switzerland, which, though they granted inheritance and other new rights to women, also included asymmetrical treatment of women and men in cases of divorce and adultery; rape was considered the violation of a male property-holder's right. (It wasn't until 2001 that those codes, which had punished women's adultery more severely than men's, were overturned—and then by critics of the secular party.) In its early years, the Kemalist regime endorsed an ideal of companionate marriage in which the sexes had complementary roles; while men participated in markets and politics, the primary duty of women was motherhood. Nilüfer Göle writes, "Women as modern housemakers, consumers of new hygienic products, and parents embodied the pedagogical civilizing mission in matters of modern living."[84]

In this regard, anthropologist Jenny White notes that "the gendered division of labor in Turkey was comparable to that in Europe."[85] And sociologist Deniz Kandiyoti remarks that the "double standard of sexuality and a primarily domestic definition of the female role" left Turkish women "emancipated but unliberated."[86] They may have been granted voting rights, but this did not translate into social or economic equality.

In Iraq, according to Sara Pursley's research, attention to women's domestic role in securing the nation's future led to a new emphasis on girls' education, one that intensified the differences between the sexes. The policies elaborated bore the influence of Western teaching. In the 1930s, she notes that a group of US-trained Iraqi educators, "influenced by the pragmatist school of pedagogy associated with the philosopher John Dewey," decided that "the Iraqi public school curriculum was not sufficiently attentive to preparing the future roles of women and men. They recommended that female students from the primary through the secondary levels, and in many cases at the college level, be required to take courses in home economics."[87] As a result, from 1932–58 the Iraqi public school experience was reshaped around gender difference. Pursley writes:

> In what might seem a paradox, the differentiation of the public school curriculum by sex was paralleled by the expansion of coeducation in Iraq at the primary and postsecondary levels during this same period. A girl entering . . . school in 1926 was certain to study in a school populated only by other girls, but she was most equally certain to study the same material and follow the same course of schooling as a boy at her grade level. A girl entering the system in 1956 might or might not find herself in a coeducational . . . school, but either way she would follow a mandatory female-only curriculum for about 20% of her time there.[88]

As in Turkey, the mixing of the sexes in public space—on the streets or in the schools—did not signal the end of the hierarchical sexual division of labor and might even intensify it.

While Turkey became an independent nation with the dissolution of the Ottoman Empire, Lebanon and Syria were placed under French mandate at the end of World War I. Although the Syrian congress granted the vote to women in 1920, three months before the arrival of French occupying forces, neither its constitution nor Lebanon's (negotiated under French tutelage) permitted women's right to vote. Feminist appeals to republican principles fell on deaf ears; their impassioned arguments that local religious authorities were violating the teaching of the Qur'an were ignored. The French High Commission preferred to leave the question of women's status in the hands of religious leaders since, according to personal status law, matters of family, marriage, women, and children belonged in the hands of those leaders. The opposition of these religious figures to women's political rights was not all that different from that of secular politicians in the metropole—they predicted that chaos would follow from any breach of the natural division of labor between the sexes. In this context, feminists sometimes tied their appeals to that division of labor, arguing that motherhood needed to be given political representation: "In motherhood a woman has the power to inspire manliness and strength in her sons to build a new nation," a Lebanese (female) union leader reminded an audience of college women.[89] The appeal to equal political rights thus rested not only on women's difference, but on the notion that it was this difference that made women a collectivity—not a collection of autonomous (male) individuals who, by definition, embodied citizenship.

In this connection it is instructive to look at India, where British imperial rule intersected with local politicians and feminists in debates about women's suffrage in the 1920s and '30s. There, Mrinalini Sinha offers a compelling analysis of the tensions in these debates, arguing that they did not follow exactly the lines of equality and difference evident among British feminists (and elsewhere in the West as well). Instead, Sinha shows that women were identified with communal interests—whether those of religious minorities (mainly Muslims) and depressed classes, or of the unified national body as a whole. In 1932, she writes, the British prime minister Ramsay MacDonald saw "women only as a plurality of collectivities nestled safely within various discrete bodies politic. His plan was to confirm these supposedly discrete political units as naturally separate communal electorates, asserting once again that women belonged only to their communities."[90] Against this vision of a religiously and economically divided country was Gandhi's nationalist vision of a unitary political community, epitomized in "the artificial transcendence of women over other social relations and identities."[91] They were the women of the nation, not representatives of Hindu or Muslim or other groupings, and in this identity they were evidence that unity was possible. "This, in effect, merely prioritized the collective contours of a reconstituted community—a unitary national community—over other political imaginations of community. Thus was the citizenship of women held hostage to competing conceptions of community."[92] In this instance, "women as a group did not lose in any simple way to men as a group. Sexual difference did not substitute for equality. The context of reinstated communal patriarchies rather than sexual difference per se, trumped the recognition of women's autonomy."[93] Nonetheless, as Sinha herself demonstrates, women were not conceived as autonomous and instead increasingly identified with "the social"—that is with a realm of concern, interest, and expertise that was said to be theirs alone. "[B]y narrowing the scope of women's collective agency to a circumscribed domain of the social, [the suffrage debate] also recast the collectivity constituted by women as 'natural' or pre-political."[94] With the ascendancy of the nationalist vision, this collective agency of women was "reoriented to usher in a unitary national political imagination whose abstract citizen was by default Hindu, upper caste, and male."[95]

Sinha argues convincingly for the need to take historical specificity and political contingency into account when thinking about women's claims for political rights. There is no question that her approach illuminates the Indian case in new and important ways. Still, it seems to me that the story I have been telling about gender asymmetry in modern nations resonates with her accounts: the identification of women with the social, even as it eventually won them the right to vote, did not dispute the naturalized explanation for their difference and the disqualifications and discriminations that followed from it.

The Political Effects of Gender Representation

It is important to note that the representation of the difference of women from men as an explanation for hierarchies of social and political organization is an idealized representation that doesn't necessarily correspond to the actual practices and beliefs of all women and men. It was a representation, moreover, that was challenged by legions of feminists and their supporters, who dismissed its premises as ill-founded and unjust. Dozens of books and articles have been written insisting on the agency of those who refused to live by the discriminatory rules imposed by emergent nation-states and who—at least in their own lives—exemplified alternative conceptions of the ways differences of sex might or might not be relevant to the conduct of social and political life. The very existence of feminist movements testifies to the inability of those who upheld the normative view of things to enforce its premises and to impose it as an uncontested way of life.

Nonetheless, it is equally important to recognize that these idealized representations (these discourses) did provide the standards for behavior—the dominant cultural norms—for inhabitants of secularizing states. Along with laws that made religion a matter of private individual conscience, that made contracts between individuals the rule for market negotiations, and that made abstraction the ground for the theory of formal political equality, these notions of difference based on sex were fundamental to the conceptualization of political modernity, and so to the formation of secular subjects, whatever the local variations. They sought to resolve what Lefort referred to as the indeterminacy of democracy—its abstractions (the individual, rights, nations, representation)—by grounding them in a seemingly concrete referent: the visible, sexed bodies of women and men. That those bodies themselves inevitably bore indeterminate meanings posed a recurring interpretive and practical dilemma for the architects of nations. There could be no uncertainty about gender (the meanings attributed to those bodies) if the social order were to remain intact, hence the ferocity with which national leaders policed the boundaries of sexual difference and invoked Nature as a guarantee that those boundaries would remain in place. At the same time, in an argument that was entirely tautological, they claimed that social and political organization demonstrated the truth of Nature's laws. The need for this double argument suggests that there was a double indeterminacy (of gender and politics) at the very heart of the discourse of secularism.

The indeterminacy of gender might be seen as doubling the value of Lefort's vision of democracy, for it leaves space for debate about "what is legitimate and illegitimate—a debate which is necessarily without any guarantor and without any end."[96] The debate, of course, doesn't take place in a vacuum but rather in the context of the pragmatic and changing demands of economy, demography, and politics—domestic and international. What is startling—and dismaying—for those of us whose goal is some form of equality (gender, racial, class) is the persistence of inequality despite changing contexts and decades of endless debate. So, for example, although those who opposed women's suffrage sought to protect the equation of citizenship with masculinity, the extension of the vote to women did not entirely invalidate the equation. Instead, it simply moved the question of men's power to another plane—as politicians, party leaders, officeholders, and guardians of the law in the political realm, as masters of markets, economies, and science elsewhere. It seems to matter less precisely where power is wielded than who wields it; the phallus (equated however mistakenly with the penis) entitles men to that right. Ultimately, Lacan reminds us, the guarantee of the phallus is the woman—de Beauvoir described her as "object and prey"—enabling man's transcendence at the expense of her own. At the end of the long struggle for women's citizenship, the dilemma captured in the title of de Beauvoir's pathbreaking book remained: women continued to be "the second sex."

CHAPTER FOUR

From the Cold War to the Clash of Civilizations

SECULARISM AS A POLITICAL discourse was eclipsed by the Cold War, although its traces and effects were not. The relationship of the state to religion was reformulated as the Soviet Union came to represent, not the embodiment of secularism as it had been defined in the nineteenth-century anticlerical campaigns but the home of what was derided as godless atheism.[1] The Christian elements always present in the secularism discourse now came to the fore as the American version of it (state neutrality defined as the protection of religion from state intervention) was increasingly emphasized. In France another notion had long prevailed—the protection of individuals and the state from the claims of religious communities. But even in France at this Cold War moment there was renewed attention to the rights of private religious conscience, something the Soviets were said to deny. It is important to note that the Soviets never entirely banned religion, even if under Stalin's reign some clergy were persecuted; the Soviet leaders not only tolerated but worked with Orthodox leaders to implement the revolution. The point is that in the Manichean scheme of Cold War polemics, the Soviets were represented as the antithesis of religious freedom in the Christian democratic West.[2]

Although Western leadership fell to the United States in the immediate postwar years (the late 1940s and the 1950s), the religious reply to communism articulated there extended to transatlantic partnerships and European integration.[3] Cold War polemics depicted the Soviets as atheists and materialists who lacked sensitivity to the necessary—even natural—spiritual dimension of human existence. Theirs was said to be a "fanatic, soulless communism."[4] The focus on religion displaced attention from Marxism's critique of capitalism—a critique to which many Europeans had long been sympathetic. One historian put it this way: in the Cold War context "religion became discursively associated in Western popular culture with 'liberty,' 'democracy,' and 'Western civilization,' and held in sharp contradistinction to the amalgam of 'atheism, barbarism, and totalitarianism' that was communism."[5] The Soviets were represented as collapsing the public/private distinction, moving to a conceptual scheme of (unnatural) gender nondifferentiation. Interestingly, although certain aspects of Western discourse remained committed to separate spheres (to spatially distinct arenas for women and men), there was a blurring of the sharp differentiation of public and private in the realms of religion and sex, particularly.

In the immediate postwar period, two distinct themes emerged: one was the importance of Christianity as the common ground of the (secular) Western powers, the other was the difference between the Soviet and Western treatment of women. There was a connection between the two themes; they were organized around the notion of freedom of choice, whether the reference was to individual religious belief (or nonbelief) and practice or to American women's ability to choose among a vast array of consumer goods as they opted to care for their husbands and children. In place of equality, there was now talk of freedom; the liberal notion of choice—in the family, the market, and politics—was offered as the answer to the Soviet state's purported denial of the rights of individual self-determination.

On the Western side, liberal democracy was represented as synonymous with individual choice; Soviet authoritarianism's compulsory system provided the negative contrast. Spokesmen for the West took freedom of choice and the objects of that choice to be universal—left on their own, they presumed, all individuals would exercise their freedom in the same way. But, as Foucault's analysis of liberalism points out, freedom and its objects are produced in specific circumstances: "[W]e should not think of freedom as a universal which is gradually realized over time, or which undergoes quantitative variations, greater or lesser drastic reductions, or more or less important periods of eclipse. It is not a universal which is particularized in time and geography. . . . Freedom is never anything other—but this is already a great deal—than an actual relation between governors and governed."[6] He goes on, "Liberalism is not acceptance of freedom; it proposes to manufacture it constantly, to arouse it and produce it, with, of course [the system] of constraints and the problems of cost raised by this production."[7] But this doesn't necessarily assume a top-down relationship from the governors to the governed. Instead, there are exchanges in which, by invoking abstract principles (equality, freedom, liberty), some of the governed demand change, which, when it is granted, comes with regulatory strings attached. So freedom isn't unconditional but qualified, its meanings brought into existence through policies and laws that at once grant and regulate it.

The objects of freedom produced in Western Cold War rhetoric that I want to explore in this chapter are religion and sex.

They are not the only ones, of course, but they are crucial for my purposes. The shape each took had profound implications for the discourse of secularism when it reemerged at the end of the twentieth century. Religious freedom and women's sexual freedom were presented as universal, though in the case of women, the meaning of freedom—women's presumed choices—changed between the 1950s and the decades following the 1960s from an emphasis on the virtues of home and family to a call for bodily autonomy and the fulfillment of sexual desire.

The celebration of freedom of religion quickly became an endorsement of Christianity. As the industrialist and diplomat Myron Taylor put it to US president Harry Truman, "The cause of Communism versus Christianity and Democracy transcends minor differences in Christian creeds. It is the *great issue* of the future and thus of today."[8] Christianity became more explicitly tied to democracy than it had been earlier, preparing the way not only for the emergence of politicized Protestant evangelicalism but for the current argument that locates the founding premises of secular democracy in Judeo-Christian values.

The woman question followed a different trajectory, from the 1950s' insistence that the home was the nation's front line against communist subversion to the explosion of the feminist challenge to that domestic ideology from the 1960s and 1970s on. In the process, the notion of choice was detached (or perhaps extended) from its market definitions and used to formulate demands for emancipation: legal, economic, political and, especially, sexual. In a way parallel to the attachment of Christianity to democracy, sexual freedom was produced as a democratic right of individuals of both sexes. Sexual freedom was a new concept in the realm of rights—which heretofore were political (a question of citizenship, of voting for and serving as representatives of the people) and economic (the right to subsistence, to a job and a living wage, perhaps to education as a means of access to paid labor). Novel (and controversial) as it was, sexual freedom—no longer a private matter—was increasingly referred to as a founding premise of secular democracy. The apparent contradiction between traditional Christian precepts and sexual liberation was not a contradiction in the reformulated secularism discourse. Instead, sexual liberation served to confirm the secularity of Christianity and, by the 1990s, international campaigns to end violence against women brought liberal feminists and Christian activists together in improbable alliances. The contrast with Muslims secured the compatibility of the two.

Freedom of Religion

In March 1946, British prime minister Winston Churchill delivered a speech at Westminster College in Fulton, Missouri, in which he coined the phrase "iron curtain" to refer to the nations under Russian domination. In it he called for an Anglo-American alliance to prevent the spread of communism in the rest of the world, and he made an explicit connection between Christianity and democracy. "Except in the British Commonwealth and in the United States where Communism is in its infancy, the Communist parties or fifth columns constitute a growing challenge and peril to Christian civilization. These are somber facts for anyone to have to recite on the morrow of a victory gained by so much splendid comradeship in arms and in the cause of freedom and democracy, but we should be most unwise not to face them squarely while time remains."[9] Two years later, British foreign secretary Ernest Bevin, seeking to downplay the Labor Party's socialist tendencies in order to secure an alliance with the United States, offered a plan: "We cannot hope successfully to repel Communism only by disparaging it on material grounds . . . and must add a positive appeal to Democratic and Christian principles, remembering the strength of Christian sentiment in Europe. We must put forward a rival ideology to Communism."[10]

The equation of "freedom and democracy" with "Christian civilization" consolidated the anticommunist alliance. Historian Samuel Moyn notes that freedom of religion soon became the organizing principle against communism. It was internationalized and Europeanized, he writes. "Soon enough, the Cold War featured a saturation of politics by Christianity in noncommunist Europe as much as transatlantically in a common project uniting 'Western' politicians and churches."[11] Important players in constructing the alliance were the World Council of Churches (founded in 1948 in Amsterdam), consisting of various Protestant denominations, and the Vatican, as well as numerous political leaders—those responsible for the increasing prominence of Christian Democratic parties in many noncommunist European countries (Italy, Germany, Austria).

The blending of religion and politics in this period is sometimes depicted as primarily an American phenomenon and, indeed, there is evidence for this in the 1950s. President Eisenhower considered it prudent to begin regular church attendance, and he defined God as essential to "the most basic expression of Americanism. Without God, there could be no American form of government, nor an American way of life."[12] In 1953 "under God" was added to the pledge of allegiance to the flag, and "in God we trust" was printed on all US currency after 1954, becoming the motto of the nation in 1956. But the movement was, from the beginning, international. As early as 1939, the Canadian prime minister Mackenzie King, referring to both fascism and communism, warned of "the forces of evil . . . loosed in the world in a struggle between the pagan conception of a social order which ignores the individual and is based upon the doctrine of might, and a civilization based upon the Christian conception of the brotherhood of man with its regard for the sanctity of contractual relations [and] the sacredness of human personality."[13] King's oration set the "forces of evil" against those of Christian civilization—pagan (primitive, polytheistic) versus civilized (monotheistic, but Christian above all). Notably, capitalism and individualism are identified in decidedly religious terms: contractual relations are *sanctified*; individual humans are *sacred*. In this way the ideological presumptions of capitalism are redefined as religious concepts, and the crusade against communism is not about competing economic and political systems but about universal moral and religious principles (good versus evil), backwardness versus progress. King's successor, Louis Saint Laurent, reiterated these ideas, stressing the Hebrew and Greek origins of Christianity, whose "very essence is freedom."[14]

Article 18 of the United Nations Universal Declaration of Human Rights (1948) was about "freedom of thought, conscience and religion" and the right "in public or private" to manifest one's belief.[15] In the debates leading up to the declaration, Soviet proposals defending the rights of "free thinkers" (that is, nonbelievers) were rejected. But the push to include God as *the source* of the rights of religious conscience was also defeated (not surprisingly) by the arguments of the French delegate, who warned that "law could have no other source than the will of the people."[16] Still, in the European context, religious freedom predominated. Moyn argues that "in certain respects Western Europeans in the Cold War years went much farther in muddying the line between publicly dominant Christianity and political life than Americans have ever done."[17] He offers as compelling evidence for this assertion the European Convention on Human Rights, enacted in 1950.[18] In the deliberations leading up to its passage, Christian Democrats played a pivotal role. Many speeches, Moyn points out, equated Western civilization with Christianity. The Irish delegate insisted, for example, that "We must make it clear that our concepts of human dignity and human rights are something different from what we see in Eastern Europe. . . . An effort is being made there to put out the light of the Church—not only of one church but of almost all churches. . . . We here in this Council of Europe can be a rallying base and a beacon light to men and women struggling against persecution of that kind."[19] To combat domestic socialism, Moyn suggests, the convention's treaty dropped many of the references to social and economic rights in the UN declaration but retained the statement on religious freedom, adding, however, the possibility for state power to limit that freedom when "necessary in a democratic society, in the interests of public safety, for the protection of public order, health or morals, or for the protection of the rights and freedoms of others."[20] This provision, Moyn points out, has today become the basis for the restriction of the rights of Muslims in the secular Christian nations of Western Europe.

Moyn maintains that the European Convention is a document intending to marginalize secularism in general—"the rejection of God and the Gospel in the sphere of social and political life" by Europeans, which Catholic philosopher Jacques Maritain concluded in 1951 had led to the "theoretical atheism of the Soviet Union."[21] I think Moyn too readily accepts the idea that secularism was somehow antithetical to religion, when, in fact, there was long a Christian component to the concept. At least some of those who attacked Soviet atheism assumed that Western secularism was not what the Russians were practicing precisely because it lacked a religious component. The distinction between atheism and secularism thus mattered, and it's one Moyn doesn't recognize. He tends to read the word atheism as synonymous with secularism—even though it wasn't in the political discourse of those years. And he often substitutes the word *secularism* when referring to a text that didn't use the word at all.[22] I think, in fact, that Dianne Kirby's different characterization of the US instrumentalization of religion in the Cold War is a better interpretation that can be extended to instances like the European Convention: "The cultivation of popular perceptions about U.S. moral leadership and benign use of power meant that religious values were increasingly represented in secular forms. It reflected a process of assimilation and translation of a religious system of values into secular ethics."[23] Kirby discerns "a similar process in Europe with the electoral success of Christian Democracy, a postwar phenomenon that remained a significant force in European politics for the rest of the century."[24] Those secular ethics had to do with political notions of freedom and democracy, and the practices associated with them (voting, separation of powers, toleration of diverse political views, freedom of the press), now seen as the inevitable legacy of Christianity but not the direct implementation of that religion—which would have been theocracy, not democracy, in the eyes of these politicians. The Christian and the democratic secular became synonymous in Cold War rhetoric in opposition to what was decried as Soviet atheism. This prepared the ground in the new century for the rejection of Islam as an unacceptable religion because theocratic and undemocratic—but not before Islam was mobilized as a religious force against the Soviets.

ISLAM IN THE COLD WAR

In the anticommunist campaigns the Russians were often described as part of the "Asiatic hordes." Secretary of the Navy James Forrestal thought that the Soviets were "essentially

Oriental in their thinking." Secretary of State Dean Acheson added that "the threat they posed to Europe" was comparable to "that which Islam had posed centuries before."[25] Orientalist images abounded in these barely veiled evocations of Christian versus Muslim crusades. A poster for the French anticommunist group Paix et Liberté depicted a dark-skinned, long-nosed Ottoman-looking man wearing a fez and armed with bloodied swords in his hands and teeth, dancing to music played on balalaikas by complicit European statesmen.[26] An anti-Bolshevik German poster depicted a similar "Asiatic" type, while an ad for a Paramount film warned that a Russian victory in the next war would lead to the sterilization of many of America's men and the rape of its women.[27] In the image a tiny, ravished woman lies cowering beneath a huge boot, and the text reads, "In case the Communists should conquer, our women would be helpless beneath the boots of the Asiatic Russians." Some scholars saw a potential link between Soviet rule and Islam. Bernard Lewis, for example, worried in 1954 that the appeal of authoritarianism "might prepare the intellectually and politically active groups [in the Muslim world] to embrace Communist principles and methods of government."[28]

A certain continuity from the Cold War to the clash of civilizations can surely be detected in these Orientalist themes, which likened Russian communism to militant Islam as forms of "Oriental despotism." But the path wasn't a direct one; polemics were one thing, strategic calculations quite another. Western powers, led by the United States, hoped to make Muslims a subversive force within the Soviet bloc—the critique of state-imposed atheism seemed a likely rallying point for any religious group. They also sought to counter the growing anticolonial, pan-Islamic nationalist movements in the Middle East (many of which were inspired by some form of socialism), and so they appealed to Muslim conservatives to join a

Christian anticommunist crusade on the moral high ground of religious freedom. The United States sought out Saudi Arabia, the home of ultraconservative Wahhabism, hoping to gain an ally against the Egyptian leader Gamal Abdul Nasser's bid to organize a Pan-Arab movement that was opposed to Western intervention in the emerging nations of the Arab world. The West's anti-leftism led it to support such authoritarian forms of political Islam against reformist (and secular) ones. In the process, liberal alternatives were suppressed as dangerously close to Soviet projects. Kirby writes that "the support of America and its allies in the region, most notably Saudi Arabia, helped create a situation in which otherwise unpopular and unrepresentative versions of Islam were able, over time, to secure a power and influence they otherwise would have been unlikely to attain."[29]

The USSR's participation in the Afghan civil war (1979–89) brought this process to a head. Within Afghanistan, opposition to the Soviets came from the mujahideen, radical Islamic fighters who, in the nineteenth century, had protested the rule of the "infidel" British colonizer of their lands. Cold War logic led the United States and Saudi Arabia to support these freedom fighters (among them the future Osama bin Laden) in their international call to arms, directing aid and weapons to them through neighboring Pakistan. This is not the place to rehearse the entire history of current conflicts in the Middle East. But it is important to note the complex relationship of the West to Islam, particularly the role played by Cold War, religiously driven, strategic policy initiatives. Kirby puts it succinctly: "In the portrayal of the Afghan War as an international jihad, bringing together volunteers from Muslim populations all over the world, there are resonances of Truman's international anti-communist religious front concept. The legacy of the religious cold war lingers around the 'Global

War on Terror.' It is presented as an extremist religious challenge to the legitimacy of the modern international system, a system designated as separate from, and yet the defender of, religion."[30]

Another way of putting this, perhaps, is that in the discourse of secularism that reemerged after the fall of communism in 1989, and more strongly after the attacks on the World Trade Center in New York City in 2001, Islam became an "extremist religious challenge" to a "modern international system" that was now understood to be democratic *and* Christian. It was in this context that political scientist Samuel Huntington, popularizer of the idea of a clash of civilizations,[31] insisted in 1993 that "historically, there has been a strong correlation between Western Christianity and democracy."[32] And President George W. Bush could justify the invasion of Iraq as a crusade in the fulfillment of God's will. "This crusade, this war on terror, is going to take a while," he said in September 2001.[33] In 2004 he defined the crusade's goal: "Freedom is the Almighty's gift to every man and woman in this world. And as the greatest power on the face of the earth we have an obligation to help the spread of freedom."[34] In a less scriptural vein, in 2007 Nicolas Sarkozy, president of France, called for a new, positive secularism: "Secularism should not sever France from its Christian roots," lest it "weaken the cement of national identity."[35] Several years later he described the French heritage as "Christianity and the Enlightenment . . . the two faces of the same civilization."[36] Angela Merkel, Germany's chancellor, urged her compatriots to pursue discussions "about the Christian view of mankind." Germans needed to attend, she said, to "the values that guide us, [to] our Judeo-Christian tradition." They were a way to bring "about cohesion in our society."[37]

The importance of Christian ethics for contemporary democracies was evident in the conversation that took place in

2004 between the German philosopher Jürgen Habermas and Pope Benedict XVI and was later published as *The Dialectics of Reason and Religion*.[38] In the face of the war on terrorism and increased conflict in the world, Habermas admitted the importance of religious traditions as the source of morality and ethics; they have "preserved intact something which has elsewhere been lost." As he wrote in *Time of Transitions*, "Universalistic egalitarianism, from which sprang the ideals of freedom and a collective life in solidarity . . . the individual morality of conscience, human rights and democracy, is the direct legacy of the Judaic ethic of justice and the Christian ethic of love. This legacy, substantially unchanged, has been the object of continual critical appropriation and reinterpretation. To this day, there is no alternative to it. . . . Everything else is just idle postmodern talk."[39] In the dialogue with Habermas, Benedict stressed the "divine light of reason" in controlling the "pathologies of religion," attributing reason to Christianity, pathologies to Islam.[40]

The incorporation of the Christian as not just an aspect but as *the source* of the democratic secular was an enduring product of the Cold War. In the clash of civilization discourse, Islam was now portrayed as an excessive form of spirituality (an "extremist religious challenge"), eclipsing the rationality that inhered in individuals—the rationality that was the source of inner Christian conscience and the freedom it expressed—in the name of an imposed collective identity. In this view Islam became a form of totalitarian politics in which shariʿa law substituted for Marxist dialectics.[41]

Sexual Freedom and the Status of Women

The classic Cold War confrontation on the woman question occurred in July 1959 during what came to be known as the "kitchen debate" between the Soviet leader Nikita Khrushchev and Vice President Richard Nixon. It took place at an exhibition in Moscow set up by the Americans as part of a cultural exchange between the United States and the USSR. In the model kitchen displaying all the latest labor-saving technology, Khrushchev scoffed at the novelty of the dishwasher; "we have such things," he insisted. Nixon ignored the comment: "This is our newest model. This is the kind which is built in thousands of units for direct installation in the houses. In America, we like to make life easier for women." Khrushchev replied, "Your capitalistic attitude toward women does not occur under Communism," perhaps referring to women's greater participation in the workforce; perhaps also, as the *New York Times* correspondent Harrison Salisbury speculated, "meaning the discrimination and exploitation of women did not occur under communism." Nixon countered: "I think that this attitude toward women is universal. What we want to do is make life more easy for our housewives."[42] The debate ended on a more agreeable note, with Khrushchev and Nixon toasting their shared admiration for the other sex.

The leaders' dialogue was the culmination of many years of disagreement about the woman question. Elaine Tyler May's book, *Homeward Bound*, offers a comprehensive discussion of the United States in the immediate aftermath of World War II. She writes that "the family seemed to offer a psychological fortress. . . . Bolstered by heterosexual virility, scientific experience, and wholesome abundance, it might ward off the hazards of the age."[43] As in the past, the center of the domestic hearth was depicted as the woman. So while US secretary of labor James Mitchell conceded that women might need to work (and they were working in increasing numbers in these years), he insisted that "No nation should ever forget that the very primary, fundamental basis of a free society is the family structure—the home—and the most vital job is there."[44] In the name of freedom of choice, Mitchell called upon women to devote themselves to their domestic, maternal roles.

Nixon emphasized the importance of choice in his replies to Khrushchev, stressing the diversity of consumer goods available to America's women, and then allying the market with democracy: "let the people choose the kind of house, the kind of soup, the kind of ideas they want." Free choice contrasted with what the Russians had. Said Nixon, "We don't have one decision made at the top by one government official. That is the difference." If left to their own choosing, his reference to a "universal" attitude implied, women would choose the home. Indeed, the US Women's Bureau offered choice as the explanation for the absence of women in politics. "The granting of equal rights to women in public life is still a question for the future," one representative observed in 1948; "this is the result of free choice on the part of most women, who evidently prefer the comfort and privacy of their own home to the grilling experiences of political campaigns and the responsibilities of major public office."[45] Free choice was now said to be the primary characteristic of democracy, and, however paradoxical, it inevitably confirmed the "universal" truth that woman's place was in the home.

Contrasting claims about the comparative status of women under capitalism and communism were evident at the United Nations, which was hammering out its position on the question of human rights in this period. One historian notes that "the status of women constituted a cold war battleground" at the United Nations.[46] The American delegates emphasized domesticity and consumer choice—the private roles of women—while the Russians touted women's equality with men in the public sphere, as shown by the numbers of women in the workforce, the provision of state-supported child care for working women, and the equal wages earned by women and men. (Historians have shown that the realities for women did not always measure up to these claims—there was a great deal of gender asymmetry in the Soviet Union—but the rhetorical contrasts had a reality of their own in the international arena where the Cold War played out.)[47] In 1953, one of the Russian representatives at the United Nations noted the refusal of the US Congress to pass an equal rights amendment (first proposed in 1923) and the absence of women in political and judicial positions.[48] In a speech to the UN Commission on the Status of Women, Soviet delegate Nina Popova noted that if "the position of women was a true measure of the democracy of any country," then "the USSR was an inspiring example to all democratic countries."[49] The Americans retorted that the family was a necessary bastion of security and that women were happier in the United States than in the USSR—happier and more beautiful than their Russian counterparts. The weekly magazine *US News and World Report* described Moscow as "a city of women—hard-working women who show few of the physical charms of women of the West. Most Moscow women seem unconcerned about their looks."[50] Needless to say, these comments didn't reflect complex realities and experiences on the ground; they served instead to portray the differences between the two systems with broad brushstrokes.

FBI director J. Edgar Hoover called upon "homemakers and mothers" to fight "the twin enemies of freedom—crime and communism." These were the true "career women," he maintained. "I say 'career' women because I feel there are no careers so important as those of homemaker and mother."[51] Hoover distrusted any group that challenged this view, and his antipathy extended from the communist-inspired organization the Women's International Democratic Federation (founded in Paris in 1945), which he and others accused of using women's rights as a "smoke screen" to further Soviet aims, to anything that smacked of feminism.[52] "The political agents of the Kremlin abroad continue to beat the feminist drums in full awareness of its disruptive influence among the potential enemies of the Soviet Union," wrote the author of a book on "the modern woman."[53] The anticommunist surveillance extended to any individuals or organizations whose behavior called into question the norms of heterosexual marriage. May writes that "[n]onmarital sexual behavior in all its forms (prostitutes, single couples, homosexuals) became a national obsession after the war."[54]

> From the Senate to the FBI, from the anticommunists in Hollywood to Mickey Spillane, moral weakness was associated with sexual degeneracy, which allegedly led to communism. To avoid dire consequences, men as well as women had to contain their sexuality in marriage, where masculine men would be in control with sexually submissive, competent homemakers at their side. Strong families required two essential ingredients: sexual restraint outside marriage and traditional gender roles in marriage.[55]

The discursive links between strong men and strong nations reinforced one another, comments historian Emily Rosenberg, as patriotism was equated with a domestic ideology of female subordination.[56] Moreover, "the social presupposition of male dominance found discursive reinforcement in Cold War foreign policies," which justified intervention by the (virile) anticommunist powers in nations deemed too weak (too feminized) to resist communist invasion.[57] It was patriotism and not religious teaching that made the case for women's primary duty to the family—these were, to be sure, secular arguments that, however, did not make their case in the language of secularism.

Unlike earlier notions of domesticity that saw motherhood as the source of women's sexual fulfillment, May notes, there was a new emphasis on women's conjugal satisfaction.[58] Historian Dagmar Herzog, in her comprehensive study *Sexuality in Europe*, points to an "eroticized model of marital domesticity" in the 1950s. "The restoration of domesticity was accompanied by heightened expectations and standards of pleasure," she writes.[59] Advocates of contraception got a more positive hearing in this climate as they framed their claims in terms of Cold War rhetoric. Margaret Sanger, whose work gave rise to the founding of Planned Parenthood in 1942, called for "national security through birth control."[60] Her followers in the United States and Europe argued successfully that "planned procreation" by eliminating unwanted pregnancies would enhance women's sexual enjoyment and so guarantee the stability of marriage. Their concern also coincided with worries about population control in the developing world, a way of addressing issues of poverty and economic exploitation to counter the communist argument that capitalism was to blame for the experiences of the poor.[61]

Except for the Catholic Church, most religious groups accepted the need for contraception; they reasoned in terms of science, health, and rational planning in order to improve women's traditional place at home. Herzog says that across Western Europe the Christian churches emphasized the importance of "mutually satisfying marital sex—no longer only legitimated by reproduction, but also for its value in nurturing the marital bond." This outlook informed at least some of the acceptance of the birth control pill, when it came on the market in 1960.[62] Although there were international feminist organizations evident in the immediate postwar period that used science to challenge the ideology of domesticity, it was not until the 1960s and '70s that matters of birth control and sexual satisfaction were associated with widespread demands for women's liberation in the West.[63] "Choice" became the motto of abortion rights organizations in this period; women's right to be free of unwanted pregnancies became an accepted line of argument, even for some reluctant legislators.

WOMEN'S RIGHTS

There was a marked difference in representations of women beginning in the mid-1960s as a result, in part, of the emergence of second-wave feminist movements in the United States and Western Europe, themselves both cause and effect of a variety of legal, social, and demographic changes associated with the extension of consumer culture, the availability of birth control, the policies of the welfare state, the need for women in the labor force, and the notion of human rights as articulated in the UN Declaration of 1948. The emphasis on rights was at the center of both feminist claims and legislative responses to them. This had the effect of bringing to the fore the question of what counted as the recognition of rights and whether equality with men was a right to which women were entitled.

Across domestic political and international lines, the debates were intense. Did rights refer to sovereign individual subjects or to collectivities based on differences of class, race, and gender? What constituted gender equality in regard to the exercise of rights? Were there natural differences that precluded equal treatment, even if men and women were defined as individuals with free will? Was homosexuality a deviation or an acceptable practice? Were sexual rights associated with the spread of capitalism or with liberation from it?[64] In the welter of discordant responses, sex was produced as a new kind of freedom, and sexual freedom became a concept parallel to religious freedom, available for incorporation into the changed discourse of secularism when it reappeared at the end of the twentieth century. As Foucault has noted, this freedom came with new regulatory implications; although (as I indicated in chapter 2) sex had long been an object of governmental concern, the movements for feminist and gay rights now brought sex from the domain of the private squarely into the realm of the public.

Even before the end of the war, welfare state policies had acknowledged the right of mothers—(re)producers of the nation's future—to state support for their efforts. Feminist Vera Brittain noted in 1953 that "the Welfare State has been both cause and consequence of the second great change, by which women have moved . . . from rivalry with men to a new recognition of their unique value as women."[65] The unique value was maternity and it required, she argued, different treatment from what men received. The postwar constitutions in France (1946), Italy (1947), and West Germany (1949) included phrases about the equality of men and women; the UN Declaration of Human Rights (1948) made equality of husband and wife in marriage one of its important principles. But it was difficult to tell what equality meant beyond the established right to vote, now granted to all adults. Predictably, perhaps, reform of civil law (divorce, child custody, challenges to paternal authority, job discrimination, access to education, affirmative action) did not follow immediately; it came slowly and unevenly, and as a result of tremendous conflict, some of which is unresolved to this day. Changing social practices, however, were clearer in demographic statistics: in the decades from 1960 to 1980 there were, overall, dramatic declines in fertility, a drop in rates of marriage, more children born out of wedlock, and a rise in divorce. Smaller families meant less time spent reproductively by women, and this was accompanied by an increase in their labor force participation and an expanded definition of womanhood itself.

In the process, women's economic and reproductive rights became public matters. There were campaigns of varying success to end gender stereotyping of jobs, to ensure equal pay for equal work, and to assign economic value to women's domestic labor. On the reproductive front, calls to legalize contraception and abortion emphasized women's right to choose and the need for the state to protect that right—here is an example of how a new freedom required new rules to define and attain it. In the course of the 1970s and '80s, many European states recognized abortion rights, with various stipulations and limitations.[66]

International conferences linked development projects for the (then designated) Third World to women's control of their reproductive activities. A major breakthrough came at the International Conference on Population and Development held in Cairo in 1994 when feminist arguments prevailed over previous strategies that had made an improvement in women's status dependent on fertility control. At Cairo, the causality was reversed and women's empowerment was made the primary focus—this meant raising women's levels of education, providing them with satisfying employment, encouraging the sharing of domestic labor with marital partners, and above all controlling their own reproductive capacities. Women so empowered, it was asserted, would choose to have fewer children, thereby slowing population growth.[67]

As Western feminists and human rights advocates turned their attention to the international scene in this period, their work was caught up in the Cold War agenda, but in a way more explicitly tied to ideas of rights than in the "kitchen debate" of 1959. The Western liberal idea of individual rights (whether applied to religion or to women) was an item for export, a way of undermining communist notions of collective, socialized responsibility and thus a way of depoliticizing issues of economic causality. Moyn notes that whereas human rights discourses in the 1940s "implied a politics of citizenship at home," in the 1970s they were concerned with "a politics of suffering abroad."[68] This was certainly true at the United Nations during the conferences held between 1975 and 1995, where debates focused on how to improve women's status in the developing world. While delegates from Western Europe and the United States focused on exporting their notions of individual rights (freedom and emancipation were the goals), those from the global South talked about social justice and the politics of discrimination—theirs was more often a language of equality, stressing the need to find alternatives to capitalism.[69]

With the end of the Cold War and the dismantling of Soviet communism, the liberal Western project came to dominate. Given the power dynamics of these encounters—where financial support came from institutions such as the International Monetary Fund, the World Bank, and NGOs, all based in the global North—it was the language of rights that prevailed. In place of debates about the relationship between economic development and social justice, attention turned increasingly to matters such as violence against women as the source of their oppression. That violence was thought to be located especially in the "underdeveloped" world, the site of honor killings, sati (widow self-immolation), and other unacceptable practices that failed to respect the bodily integrity of women and girls. I will return to the ways in which "violence against women" set the terms for the anti-Muslim impetus of the secularism discourse in the twenty-first century. For now, though, I want to simply point out that the emphasis on bodily integrity, individual choice, and sexual rights meant that women (referred to as "the sex" in the nineteenth century) were once again being represented as primarily sexual beings, a representation that could be interpreted in a variety of ways.

SEXUAL FREEDOM

Herzog notes that "the twentieth century is often called the 'century of sex,'" and, although she cautions that a progressive narrative oversimplifies that characterization (there were setbacks and ambivalences), she thoroughly documents the "amplified political significance of sexuality" in the countries of the West in the course of those many decades.[70] Although there were distinctive histories by nation, sex was a central preoccupation whether in novels, films, advertising, other cultural media, or politics. Associated with Bohemian movements of artists, writers, and intellectuals in the early part of the century, sexual liberation became a mantra in the 1960s.[71] For some student movements—Berkeley in 1964—free love was a form of free speech. During the May '68 uprising in France, the walls were plastered with invocations to love and sex: "Orgasm without limits." "The more I make love, the more I make revolution." In West Germany, protestors insisted that "Pleasure, sex and politics belong together."[72] In the United States, opponents of the Vietnam conflict called upon us to "Make Love, not War." On the left, some activists turned to the theories of the Austrian Freudian Marxist Wilhelm Reich for inspiration. His writings from the 1920s and '30s were republished and retranslated in the 1960s. In them Reich maintained that "social justice and the pursuit of pleasure were mutually enhancing projects."[73] Others found inspiration in research by Americans Alfred Kinsey and William Masters and Virginia Johnson, whose reports on human sexuality documented a variety of sexual practices at odds with normative expectations.[74] Homosexuality received new attention in this period, and the rise of the gay rights movement challenged the association of same-sex practices with perversion. The capitalist market was quick to cash in on the new attention to sex, churning out manuals to improve technique, implements to enhance pleasure, and ads that appealed to the new identities in play.

Attention to physical pleasure and erotic exchange replaced older models of heterosexual coupling (ones focused on reproduction or complementarity), but sexual freedom (even as it expanded the definition of the couple to include same-sex partners) was not necessarily synonymous with gender equality. It did, however, open the space for a feminist critique of prevailing norms and for campaigns to end the oppression and discrimination that were defined as freedom's antithesis (among them misogyny, male domination, sexual harassment, rape, domestic violence, and homophobia).[75]

Within feminist and gay liberation movements, there were enormous debates about what sexual freedom might actually mean and whether laws were needed to guarantee it as a human right: "Is monogamy a possibility of sexual liberation or will it wither away like the state?"[76] Was the heterosexual sex act itself an inevitable form of alienation for women?[77] Was lesbianism a matter of private sexual preference or a political alternative to the heterosexual matrix? Were lesbians women?[78] Were reproductive technologies the only way to emancipate women from their primary role as mothers?[79] Was pornography an acceptable expression of desire or a stimulus to violence that must be outlawed? Was prostitution freely chosen sex work or sexual and economic exploitation?[80] And what about feminism itself: Should women claim equality (a basic human sameness) or difference (a distinctive set of feminine traits) as the ground for the recognition of their rights?[81] Would change come from consciousness-raising or did it require some kind of socioeconomic revolution?[82] What were the implications of an appeal to the state to recognize these rights? The answers to these questions differed radically and gave rise to factions and fractures that endure to this day, but they were also signs of a shared belief that there was something to aspire to that was called sexual freedom and that it was a universal human right.

"Sexual feelings and responses," wrote the authors of *Our Bodies, Ourselves* (1971), are "a central expression of our emotional, spiritual, physical selves."[83] The editors of a pathbreaking collection of essays, *Powers of Desire: The Politics of Sexuality* (1983), summed up the notion of freedom embraced by feminists of every stripe in this period:

> Those who created the modern women's movement could choose sex because it did not carry the same punitive consequences that it carried for previous generations of women and we *have*, by and large, chosen sex. This is a victory, one both furthered and truncated by historical circumstances, but one, certainly, that we grasped for ourselves, not out of false consciousness but out of desire and the impulse for freedom. This is not to imply that sexual violence does not continue to limit and shape our possibilities. But it is to affirm, at the same time, women's potential for autonomy and power. . . . We are on a long march.[84]

This vision of sexual freedom and women's autonomy was articulated by feminists within the terms of liberal democracy's progressive narrative at a precise moment in the history of Western feminism and of neoliberal capitalism. Emily Martin suggests that the end of Fordist mass production and the advent of "an era of flexible accumulation" based on mass consumption led to a transformation in perceptions of bodies.[85] In the process, she writes, the sexed body replaced the laboring body and the discourse of sexual freedom emerged. It became incorporated into a more general public discourse through advertising and the media. This radical restatement of women's agency presumed universality even as its historical context was acknowledged: there was a natural desire—an "impulse for freedom"—enabled, to be sure, by historically specific new reproductive technologies and legal reforms. According to the editors of *Powers of Desire*, modern women don't face the "same punitive consequences"—that is, unintended pregnancies or, in the case of lesbians, criminal proceedings—that follow from unregulated sexual encounters. As a result, women are finally able to realize a long-deferred dream in which sex is driven by an individual woman's desire—her choice alone—not by her need to define her femininity as an object of men's desire.

The assertion of a right of sexual citizenship in terms of individual women's sexual agency came with a claim of universality that troubled some critics, not the least because it became the standard for international regulation in protocols of the United Nations, NGOs, and other agencies. Leticia Sabsay, following Foucault, notes that "the reification of the sexual rights-bearing subject presumes that gender and sexuality are universal entitlements rather than the specific outcome of social and political struggles."[86] We might add that the emphasis on sexual agency was seen as overshadowing the equally pressing matters of economic, political, and social agency. The universal dimension of this freedom was "essential to the consolidation of European and Euro-American identity," notes Joseph Massad in a searing critique of Western liberalism.[87] Along these same lines Sabsay adds that sexual citizenship (the enjoyment of the rights of sexual freedom) becomes "a marker that distinguishes the so-called advanced Western democracies in opposition to their 'undeveloped others.'"[88] What for some was a measure of all women's autonomy from the restrictions of patriarchy, for others became a sign of civilizational superiority.

The most dramatic turn in the international campaign for women's rights came with the emergence of the issue of "violence against women." Massad links the change to the declining power of the USSR (with its advocacy of economic and structural change) and the ascendancy of the United States (with its emphasis on individual rights), and he identifies a UN conference in Nairobi in 1985 as the beginning of the switch from a focus on social justice and economic development to the issue of violence against women.[89] In the course of the 1990s, violence against women became the defining humanitarian endeavor for an unlikely alliance of secular feminists and evangelical Christians. However different their outlooks, writes the sociologist Elizabeth Bernstein, these groups joined forces to encode issues "such as rape, sexual harassment, pornography, sexual violence, prostitution, and . . . trafficking into federal and . . . international criminal law." It was trafficking, particularly, that became the object of global campaigns:

> Anti-trafficking discourses have been pushed forward by a remarkably diverse coalition of social activists and policy makers—one which spans from left to right, and which comprises secular feminists, evangelical Christians, human rights activists of diverse stripes, and a cadre of prominent celebrities and corporate officials. Despite longstanding disagreements around the politics of sex and gender, these groups have come together to advocate for harsher criminal and economic penalties against traffickers, prostitutes' customers, and nations deemed to be taking insufficient steps to stem the flow of trafficked women.[90]

Trafficking was described as "sexual slavery," the antithesis of "sexual freedom." "Freedom" gestured to the radical vision of sexual autonomy (as expressed in *Powers of Desire*), as well as to more staid Christian notions of monogamous marriage, but it lacked the strong emphasis on equality (and economics) that had impelled so many second-wave feminists. In this discourse, violence became the cause of women's dependency rather than one of its effects, the reason for their sexual, economic, and social disempowerment. Women's freedom was to be won through a moral crusade: criminalization of some of them and, especially, of those (men) who exploited them. Their salvation would come from employment in the regular labor market (however menial their jobs) and in marriages (however asymmetrical the gender roles). Bernstein cites many examples of the kinds of work (low-paying textile and clothing manufacturing among them) and marriages (hardly egalitarian) that "rehabilitated" women were offered—they did not enable the kind of autonomy feminists once envisioned.

The discourse of sexual slavery was pressed into the service of a rescue operation of non-Western women especially. This approach, Massad points out, brings non-Western states "in line with the neoliberal order," because the rescue of women serves the interests of global capitalism: not only are women a desirable source of cheap labor in the textile and care industries, but—more broadly—the press for legislation against violence moves the question of the state's role in promoting gender equality from one of provision of economic and social services to one of criminal enforcement against perpetrators of violence, and also of women defined as deviant (sex workers are a prime target).[91] Inderpal Grewal notes that the idea that gender inequality would be resolved by ending violence against women became "the tactics through which the question of violence posed by feminist movements became governmentalized."[92] This led, she adds, to the reshaping of relations between the West and non-West along liberal lines. Sexual freedom was a characteristic of the West; sexual violence or sexual slavery of the non-West. The explicit link to Islam was there to be made. The rhetoric of sexual freedom, notes Eric Fassin, "may . . . be the price that many conservatives are willing to pay so as to provide a modern justification to anti-immigration politics that could otherwise appear merely as reactionary xenophobia."[93]

Fassin makes the connection I have been exploring between the emergence of sex as a realm of freedom and the discourse of secularism that aimed its animus at Muslims. As is usually the case with rhetorical polemics, phrases associated with very different projects become detached from their contexts and put to uses different from (indeed antithetical to) the ones initially envisioned. So it was that in the course of the Cold War and its aftermath, when women's freedom was defined as their sexual agency—and freedom was associated with (Christian) democracy—women's sexual freedom could then become the emblem of the superiority of all of Western civilization to its new rival in the (Middle) East.

POSTCOMMUNIST EASTERN EUROPE

In Eastern Europe the legacy of the early Cold War years was apparent in postcommunist rhetoric, which took up the themes linking democracy, Christianity, and the return of women to their more "natural" roles in the private sphere. State socialism, with its definition of equality as women's workforce participation, was denounced as having been antithetical to nature, "a critique based on the notion that the bedrock of a healthy society is sexual essentialism."[94] "Ironically," write Susan Gal and Gail Kligman, "standard communist propaganda in many East Central European countries before 1989 echoed Western neoconservative views of the family," but in the postcommunist moment, the family was construed as a long-standing "site of resistance" to communism.[95] Although there were, to be sure, important differences among the former nations of the Soviet bloc, nationalist politicians led the way in defining their policies of marketization and privatization as the advent of democracy. In this they were joined by religious authorities who, in some cases, resorted to "scientific" rather than biblical invocations in their opposition to nontraditional gender roles.[96] Their celebration of religious freedom after what were said to be decades of suppression (ignoring a more complex history), and their celebration of freedom for women to pursue traditional family roles, went hand in hand.

The politicians' attention to the restoration of what was taken to be a universal system—men at work, women at home—was one way of avoiding discussion of increases in unemployment and in social inequality. Debates about abortion and an insistence on women's primary reproductive roles became, Gal and Kligman write, "a substitute for debate about democratic politics."[97] In public discourse, they add, "the family is generally sacralized, and not only by nationalists. . . . The private household continues to be valued as the place where people live their honest, authentic, and meaningful lives."[98] As unemployment rose with the return to capitalist practices, bringing with it increases in social inequality and the loss of state support for schools, health care, and households, "the image of the stable, autonomous family survive[d], despite . . . profound changes in divorce rates and in single parenting, as well as decreases in fertility and in the public subsidizing of childbearing and child rearing."[99] This idealized family became relentlessly heterosexual, but now with a sexualized wife/mother at its center looking to her breadwinner husband for material support. In Hungary, Katalin Fabian noted, "a polarization of opinion as to the appropriate behavior of men and women" was translated into a "hyper-masculinization and a hyper-feminization."[100]

Researchers have noted "a new emphasis on individuation in . . . magazines, and the sexualization of femininity" in Poland, Germany, Croatia, Romania, and Bulgaria. This new media emphasis—"sexualized individualism," Gal and Kligman call it—has distressed many women in the region, particularly those who grew up with a different sense of self under communism, and also those feminists who insist that achieving equality is a matter of changing economic, political, and social structures—something that communism promised, even if it didn't always deliver it. It has, nonetheless, had a powerful impact, not only on younger generations of women but also as a way of defining a postcommunist discourse of "freedom." That is the freedom to return to clear distinctions between public and private and so to "natural" systems of gender asymmetry, but with a new erotic dimension. Some of this emphasis is ironic, given reports by Western feminists in the 1990s of a reluctance to discuss sexual issues on the part of their East European counterparts. It also ignores the important developments of feminist and gender studies in this region.[101] But while feminists were organizing gender studies, media were celebrating the return of true femininity.

In response to what was reputed to be the suppression of true femininity under communism, there was an outpouring of magazines "discussing feminine strategies, eroticism, sex, cosmetics, beauty, and fashion," and products of all kinds for sale. In Romania, "the first and most successful small businesses have been the cosmetic and designer clothes boutiques."[102] In Poland, sexual freedom for some meant the availability of cosmetics and plastic surgeons (for nose jobs and breast enlargement). One woman, interviewed by a reporter, explained why she had enrolled in a charm school: "We were told under communism that looks didn't matter, that the bigger goal did, but of course, that was just a big lie."[103] In Croatia, media reporting presented sex shops, pornography, and telephone sex as "evidence of having achieved the hallowed fruits of Western civilization."[104] A former East German magazine dropped its earlier coverage of working women as icons of feminine beauty and power, replacing them with young fashion models, "emodying seductive, feminine beauty."[105] The "erotic boom" in Russia, as one sociologist there dubbed it ("beauty pageants, rock culture, jeans, pornography, personal ads, and prostitution"), was a response to "the desexualization of life under communism, the recognition of one's bodily self as an inseparable part of one's identity."[106] Anastasya Posadskaya, of the Moscow Center for Gender Studies, talked of the sexual revolution in her country. "Well, it's certainly the case that young people at the moment are extremely interested in sex."[107] She thought the "rampant spread" of pornography was "an inevitable stage that society has to go through. Taboos on representations of the naked body and on the public discussion of sex were built into the totalitarian system, but interest in these matters hasn't ceased to exist just because of the silence."[108]

There was no unanimity about the advent of free sexuality in postcommunist society; indeed, there was opposition to it on the left and on the right. Some feminists associated it with misogyny—they objected that women were to be compensated for the loss of vital social supports for child care and employment by a newly found and frivolous femininity; others saw free sexuality as the cover for capitalist exploitation and the denial of economic and political equality, which had prevailed under state socialism; still others, like Posadskaya, took it as a sign of a welcome liberation.[109] On the right, some politicians and clerics condemned the sexual revolution as the invasion of corrupt Western commerce into what they hoped would be more traditional (that is pre-Soviet) ways of organizing gender relations. The tolerance, or not, of homosexuality was deeply ingrained in debates that invoked religious teachings (Catholic, Orthodox) in defense of the heteronormative nuclear family. In this view of it, freedom of religion and restored gender "normalcy" went hand in hand. Whatever the position taken, however, it was clear that a newfound sexual freedom was an object of intense interest. In Foucauldian terms we might say that sex was *produced* as a freedom—as an unquestioned individual right—in this context.

What is important for my argument about the emergence in postcommunist Eastern Europe of this "sexualized individualism" is that, despite the disagreements, the "new sense of self, uses of the body, and ideas about sexuality" were not at odds with the emergence in the West of the discourse of sexual freedom during the last decades of the twentieth century.[110] These ideas about sexuality in Eastern Europe were either an explicit endorsement of the Western theme or a variant on it, and they became part of the polemic against Muslims in those countries. The equation of sexual autonomy and democracy led to the suppression of a much more complicated history of women's status and agency under communism—a history that is only now being explored in all its nuance.[111]

Freedom Redefined

Just as Christianity became associated with democracy in the Cold War period and beyond, so women's (and, in some instances, gay) sexual freedom became a democratic attribute in the same era. The definitions of freedom were multiple and not without conflict; they cannot easily be reduced to a single set of beliefs. But as abstract rhetorical slogans (Freedom! Democracy! Sexual liberation!), they were available for recuperation. And that was exactly what happened in the new discourse of secularism that defined itself in opposition to Islam in the late twentieth and early twenty-first centuries.

CHAPTER FIVE

Sexual Emancipation

THE DISCOURSE OF SECULARISM returned late in the twentieth century, carrying with it the traces of Cold War definitions of freedom as equivalent both to Christianity and to women's sexual emancipation. Secularism was raised to a primordial principle in France in 1989 during the commemoration of the bicentennial of the French Revolution. There a group of prominent intellectuals, recalling the capitulation to the Nazis, warned that tolerating Islamic practices would amount to a second Munich for France and Europe.[1] The notion of a "clash of civilizations" came into wide international prominence in the years that followed, ascribing totalitarianism and sexual repression to Islam and equating democracy with Christian values *and* the rights of women.

According to sociologists Ronald Inglehart and Pippa Norris, writing in 2003, the "true clash of civilizations" was about "gender equality and sexual liberalization." "A society's commitment to gender equality and sexual liberalization proves time and again to be the most reliable indicator of how strongly that society supports principles of tolerance and egalitarianism."[2] The elements of this commitment were women's access to jobs and education, the availability of abortion and divorce, tolerance for homosexuality, and values of individual autonomy and self-expression. They were said to be the fruits of modernization: "Modernization compels systematic, predictable changes in gender roles."[3] Nothing was said about the economic conditions that might or might not make sexual liberalization possible, nor about what the measures of gender equality might be.

Inglehart and Norris limited their definition of sexual liberalization to things like abortion and divorce while others went further, insisting that the fulfillment of sexual desire in any form was a basic human right. Indeed, a claim for the universality of sexual rights became one of the mantras of the clash of civilizations polemic. In it, Western women are deemed autonomous, free to pursue their desire, in contrast to Muslim women, whose sexuality is literally under wraps, confined as it is by garments that hide their beauty and symbolically signal their status as subordinate to men. Western sexual freedom is represented as fulfilling the natural inclinations of all women, whereas Islam denies their innate femininity. In some countries (notably the Netherlands) the logic of sexual liberalization extends to homosexuals, who are said to be free to realize the truth of themselves as individuals. In this discourse, sexual desire is reified; it becomes a natural law outside of history. Since it is the defining attribute of the human, the fulfillment of sexual desire is the most important element of human freedom. So Martha Nussbaum, looking to improve the lot of impoverished women in the global South, asserts that "sexual satisfaction" defines "the truly human."[4]

But what counts as sexual satisfaction? And how does it lead to gender equality? The twenty-first-century discourse of secularism rests on an opposition between the West and Islam articulated in terms of a contrast between uncovered and covered women's bodies. Uncovered women are presumed free to follow their desire, whereas covered women are not. But uncovered women's desire is most often presented as the choice to conform to prevailing norms that define femininity in terms of male desire. So the leadership of the secular Muslim group in France, Ni Putes Ni Soumises (Neither Whores nor Doormats), defined their freedom this way: "It's better to wear a skirt and take up one's femininity than to hide it behind a veil in order to avoid the gaze of others."[5] Referring to women who refuse to wear the veil, a member of the group writes of how "they try to resist by being themselves, by continuing to wear revealing clothing, by dressing in fashion, by using makeup."[6] The femininity evoked here is not the dream of those second-wave feminists who were intent on unleashing "the powers of desire" free of the male gaze; it is instead a more conventional notion that defines women as the object of men's desire. Mayanthi Fernando notes that these women equate "a particular mode of heterofemininity with individual autonomy and sexual equality—values that define the modern, secular woman" and they "propose that to be secular is to be sexually normal."[7] The contrast between covered and uncovered bodies is not about women exercising their independent sexual agency but about advertising their sexual availability, and so appealing to longstanding gender asymmetries. There are many examples of the continued objectification of women in Western democracies, among them accounts by women required by employers to conform to dress codes that emphasize their sexuality.[8] In the current discourse of secularism, "the many and varied feminist struggles of the 1970s have been selectively filtered" to serve the ends of global capital, comments Hester Eisenstein, and (I would add) to further the notion of a clash of civilizations.[9]

Subjects/Objects of Desire

The popular Western representation of Muslim women portrays them as sexually repressed while their secular Western counterparts are sexually liberated ("they" are trapped in a past from which "we" have escaped; "they" lack access to the truth that "we" know how to discover). The focus is on women (and, in some countries, also on homosexuals) as the embodiment of Western liberation on the one side, and as victims of Islamic oppression on the other. Women, once "the sex" and excluded from citizenship on those grounds, now—still as "the sex"—provide the criteria for inclusion, the measure of liberated sexuality, and, ironically, for gender equality. Ironically, because this equality usually rests not on the notion of the inherent sameness of individuals but precisely on the difference of women from men, on the complementarity of normative heterosexuality. Equality in the rhetoric of politicians as often means the equality of immigrant women with native French or German or Dutch women as it does women with men. "Let us make sure that the rights of French women also apply to immigrant women," said Nicolas Sarkozy, then minister of the interior in 2005.[10] In his view, these rights include not only abortion and divorce but also the "right" to wear sexy clothing and to sleep with men who are not their husbands. Significantly, these rights do not include jobs and social support for all classes of women. The focus on liberated sexuality (whether hetero- or homosexual) echoes with the notion of consumer desire as the motor of the market and serves to draw attention away from the economic and social disadvantages that result from discrimination and structured forms of inequality.

Dina Siddiqi analyzes a "Made in Bangladesh" ad by the company American Apparel in these terms. The ad uses as a model Maks, a "liberated" Bangladeshi woman whose brown, nude body signals her escape from Muslim oppression (recounted in a text that accompanies the ad).

> The surest sign of Maks's distancing herself from her "Islamic faith" is the exercise of her right to uncover her body to the male gaze. The not so subtle message is that ultimate freedom for Muslim women lies in literally unveiling themselves. . . . Sexuality is essential to her freedom. The emphasis on individual agency works to erase history, meanings and contexts in which images of Muslim women are produced and circulated. They also do great epistemic violence to the real lives of Bangladeshi garment workers. This is a neoliberal twist on older narratives of rescue. The difference today is that feminism is big business, quite literally. The formerly Muslim model is saved from Islam to the world of the free market where she can "sell" her body to sell clothing. Freedom, it seems, is up for sale.[11]

Writing about France, Eric Fassin notes that "equality is now defined exclusively in terms of gender, thus leaving out race or class. In the same way, *laïcité* is primarily understood as sexual secularism, insofar as it pertains to women and sexuality rather than the separation of church and state in schools, as was the case from the Third Republic until the 1980s."[12] Anne Norton, in her book *On the Muslim Question*, comments that sexual pleasure is now offered as secular redemption.[13]

In the new discourse of secularism, the secular and the sexually liberated are synonymous. The old distinction between public and private is erased; sex has become a public activity ("the personal is political" was a slogan of second-wave feminism). It is useful in this connection to return to volume 1 of *The History of Sexuality* for critical insight into the ways in which the concept of sexual liberation operates. There Foucault argued that the idea that sex had been long repressed served not only to naturalize it but to set it up as the antithesis of power (a natural trait, outside social and other constraints), rather than as what it in fact was—an instrument of power. "What I want to make apparent," he explained to some interviewers, "is that the object 'sexuality' is in reality an instrument formed a long while ago, and one which has constituted a centuries-long apparatus of subjection."[14] He put it this way in *The History of Sexuality*: "Sexuality must not be described as a stubborn drive, by nature alien and of necessity disobedient to a power which exhausts itself trying to subdue it and often fails to control it entirely. It appears rather as an especially dense transfer point for relations of power."[15] The explosion of discussions of sexuality (and of the sex presumed to be driving it) established them as objects of knowledge and so of regulation. By the end of the eighteenth century, "the sexual conduct of the population was both an object of analysis and a target of intervention."[16] Sex was, Foucault writes, "a means of access both to the life of the body and the life of the species."[17] In the West, sex has been offered as the answer to who and what we are. We have been brought almost entirely—"our bodies, our minds, our individuality, our history—under the sway of a logic of concupiscence and desire."[18] In the process, sex became the foundation for the state's regulation of populations, the disciplining of bodies, the surveillance of children and families, distinctions between the normal and the perverse, and the classification of identities (chapter 2). We must not think that by saying yes to sex," Foucault warned, "one says no to power; on the contrary, one tracks along the course laid out by the general deployment of sexuality."[19]

For Foucault, genuine emancipation would involve a "veritable movement of de-sexualization," a refusal to be pinned down to sex as the key to identity. For this reason he considered women's liberation movements to have "much wider economic, political and other kinds of objectives than homosexual" liberation movements, because they could more easily refuse the "sexual centering of the problem."[20] While homosexual movements had no choice since it was their "sexual practice which is attacked, barred, and disqualified as such," the need to limit their claims to their sexual specificity made it much more difficult to escape the "trap" of power. "Bodies and pleasures," an intentionally vague formulation, was Foucault's alternative to the identity politics that took shape in the wake of the science of sex and sexuality. Foucault refused a positive detailing of emancipation; the point was a negative one: to be emancipated from sex, not to be defined by it.

None of this has changed much since Foucault wrote, although the types of regulation and the definition of norms have been adjusted differently (around issues of sexual harassment, abortion, contraception, HIV/AIDS, gay marriage and adoption, and the like), depending on the outcomes of specific campaigns and contests, in different countries of the West. I don't want to deny the importance of the reforms that have been instituted, but I do want to remind us of a dimension we sometimes forget. The debates about these issues and the reforms resulting from them have intensified the hold of "the logic of concupiscence and desire" on the modern Western imaginary, in the politics of both the Right and the Left.[21] Whether evangelicals argue that sex should be enjoyed only in monogamous heterosexual marriages or secularists insist that sex is the latest recreational activity, whether prostitution is deemed a criminal activity or just another form of wage labor, sex remains "a dense transfer point for relations of power" in Western emancipatory discourse.[22]

The meaning of democracy now includes "sexual democracy," usually understood, paradoxically, as the free reign of individual desire within normative constraints unacknowledged as such. The normative constraints are obscured by defining them in opposition to some excess: predatory rapists in urban ghettos and African militias, sex traffickers, polygamists, promiscuous (as compared with monogamous) gay men, honor killings, genital mutilation. The excesses go both ways: sexual overindulgence on the one side, and sexual repression on the other. In the Muslim case, men are the embodiment of sexual excess (polygamy, gang rape of nonconforming daughters and sisters) *and* the vehicles for the sexual repression of women and homosexuals (stoning, honor killings, forced wearing of veils and burqas, jailing and murder of gay men and women). These negative representations offer an "unnatural" contrast to what is deemed "natural" and thus unquestionable. So that, as in the French instances I cited earlier, "liberated" women are expected to conform to established norms that make flaunting one's body a demonstration of femininity's "natural" attraction to the opposite sex. And in the Netherlands, where gay marriage has been legal since 2001, Pim Fortuyn's comment about liking to fuck young Moroccan boys without interference from backward imams stands as a call for tolerance (of homosexuality), while its emphasis on the availability of brown bodies articulated in the language of colonial orientalism is normalized in the process.[23] Similarly, in Israel, a public relations campaign to promote Tel Aviv as a gay tourist destination—"pink washing," its critics call it—seeks to identify Israel as a modern (Western) tolerant nation (suppressing all mention of the daily violence committed against Palestinians and the Orthodox rabbinical condemnation of homosexuality) in contrast to the rest of the Middle East, which Benjamin Netanyahu told the US Congress was "a region where women are stoned, gays are hanged, and Christians are persecuted."[24] Norton comments that the tolerance of homosexuality becomes "a license for the intolerance of Muslims."[25]

This intolerance rests in part on a contrast between self-determining individuals (women in the West) and those without such agency (Muslim women). But as Foucault reminds us, there is no such thing as a self-determining individual; there is only the fantasy of self-determination. The fantasy is a way of denying the constitutive force of cultural norms in any society. Or, as Saba Mahmood puts it, there is a "paradox of subjectivation": "the very processes and conditions that secure a subject's subordination are also the means by which she becomes a self-conscious identity and agent."[26] Individuality is not an inherent capacity but rather that which is attributed to subjects; "'agency' is the product of authoritative discursive traditions whose logic and power far exceeds the consciousness of the subjects they enable."[27] It involves the forceful, sometimes violent disciplining of mind, body, and soul. This is true for both secular and religious women, although the terms are different. Mahmood analyzes the agency of pious Muslim women from this perspective; the realization of a self involves submission to the external authority in the form of "moral codes that summon [her] to constitute herself in accord with [their] precepts."[28] For Nilüfer Göle, religion becomes a mode of self-fashioning for those who "seek to restore piety to modern life"; modest dress and decorum are the means by which a desirable self is enacted. Secular women are no less subjectivated, Göle reminds us.[29] "Secular self means a set of bodily practices to be learned, rehearsed and performed, ranging from ways of dressing (and undressing), talking and socializing with men to enacting in public. The habitations of the secular are not transmitted 'naturally' and implicitly, but on the contrary become part of a project of modernity and politics of self that require [for those coming from outside] assimilation and 'acculturation' to Western culture."[30] The particularity of this Western culture has become more visible,

Göle suggests, in the heated contests over appropriate dress for women on the streets of European cities. "Islam provides an alternative repertoire for self-fashioning and self-restraint by means of disciplinary practices, which range from supervision of the imperatives of faith and control of sexuality, both in mind and body."[31] She continues, "the Islamic veil, when it is not enforced on women by state power or communitarian pressure, and expresses the personal trajectories of women and their self-fashioning piety, presents a critique of the secular interpretation of women's emancipation."[32] This is a critique that the proponents of a clash of civilizations refuse to acknowledge, insisting instead that self-determination exists only on the secular side.

Sara Farris suggests that there is another important dimension to the insistence on Muslim women's assimilation to Western sexual standards. Not only does capitalism require the development of their capacity for endless consumerism (and thus a self-concept as individuals freed of the communitarian constraints that inhibit the fulfillment of their desire), it also insists on their thinking of themselves as commodities, displaying what they've got to sell. Citing the work of Alain Badiou and Frantz Fanon, she concludes that "the emphasis on the unveiling of Muslim women in Europe . . . combines . . . the Western male's enduring dream of 'uncovering' the woman of the enemy, or of the colonized, and the demand to end the incongruence of hidden female bodies as exceptions to the general law according to which they should circulate like 'sound currency.' "[33] We might extend this insight to the tolerance of homosexuality: desiring individuals of whatever sexuality make better consumers—their particular tastes can be translated into lucrative market niches—and the commodification of their (once unacceptable) desire attests to the infinite expandability and adaptability of the market.[34]

The market is crucial these days, writes A. K. Kordela, blending Marx and Lacan, not just as an economic vehicle but as a source of psychic assurance. Consumerism—shopping—has become what she calls a form of "surplus enjoyment" that "adjoins itself to immortality," "just like surplus value adjoins itself to capital."[35] "As surplus-enjoyment enables infinity to conquer life, shopping, albeit central, is just one among many biopolitical mechanisms—in this case, a frustration machine—through which the illusion of immortality can be sustained."[36] Whereas once reproduction served this end in the discourse of secularism (one's children were one's posterity), increasingly, the pursuit of desire has taken its place.

The pursuit of desire, however, says nothing about the nature of the relations between the sexes. In that sphere, the asymmetry described by Freud and Lacan remains (chapter 3). It is only by ignoring the psychic dimensions of sexual experience—the signification of the phallus (penis) and its association with power—that desire and equality can be considered equivalent.

The Muslim Question

The terminology of emancipation and equality is central to the secularism discourse that addresses the place of Muslims in the historically Christian/secular countries of Western Europe. In some ways, it's a rehearsal of the nineteenth-century "Jewish Question" about which Marx wrote his famous essay in reply to Bruno Bauer. Were Jews to be emancipated (that is, given political recognition) as Jews or as individuals? Were they a religious or ethnic entity? Did all Jews necessarily practice the religion ascribed to them? Did their religious commitments preclude the possibility of inclusion in a supposedly neutral political state? Or, in the formulation of the earlier debate during the French Revolution, were they to be treated as individuals or as "a nation?"[37] If the question then was about the grounds for exclusion, today it focuses on the need for assimilation, on the willingness or not of Muslims to shed what is referred to as their "culture" in order to become European (or American, Australian, etc.).

It was not just that historically religion was antithetical to the secular politics of the nation-state—Christians, after all, did not present the same dilemma. For purposes of citizenship they could be abstracted from the religion they continued to practice, even if (as was the case with French Catholics) theirs was not the privatized form of conscience associated with Protestantism. It was the status of Jews as a long-reviled "foreign" minority that mattered; in the course of the nineteenth century, their religious difference was increasingly cast in racial terms, and race, like sex, was seen not to be susceptible to the abstraction required for the political equality deemed to underlie national identity. Even for assimilated Jews, the taint of particularity did not disappear, as was evident in France in the Dreyfus affair, and in many other European countries in the 1930s and '40s.

The "Muslim Question" is today's version of the "Jewish Question," even as references (by the pope, Angela Merkel, Nicolas Sarkozy, and many others) to an enduring Judeo-Christian European tradition (with shared values, moralities, and practices) have tended to efface the long and tortured history of European anti-Semitism. Norton points out that "the refusal of Muslims is marked by a symbolic (but only a symbolic) embrace of the Jews. . . . The refusal of one anti-Semitism becomes the occasion for another. . . . In this way, hatred becomes the required sign of love."[38] These days, a racialized Islam (expressed in the language of "culture") now holds the place, once assigned to Jews, of the inassimilable

Other, and the problems it presents to its European hosts are couched in similar terms. In the current discourse of secularism, the question of religion as an obstacle to emancipation focuses largely on Islam; other religions (Christian, Jewish) have proven compatible with democracy—a point established conclusively during the Cold War (chapter 4).

Of course, despite the fact that in liberal theory it was abstraction that created individuals (whatever their commitments or social standing) and made them equal for the sole purpose of political representation, there were always prerequisites. Property-holding white males were initially the only conceivable individuals; later a more generalized masculinity was the criterion. The different histories of the extension of suffrage in the countries of Western Europe and the United States demonstrate the limits of abstraction as an instrument of even a narrowly political equality. It might serve as a potent ideal for groups claiming the rights of citizenship, but it was hardly a guarantee that the particularities of their differences would be automatically lifted.[39] For one thing, the discursive constitution of the abstract individual rested on its concrete physical antithesis—women as "the sex," blacks as indelibly marked bodies. Saidiya Hartman, writing of the political possibilities for former slaves in the United States, refers to "the prison house of flesh . . . the purportedly intractable and obdurate materiality of physiological difference."[40] For another, the terms of national identity and the imperatives of capitalism established physical or cultural prerequisites; only certain kinds of people were eligible for the abstraction that conferred citizenship.[41]

In one sense, then, the current demand that Muslims conform to certain rules of eligibility is not new. What is striking today is the nature of those rules and the way the vocabulary of emancipation and equality is employed to articulate them.

The issue is not so much whether to confer rights on, or to extend equality to, these newer residents of European nations, but whether they are psychologically sufficiently emancipated and/or egalitarian to be eligible for full membership and permanent inclusion. In the secularism discourse, interiority is taken to be a condition, not a state to be realized but something natural that simply needs to be unveiled. No longer is emancipation about the legal removal of obstacles or impediments to freedom. Nor is equality to be achieved by abstraction from social or other differences. And neither emancipation nor equality are considered to be the consequences of state action (although they are qualities said to thrive in secular democracies). Rather, emancipation and equality are traits presumed to inhere in individuals, establishing their agency—their very humanity—and so their eligibility for membership in the community of the nation.

In this view, the secular democratic nation-state provides only a context for the already emancipated by protecting their exercise of self-determination. But it cannot instill that quality in people who lack it. Indeed, the presence of the unemancipated constitutes a threat to the very life of Western civilization, a threat that must be contained or eliminated. Ayaan Hirsi Ali tells the story of the murder of Theo van Gogh and of the attacks of September 11, 2001, in these terms; ultimately she attributes the deaths and destruction not to a single murderer or group of murderers but to murderous Islam itself.[42] "The veil is a terrorist operation," warns the philosopher André Glucksmann in 1994. "Wearing the veil is a kind of aggression," says French president Jacques Chirac in 2003 on the eve of the passage of the law forbidding the wearing of headscarves in state schools.[43] Recently, the niqab has been outlawed in a number of countries on the grounds that it constitutes a threat to public security. After all, some feminists argue, "a veil can hide a beard."[44] The suggestion here is that there is a necessary link between "covered" sexuality and the violence of political terrorism.[45]

The representation of veiled women as terrorists has many contradictory implications. On the one hand, these women are depicted as aggressive, their veil taken as the flag of a terrorist insurgency. On the other hand, they are cast as the victims of their male relatives, barbarians who use women to further their own ends. In either case, the veil is taken to be the ultimate sign of women's lack of emancipation, of their forced or willing submission to a culture in which an inegalitarian system of gender relations prevails. The calls to outlaw headscarves, veils, and niqabs (and most recently, burkinis) are all uttered in the name of women's right to self-determination and equality between the sexes.

The Genealogy of Emancipation

Sexual liberation and gender equality became synonymous in the discourse of secularism—this despite the fact that there is no necessary equation between emancipation and equality. In fact, historically emancipation, freedom, and equality are not equivalents. I want to explore their differences in order to critically appreciate what is at stake in the emergence of the notion of sexual emancipation as a key to gender equality. To do this, it is useful to begin with a quote from Karl Marx on the question of emancipation: "It was by no means sufficient to ask: Who should emancipate? who should be emancipated? The critic should ask a third question: what kind of emancipation is involved?"[46]

Emancipation is a complex word. According to the *Oxford English Dictionary*, it denotes the lifting of "restraints imposed by superior physical force or legal obligation."[47] In

Roman law emancipation referred to the freeing of women or children from the *patria potestas*—the father's power. In English civil law Catholics were enfranchised by the Catholic Emancipation Act of 1829. Slaves in the United States were manumitted in 1863, the terms set forth in Abraham Lincoln's famous Emancipation Proclamation. (Although emancipation and manumission are now used synonymously, in ancient Rome, manumission referred specifically to slaves or servants, emancipation to family members.) Figuratively, the word has been extended to mean liberation from "intellectual, moral, or spiritual fetters."[48] In either definition, to be emancipated is to get out from under, to be able to press ahead with no obstacles in one's path, to enjoy some measure of unencumbered thought or movement, from a situation of constraint to one of some kind of freedom.

Historically, the word emancipation has often been synonymous with liberation or freedom, *but not with equality*. So, for a Roman son or wife, emancipation would more often mean disinheritance than the possibility of assuming equal standing with a father or husband. And while English Catholics won certain civil rights in the nineteenth century, they hardly acquired the social and economic privileges enjoyed by members of the Protestant Church of England. Although former slaves in postbellum America were viewed as owners of their own labor power, they were not understood to be in the same category as white workers or, for that matter, as white citizens. "From this vantage point," writes Hartman, "emancipation appears less the grand event of liberation than a point of transition between modes of servitude and racial subjection."[49] The legal regimes of industrial capitalism considered employers and workers as equal parties to labor contracts, but their social and economic statuses were never equivalent. Similarly, the achievement of suffrage for women in the twentieth century did not erase the lines of sexual difference that had long justified the denial of their right to vote (chapter 3). When the Industrial Revolution brought more jobs for women, they did not thereby gain economic parity with men. Nor did the "consciousness-raising" movements of second-wave feminism usher in a new regime of gender equality. The end of legal and/or psychological subjugation has not always conferred social, economic, or even political equality upon those who once held the reins of power or those who were never subjected to similar forms of domination.

That emancipation and equality are not synonyms results from the classic tension in liberal theory between formal and substantive rights. This was Marx's critique of Bauer's essay, "On the Jewish Question." There Marx addressed the issue of emancipation in these terms:

> The state abolishes, after its fashion, the distinctions established by birth, social rank, education, occupation, when it decrees that [these] are non-political distinctions, that every member of society is an equal partner in popular sovereignty. . . . But the state, more or less, allows private property, education, occupation, to act after their own fashion, namely as private property, education, occupation, and to manifest their particular nature. Far from abolishing these effective differences, it only exists so far as they are presupposed; it is conscious of being a political state and it manifests its universality only in opposition to these elements.[50]

In other words, it is through abstraction that individuals become the same—that is, equal—but only for the limited purpose of political membership and legal standing. The universality of national sovereignty depends on its distinction from social particularities. Equality before the law works by abstracting individuals from the power relationships in which they are located. The extension of emancipation to previously excluded groups does not alter structures of domination and inequality in the social realm. Instead, it naturalizes those structures by relegating them to civil society, removing them as objects of political attention. Marx reminds readers that "The political suppression of private property not only does not abolish private property; it actually presupposes its existence."[51] Private property in this way becomes a fact of life rather than an object of social and political dispute.

Arguably, it is liberalism's notion of the abstract individual that has conflated the definitions of emancipation and equality, leading to the conclusion that because they are deemed equal before the law, individuals are similar in all areas of life. The basis for sameness has varied among political theorists and has included dignity, empathy, godliness, the mutual capacity to kill one another, reason, self-interest, and passion. Abstraction attributes some universal traits as the basis for individual sameness; this is a fictional necessity of the political theory, historically the grounds for the inclusions and exclusions of citizenship.

There is a history still to be written about representations of the individual as the basic social unit, the various morphings of the abstract individual of political theory into a social and economic being at different moments in time. Marx links the political idea of formal equality to the economic concept of labor power. Once individuals are conceived abstractly, "all kinds of labour are equal and equivalent."[52] Abstraction removes social inequalities from consideration; it is a way of concealing and depoliticizing differences of substance and value. Along the way in this history of the abstract individual, there have been important objections and modifications: group identity as foundational for the formation of subjectivity (class, race, ethnicity, gender, sexuality, religion) and so a ground for political mobilization and political representation (labor parties, quotas, pillars in Belgium and the Netherlands, the law on *parité* in France); ideas of collective responsibility implemented in welfare states; affirmative action (or positive discrimination) as a corrective for discrimination based on negative stereotyping; and cooperation rather than competition theorized as a basic human attribute. But the individual has remained at the center of Western liberal discourse, returning with a vengeance in this neoliberal age.[53]

The late 1970s ushered in an age of heightened individualism in the neoliberal policies of Margaret Thatcher in England and Ronald Reagan in the United States. These days, in the era of globalization, all aspects of life have become increasingly "marketized," and the state's role is narrowed to a protector of market forces and individual self-determination. Society is conceived to be a mass of self-actualizing individuals, their fortunes a reflection of their choices, the condition of their lives a measure of the responsibility they have (or have not) taken for it.[54] Self-determination, once a term associated with the emancipation of former colonies from imperial rule (and their achievement of national sovereignty), is now part of psychology's lexicon. "Self-determination theory" (SDT), a relatively new field of social psychology, maintains that the human need for "competence, autonomy, and relatedness" is "universal and innate." Autonomy, according to the empirical researchers who defined the field, is the "universal urge to be causal agents of one's own life and act in harmony with one's integrated self."[55] SDT offers the fantasy of the self-directed individual of modern, secular, Western political theory as the universal human, the standard model for all civilized behavior. Evolutionary psychology grounds this fantasy in species biology: the modern individual is taken to be the outcome of a long process of "natural selection." From this perspective, emancipation is not a matter of being free of prior impediments but of understanding oneself in modern Western terms, and equality suggests a sameness of free, self-actualizing individuals.

The Reification of Desire

What are we to make of the fact that the rhetoric of democracy in the service of global capital now includes the language of sexual emancipation and its imagined equation with gender equality? What work is that language doing? Kevin Floyd's use of the notion of reification is useful for answering these questions. Floyd takes the term from the Frankfurt School philosophers who used it to refer "to a certain misapprehension of capitalist social relations; it identifies the very process of social differentiation within capital as fundamentally and objectively mystifying, as preempting any critical comprehension of the social."[56] I use it in this sense to refer, in part, to the racialized and cultural "othering" of Muslims and the normalizing and naturalizing of "our" secular, Western way of life, and also to the continuing influence of Christian moral principles on the discourse of secularism. The notion of reification can be used to understand as well the co-optation of the ideals of social movements (and, indeed, of the social movements themselves) in the service of conservative nationalist agendas. But there's yet another way I want to use it: to ask what the equation of sexual emancipation and gender equality reveals about the terms of the current discourse of secularism.

What interests me in the deployment of the rhetoric of emancipation and equality is the way in which sexual desire has been singled out (reified) as the defining universal feature of the human, eclipsing other attributes such as hunger, spirituality, or reason. Eli Zaretsky suggests that, in the course of the twentieth century the turn to sexuality offered a critique of capitalist society that postulated a "natural life of men and women outside society's domination."[57] (Something of this can be seen in the work of Wilhelm Reich, Norman O. Brown, and Herbert Marcuse.) These ideas have been taken up in the discourse of secularism that counts those most able to act on and realize their desire (always within the normative limits I discussed above) as best suited for citizenship; those in whom such action is said to be regulated or suppressed by alien cultural proscription are ineligible. In the place of the equality of abstract individuals (historically coded as masculine), we now have the equality of sexually active individuals (represented by a feminine or feminized figure); agency is located not in the reasoning mind but in the desiring body.

Desiring bodies have a materiality that abstract reason does not, but sex as the natural common denominator for the human, like reason, still permits abstraction from the social determinants of consciousness and material life—and also, of course, if we think psychoanalytically, from all the influences (cultural, familial, social, economic, political, legal, religious, etc.) that are (phantasmatically) incorporated into the unconscious aspects of desire and that give its articulation a history. It also evades the question of regulation in the articulation of desire. The very freedom ascribed to it carries limits, as Foucault has pointed out.[58] Moreover, desire alone does not make humans equal; the explanations for sexual difference that posit the meanings of masculinity and femininity can lead to very different—and unequal—paths for fulfillment.

Sexual self-determination is as much a fantasy as rational self-determination, but there is a difference: the one implies a plethora of enactments, the other a single measure of performance. While sex is synonymous with excess and pleasure, reason connotes discipline and control. (It is precisely those qualities once valued as expressions of rationality—regulation and disciplined control of the self—that are now decried as repressive instruments of Islamic fundamentalism, even as Muslims are depicted as bloodthirsty terrorists, lacking morality and compassion.)

The rhetoric of sexual emancipation and gender equality, so evident in the debates about the "integration" of Muslims into the nations of Western Europe, is symptomatic of a larger change in the way the discourse of secularism represents the human. As they are used in the prevailing discourse, emancipation and equality dissolve the private/public distinctions and bring an explicit market logic into the political realm: labor power is replaced by sexual power, and liberated sexuality has little to do with the reproductive mandate typically associated with heterosexual couples. Humans are the subjects and objects of desire, at once consumers and commodities, naturalized as such. The collapse of the distinction between public and private, the entry into the public arena of the formerly private feelings and practices of sex does not necessarily politicize sex. Of course, issues of reproductive rights and the recognition of gay sexuality are intensely political, but at the same time, the idea that sex itself is natural (and so presocial) is depoliticizing. The question of what counts as desire is removed from contests over its regulation. Sex and the desire that expresses it then have no connection to the social or cultural values that define it; in this way a specifically Western notion achieves universality.

The difference between action motivated by reason and action motivated by desire is crucial here; it is the difference between politics and the market. The state is no longer the regulator but the facilitator of the interactions of desiring individuals. The sign of their emancipation is the freedom to enact and to seek to fulfill their desire (in terms of varieties of pleasures and tastes) in whatever market it is pursued.[59] There is no guarantee of social equality—gender or otherwise—in this definition of freedom. Equality refers only to the possibility that each individual has of acting on his or her desire; it does not take into account the psychic, economic, and social limits on that action, or the fact that what counts as liberated action is measured in idealized Western terms. Again, it is useful to cite Norton here: "sexual freedom," she says (referring to Pim Fortuyn, but in a comment that is more generally applicable), "became not a metonym for political freedom, but a substitute" for it.[60]

I have been suggesting that the deployment of the language of sexual emancipation and gender equality to dismiss Muslim claims for recognition as full members of the nation-states of Western Europe, in which so many have now for so long resided, is not simply Islamophobia (which it certainly is) but has a larger resonance. The substitution of sexual desire for abstract reasoning replaces the workings of the mind with the materiality of the body; the abstract individual becomes a pulsating, lusty person. But if that substitution seems to bring the social into the realm of politics (as the language of emancipation and equality suggests), it does not. Rather, it introduces another universal human quality (the sex drive, desire, sexual identities) that is understood to be presocial, and whose satisfaction is neither a relative matter (defined historically or culturally) nor an issue open to contest (politics). There is only one route to satisfaction: the one said to prevail in the modern democracies of the West—even if in those countries what counts as satisfaction has taken many different and even contradictory forms, and even if, as continues to be the case, there is an asymmetrical relationship between the sexes. But contradiction is eliminated when the West is compared to the East, the Christian secular to the Muslim religious. When emancipation and equality are taken to be synonymous and defined as expressions of a universal and reified sexual desire, they are no different from formal political equality. Here we can return to a version of Marx's critique: they are instruments for the perpetuation of the subordination and inequality of women in the West, as well as of disadvantaged minority populations—in this instance Muslims—and for their continued marginalization in the secular and Christian democracies of the West.

Sex and Secularism

As I have studied it here, secularism is not an objective description of institutions and policies but rather a polemical term whose meanings change in the different contexts in which it is deployed. In this book I have tracked the changes in those meanings and the political uses to which the discourse of secularism has been put. The questions historians and others must ask are not what has secularism always meant and where can it be found, but instead what work does the appeal to secularism do in historically specific circumstances, how does it organize our perception, and with what effects and to what ends?

The question to ask about gender is similar because the categories of male and female, masculine and feminine, are also mutable, defined within particular contexts of nation building, racial identities, religious teachings, and social and political movements. Gender and the sex and sexuality to which it refers—and whose meanings it produces—are mutable concepts because they refer to an intractable psychic dilemma: there is no ultimate sense that can be made of differences of sex. Appeals to timeless, natural, or biologically determined differences between men and women are attempts to assuage the anxiety that comes with this indeterminacy and to provide a model for social and political organization. Gender does not ascribe its social roles based on the imperatives of physical bodies; rather, it is a historically and culturally variable attempt to provide a grid of intelligibility for sex, and—beyond sex—for the intelligibility of systems of political rule.[61] It is not that gender and politics as established entities come into contact and so influence one another. Rather, it is that the instability of each looks to the other for certainty: political systems invoke what is deemed the immutability of gender to legitimize asymmetries of power; those political invocations then "fix" differences of sex, in that way denying the indeterminacy that troubles both sex and politics.

This book has tracked the mutually constitutive operations of gender and politics by examining the discourse of secularism from its nineteenth-century anticlerical origins to its current deployment in anti-Muslim campaigns. As the historical contexts and targets of secularists changed, so did representations of sexual difference. This was particularly true of the status and situation of women. In the nineteenth and early twentieth centuries, the cultural and racial superiority of women in Western nation-states to their counterparts in the past and in the colonies had to do with their loving consent to subordination, the acceptance of their role as childbearers and domestic managers, providing the healing antidote (the "haven in a heartless world") to the ravages of politics and the market in which their fathers, husbands, and sons toiled. The distinction between the private and the public, female and male spheres of activity, was central to this representation, as was the insistence that women's sexuality be directed exclusively to procreation. A contrast with the promiscuous sexuality of women of other races and cultures (slaves, "Hindoos," Arabs, Africans, Muslims) helped secure this vision of the superior morality of white Christian women. In the nineteenth and early twentieth centuries, gender equality was *not* a "primordial" feature of the supposed religious neutrality of modern Western nation-states; gender *in*equality was.

In the twenty-first century, the public/private divide has disappeared, and women in the West are depicted as sexually liberated, free to fulfill their desires however they wish, and this is said to be a measure of the equality brought by "secularism"—by which is sometimes meant a greater openness to a diversity of sexual practices ("sexual democracy"), sometimes an antireligious stance, sometimes an explicitly Protestant notion, and usually a liberal conception of freedom as autonomous, self-willed, individual action. Exactly how this constitutes equality—and in what realms—is rarely spelled out. Indeed, I have been arguing that this vision of sexual emancipation is not the realization of a universal freedom but is instead a historically specific creation: a Western middle-class notion of what it means to be free. It is, moreover, a freedom that does not necessarily confer equality—the asymmetry of the difference of sex continues both in the most intimate of relationships as well as in the marketplace of jobs and ideas. It is only in the contrast with Muslim women's fate (they are depicted as sexually oppressed, victims of male violence, deprived entirely of agency in matters personal and religious) that the idea achieves its sense. In the extremity of the French case, an entire vision of national identity is said to rest on the visual availability to men of women's sexualized bodies—hardly an indicator of equality in any structural sense of the term but defined as such in the programs endorsed by even some socialist politicians.[62]

The contrast of East/West is a feature of the discourse of secularism, from its earliest formulations to the present. There are continuities and changes. The continuities have to do with the centrality of sexual difference (I have elsewhere referred to this as "sexularism"), with a particular focus on the place of women, and with the liberal notion of individual choice or consent. There is also a persistent Christian dimension in this discourse. The changes have to do with the substantive content of those concepts: from sex in the interests of the reproduction of family, race, and nation to sex as the fulfillment of individual desire; from women as private, passionate creatures to women as public agents exercising free choice; from an emphasis on the complementarity of the sexes to "equality" between them. These idealized visions are secured less by references to the psychic and structural realities of the lives of men and women than by contrasts with an equally fantasized foreign "other"—the Muslim woman of the East. Always deprived of individual agency, she was first presented as the embodiment of wasteful sexuality, now as its unnatural repression. She is promiscuously aggressive in the nineteenth-century depictions, now more often described as the passive instrument of her terrorist fathers and brothers. Her purported state of abjection is the antithesis of whatever "equality" means in the West—indeed, Muslim women's purported abjection functions to define Western equality in general terms, stressing some things (the right to vote, access to education, sexual freedom of choice) and not others (economic inequality, glass ceilings, misogyny, domestic violence).

Despite a vast body of literature that has contested these images as stereotypes that misrepresent the experience and the agency of Muslim women and the freedom of women in the Christian secular West, the discourse of secularism continues to offer them as proof of the superiority of "our" way of life. The power of this discourse matters because of its influence on politicians and the media, as well as on ordinary people.

The aim of this book has been to offer a more nuanced understanding of the operations of the discourse of secularism, a critique of its exaggerated claims and their political implications. Above all, I think it is important to see how invested the current discourse has been in contrast to a caricatured "East," and then to ask how we would understand secularism's claims if they were detached from that contrast and treated as products of history. What would we see that is now obscured? What difficulties and intransigencies would become apparent?

First, of course, we would see that secularism is not an eternal set of principles but a polemical term put to work differently in different contexts. Next, gender would be understood as the insistent but ultimately vain attempt to resolve the enduring conundrum presented by the difference of sex. Its connection to politics would also become clear as the preferred solution to what Claude Lefort deemed the indeterminacy of representative government (see chapter 3). My analysis of the history of the discourse of secularism shows how politics invokes gender and, reciprocally, how gender is secured by politics. Gender and politics have used each other to establish their legitimacy and to enforce their rules, justifying inequalities as natural phenomena—inequalities that extend beyond gender to race, class, ethnicity, and religion. Untangling the operations of this interconnection in the discourse of secularism has been for me a critical project, and not only because it exposes the way certain claims about equality have served to perpetuate inequality. What is also at stake in insisting on the historicity of this discourse, and on the indeterminacy of the meanings of gender and democratic politics upon which it rests, is that those meanings are perpetually and irresistibly open to change. In this way, critique allows us to think otherwise about the relationship of past to present and about the difficulties we face in acting to realize more just and egalitarian futures.

NOTES

Introduction: The Discourse of Secularism

1. Samuel Huntington, "The Clash of Civilizations?" *Foreign Affairs* 72:3 (1993): 29–30.

2. Cited in Dominic McGoldrick, *Human Rights and Religion: The Islamic Debate in Europe* (Portland, OR: Hart, 2006), 89.

3. Ronald Inglehart and Pippa Norris, "The True Clash of Civilizations," *Foreign Policy* 135 (2003).

4. Oates's Twitter quote ("Where 99.3% of women report having been sexually harassed & rape is epidemic—Egypt—natural to inquire: What's the predominant religion?") was written about in Frank Bruni's op-ed piece, "Tweeting Toward Sacrilege," *New York Times* online, July 13, 2013.

5. Riposte Laïque, November 26, 2012, http://ripostelaique.com/; see also, *Droite(s)-Extrême(s)* blog, http://droites-extremes.blog.lemonde.fr/2010/09/05/ce-quest-vraiment-riposte-laique/.

6. For their help in clarifying my thoughts on this question, I am grateful to the students in a graduate seminar in Anthropology at UC Berkeley in the fall of 2016—Brent Eng, Aaron Eldridge, Basit Iqbal, Mohamad Jarada, and Philip Balboni, and to the co-instructor, Mayanthi Fernando. They may not entirely agree with what I've said here, but the conversations we had helped me to think better about this.

7. A few among many examples: Ronald Inglehart and Pippa Norris, *Sacred and Secular: Religion and Politics Worldwide* (Cambridge: Cambridge University Press, 2004); Charles Taylor, *A Secular Age* (Cambridge, MA: Harvard University Press, 2007); John Lardas Modern, *Secularism in Antebellum America* (Chicago: University of Chicago Press, 2011); Linell E. Cady and Elizabeth Shakman Hurd, eds., *Comparative Secularisms in a Global Age* (New York: Palgrave Macmillan, 2010); Rajeev Bhargava, ed., *Secularism and Its Critics* (New Delhi: Oxford University Press, 1998); and most contributors to the Social Science Research Council website, the Immanent Frame, http://blogs.ssrc.org/tif/.

8. For a useful distinction between word and concept, see Reinhart Koselleck, *The Practice of Conceptual History: Timing History, Spacing Concept*, trans. Todd Presen, Kersten Behnke, and Jobst Welge (Stanford, CA: Stanford University Press, 2002).

9. Charles Taylor, *A Secular Age*, 167.

10. Talal Asad, *Formations of the Secular: Christianity, Islam, Modernity* (Stanford CA: Stanford University Press, 2003), 25.

11. Saba Mahmood, *Religious Difference in a Secular Age: A Minority Report* (Princeton: Princeton University Press, 2016), 21.

12. Kathleen Davis, *Periodization and Sovereignty: How Ideas of Feudalism and Secularization Govern the Politics of Time* (Philadelphia: University of Pennsylvania Press, 2008), 11.

13. Ibid., 77.

14. Tomoko Masuzawa, *The Invention of World Religions, or How European Universalism Was Preserved in the Language of Pluralism* (Chicago: University of Chicago Press, 2005). See also Pamela Klassen, "Christianity as a Polemical Concept," in *The Companion to the Anthropology of Religion*, ed. Janice Boddy and Michael Lambek (Chichester, UK: Wiley-Blackwell, 2013), 344–62.

15. Asad, *Formations of the Secular*, 1.

16. Jordan Alexander Stein, "Angels in (Mexican) America," *American Literature* 86:4 (December 2014): 684. See also Peter Coviello and Jared Hickman, "Introduction: After the Postsecular" in the same issue.

17. Edward Said, *Orientalism* (New York: Vintage Books, 1978; 1994), 2–3.

18. Sara Farris, "Femonationalism and the 'Regular' Army of Labor Called Migrant Women," *History of the Present* 2:2 (2012): 196.

19. "Séculaire" and "Sécularisation," *Encyclopédie, ou dictionnaire raisonné des sciences, des arts et des métiers*, 17 vols., ed. Denis Diderot (co-ed. Jean le Rond d'Alembert through 1759) (Neufchâtel, 1751–66), 14:881–83.

20. Cited in Laura Schwartz, *Infidel Feminism: Secularism, Religion and Women's Emancipation, England, 1830–1914* (Manchester: Manchester University Press, 2015), 8. Schwartz writes of the difficulty feminists had within the secularist movements of contesting natural law arguments about women's place.

21. *Le Grand Robert de La Langue Française*, 2nd ed. (Paris: Dictionnaires Le Robert, 1987), 5:915.

22. *Encyclopédie*, 14:881.

23. *The Compact Edition of the Oxford English Dictionary* (New York: Oxford University Press, [1971]), 2:2704.

24. José Casanova, "Secularization," in *International Encyclopedia of the Social and Behavioral Sciences*, ed. Neil Smelser and Paul B. Baltes (Amsterdam: Elsevier, 2001), 13787–791.

25. Ibid.

26. *Encyclopédie*, 14:881.

27. Talal Asad, *Genealogies of Religion: Disciplines and Reasons of Power in Christianity and Islam* (Baltimore: Johns Hopkins University Press, 2009), 28.

28. Joan Wallach Scott, *Parité: Sexual Equality and the Crisis of French Universalism* (Chicago: University of Chicago Press, 2005).

29. Conseil d'Etat, *Réflexions sur la laïcité* (Paris: Conseil d'Etat, 2004), 295. Gender equality came into focus in relation to *laïcité* for the first time in 1987 when, seeking to bring French practice into conformity with the European Convention's prohibition of sex discrimination, the Conseil decided that Catholic women's religious orders must be treated in the same way as those of men.

30. Ibid., 341.

31. Cited in ibid., 128; see also 206. *Dahlab v. Switzerland*, Application No. 42393/98 ECHR (2001).

32. Cour Européenne des Droits de l'Homme, Grand Chambre, *Affaire Lautsi et autres, c. Italie* (Requête no. 30814/06), March 18, 2011, 15:11.9.

33. Joseph Ratzinger and Jürgen Habermas, *The Dialectics of Secularization: On Reason and Religion* (San Francisco: Ignatius Press, 2007). This insistence on the Christian heritage of Western European states is not the same as the arguments of political theorists about the theological character of nations. Those arguments suggest that nationalism is the functional equivalent of religion, not that certain religions are literally the foundation for secular states.

34. There are, of course, exceptions, as pointed out in Karla Mallette's study of the ways in which some Southern European philologists in the nineteenth century sought to prove the Arab origins of European civilization. Instead of Europe's "other," Arabs were identified as its predecessors. Karla Mallette, *European Modernity and the Arab Mediterranean: Toward a New Philology and a Counter-Orientalism* (Philadelphia: University of Pennsylvania Press, 2010).

35. Ernest Renan, *De la part des peuples sémitiques dans l'histoire de la civilization* (1862). See also Renan, "L'Islamisme et la Science" (1883), in his *Discours et Conférences* (Paris: Calmann-Lévy, 1887). In it he talks of the "inferiority of Muslim countries, the decadence of states governed by Islam, the intellectual nullity of those who receive their culture and education from this religion" (377).

36. Masuzawa, *The Invention of World Religions*, 20.

37. Ibid., 179.

38. Gil Anidjar, "Secularism," *Critical Inquiry* 33 (2006): 66.

39. Cited in Timothy Mitchell, *Colonizing Egypt* (Berkeley: University of California Press, 1991), 111.

40. Racial difference that is focused on the differences between white and black women has a long history, dating back at least to the sixteenth century. Jennifer Morgan writes that whether in North America or Africa, "indigenous women bore an enormous symbolic burden as writers from Walter Raleigh to Edward Long employed them to mark metaphorically the symbiotic boundaries of European national identities and white supremacy." Jennifer Morgan, " 'Some Could Suckle over Their Shoulder': Male Travelers, Female Bodies, and the Gendering of Racial Ideology, 1500–1770," *William and Mary Quarterly*, 3rd series, 54:1 (January 1997): 169.

41. Frantz Fanon, "Algeria Unveiled," in *A Dying Colonialism*, trans. Haakon Chevalier (New York: Grove Press, 1965), 177.

42. Ibid., 165.

43. Ann Laura Stoler, *Carnal Knowledge and Imperial Power: Race and the Intimate in Colonial Rule* (Berkeley: University of California Press, 2002), 13.

44. See Linell E. Cady and Tracy Fessenden, eds., *Religion, the Secular, and the Politics of Sexual Difference* (New York: Columbia University Press, 2013); Janet R. Jakobsen and Ann Pellegrini, eds., *Secularisms* (Durham, NC: Duke

University Press, 2008). See also Andrew Parker, Mary Russo, Doris Sommer, and Patricia Yaeger, eds., *Nationalisms and Sexualities* (New York: Routledge, 1992).

45. Alenka Zupančič, *Why Psychoanalysis?* Summertalk series (Natchitoches, LA: Northwestern State University Press, 2008), 7.

46. Sylvia Wynter, "1492: A New World View," in *Race, Discourse, and the Origin of the Americas: A New World View*, ed. Vera Lawrence Hyatt and Rex Nettleford (Washington, DC: Smithsonian Institution Press, 1995), 5–57. Wynter argues that "From this ultimate mode of otherness based on race, other subtypes of otherness are then generated—the lower classes as the lack of the normal class, that is the *middle class*; all other cultures as the lack of the normal culture, that is, *Western culture*; the nonheterosexual as the lack of *heterosexuality*, represented as a biologically selected mode of erotic preference; women as the lack of the normal sex, *the male*. So, while serving as units of an overall totemic system, all were themselves generated from the central and primary representation of the black physiognomy as 'proof' of the represented evolutionarily determined degrees of genetic perfection" (42; italics in original).

47. Thanks to Brian Connolly for this suggestion. See also Jacqueline Stevens, *Reproducing the State* (Princeton: Princeton University Press, 1999); and Jennifer Morgan, "'Some Could Suckle over their Shoulder,'" 169n8: "I would posit that, rather than creating a hierarchy of difference, simultaneous categories of analysis illuminate the complexity of racialist discourse in the early modern period."

48. Claude Lefort, *Democracy and Political Theory*, trans. David Macey (Cambridge: Polity Press, 1988).

49. Michel Foucault, *History of Sexuality* (New York: Vintage Books, 1980), 1:103.

50. Kevin Floyd, *The Reification of Desire: Toward a Queer Marxism* (Minneapolis: University of Minnesota Press, 2009), 6.

51. Nancy Armstrong, *Desire and Domestic Fiction: A Political History of the Novel* (New York: Oxford University Press, 1987), 89.

52. Denise Riley, *"Am I that Name?" Feminism and the Category of "Women" in History* (London: Macmillan, 1988), 8.

53. G. J. Barker-Benfield, *The Culture of Sensibility: Sex and Society in Eighteenth-Century Britain* (Chicago: University of Chicago Press, 1996), xxvi.

54. Isabel Hull, *Sexuality, State, and Civil Society in Germany, 1700–1815* (Ithaca: Cornell University Press, 1997), 296.

55. Susan Juster, *Disorderly Women: Sexual Politics and Evangelicalism in Revolutionary New England* (Ithaca: Cornell University Press, 1996), 216.

56. Elizabeth Maddock Dillon, *The Gender of Freedom: Fictions of Liberalism and the Literary Public Sphere* (Stanford, CA: Stanford University Press, 2007), 3.

57. Afsaneh Najmabadi, *Women with Mustaches and Men without Beards: Gender and Sexual Anxieties of Iranian Modernity* (Berkeley: University of California Press, 2005), 3.

58. Wendy Brown, *Undoing the Demos: Liberalism's Stealth Revolution* (Cambridge, MA: Zone Books, 2015).

Chapter One: Women and Religion

1. Hubertine Auclert, *Le vote des femmes* (Paris, 1908), 56–57.

2. Hubertine Auclert, *Les femmes arabes en Algérie* (Paris, 1900), 63.

3. Auclert, *Vote des femmes*, 56–57.

4. Elizabeth Shakman Hurd, *The Politics of Secularism in International Relations* (Princeton: Princeton University Press, 2008).

5. Ibid.

6. Owen Chadwick, *The Secularization of the European Mind in the Nineteenth Century* (Cambridge: Cambridge University Press, 1975), 93.

7. Paul Seeley, "Ô Sainte Mère: Liberalism and the Socialization of Catholic Men in Nineteenth-Century France," *Journal of Modern History* 70:4 (December 1998): 866.

8. Olwen Hufton, "Women in Revolution," *French Politics and Society* 7:3 (Summer 1989): 66. This is not to say that women were not already (during the ancien régime) identified as evincing greater religiosity than men, only that in the discourses of anticlericalism in the nineteenth and twentieth centuries, the Revolution of 1789 was taken to be an originary moment. On this, see Robert Kreiser, "Enthusiasm in Early Eighteenth-Century Paris: The Convulsionaries of Saint-Médard," *Catholic Historical Review* 61:3 (July 1975): 353–85; Frank Tallett, "Dechristianizing France," in *Religion, Society, and Politics in France since 1789*, ed. Frank Tallett and Nicholas Atkin (London: Hambledon Press, 1991); Keith Thomas, "Women in the Civil War Sects," in Trevor Ashton, ed., *Crisis in Europe, 1560–1660* (New York: Basic Books, 1965), 317–40.

9. Cited in Richard Cobb, *Les armées révolutionnaires: Instrument de la terreur dans les départements, avril 1793-Floréal an II* (Paris: Mouton, 1961–63), 450.

10. Tallett, "Dechristianizing France," 26.

11. Moreau quoted in *A History of Private Life*, vol. 4, *From the Fires of Revolution to the Great War*, ed. Michelle Perrot, trans. Arthur Goldhammer (Cambridge, MA: Harvard University Press, 1994), 44.

12. Maurice Agulhon, *Marianne au combat: L'imagerie et la symbolique républicaine de 1789 à 1880* (Paris: Flammarion, 1992).

13. Zrinka Stahuljak, *Pornographic Archaeology: Medicine, Medievalism, and the Invention of the French Nation* (Philadelphia: University of Pennsylvania Press, 2012).

14. Sarah A. Curtis, "Charitable Ladies: Gender, Class and Religion in Mid-Nineteenth-Century Paris," *Past and Present* 177 (2002): 121–56. The information on women and the Catholic Church can also be found in Linda Clark, *Schooling the Daughters of Marianne: Textbooks and the Socialization of Girls*

in Modern French Primary Schools (Albany: SUNY Press, 1986); Michela Di Giorgio, "The Catholic Model," in *A History of Women in the West*, vol. 4, *Emerging Feminism from Revolution to World War*, gen. ed. Georges Duby and Michelle Perrot, trans. Arthur Goldhammer (Cambridge, MA: Harvard University Press, 1993); Ralph Gibson, "Le catholicisme et les femmes en France au XIXe siècle," *Revue d'histoire de l'Église de France* 79 (1993): 63–94; Carol Harrison, "Zouave Stories," *Journal of Modern History* 79:2 (2007): 274–305; Claude Langlois, "Catholics and Seculars," in *Realms of Memory*, ed. Pierre Nora, trans. Arthur Goldhammer (New York: Columbia University Press, 1996); Hazel Mills, "'La Charité est une mère': Catholic Women and Poor Relief in France, 1690–1850," in *Charity, Philanthropy and Reform*, ed. M. Cunningham and J. Innes (London: Macmillan, 1998); Paul Seeley, "Ô Sainte Mère," 862–91; Judith Stone, "Anticlericals and Bonnes Soeurs: The Rhetoric of the 1901 Law of Association," *French Historical Studies* 23:1 (Winter 2000): 103–28.

15. Seeley, "Ô Sainte Mère," 891.

16. Jules Michelet, *La Femme* (1859), in his *Oeuvres Complètes*, vol. 18 (Paris: Flammarion, 1985).

17. Jules Michelet, *Du Prêtre, de la femme, de la famille*, 3rd ed. (Paris: Hachette, 1845), vi. Further references to this book are given by page number in the text. See also Timothy Verhoeven, "Neither Male nor Female: The Jesuit as Androgyne, 1843–70," *Modern and Contemporary France* 16:1 (2008): 37–49.

18. Jules Michelet, *L'Amour* (1858), in his *Oeuvres Complètes*, vol. 18 (Paris: Flammarion, 1985), 221–23.

19. Cited in Roland Barthes, *Michelet* (New York: Hill and Wang, 1987), 148.

20. Steven C. Hause with Anne R. Kenny, *Women's Suffrage and Social Politics in the French Third Republic* (Princeton: Princeton University Press, 1984), 240. See also 236–41.

21. Françoise Mayeur, "The Secular Model of Girls' Education," in *A History of Women in the West*, vol. 4, *Emerging Feminism from Revolution to World War*, gen. ed. Georges Duby and Michelle Perrot, trans. Arthur Goldhammer (Cambridge, MA: Harvard University Press, 1993).

22. J. P. Daughton, *An Empire Divided: Religion, Republicanism, and the Making of French Colonialism, 1880–1914* (Oxford: Oxford University Press, 2006), 124.

23. Tisa Wenger, "The God-in-the-Constitution Controversy: American Secularisms in Historical Perspective," in *Comparative Secularisms in a Global Age*, ed. Linell E. Cady and Elizabeth Shakman Hurd (New York: Palgrave Macmillan, 2010), 91.

24. John Lardas Modern, *Secularism in Antebellum America* (Chicago: University of Chicago Press, 2011), 75.

25. Max Weber, "The Social Psychology of the World Religions," in *From Max Weber: Essays in Sociology*, ed. and trans. H. H. Gerth and C. Wright Mills (New York: Routledge, 1998), 295.

26. Modern, *Secularism*, 20.

27. Brian Connolly, *Domestic Intimacies: Incest and the Liberal Subject in Nineteenth-Century America* (Philadelphia: University of Pennsylvania State, 2014), 83.

28. Susan Juster, *Disorderly Women: Sexual Politics and Evangelicalism in Revolutionary New England* (Ithaca: Cornell University Press, 1996), 7.

29. Ibid., 109.

30. Ibid., 128.

31. Ibid., 112.

32. Susan Juster, *Doomsayers: Anglo-American Prophecy in the Age of Revolution* (Philadelphia: University of Pennsylvania Press, 2003); Barbara Taylor, *Eve and the New Jerusalem: Socialism and Feminism in the Nineteenth Century* (New York: Pantheon, 1982); E. P. Thompson, *The Making of the English Working Class* (New York: Vintage, 1966).

33. Seth Moglen, "Excess and Utopia: Meditations on Moravian Bethlehem," *History of the Present* 2:2 (2012): 136.

34. Ibid., 140–41.

35. The quote is from a private e-mail correspondence from Moglen to me.

36. Modern, *Secularism*, 3, 26.

37. Ann Douglas, *The Feminization of American Culture* (New York: Knopf, 1977). On feminization and religion in Europe, see Derek K. Hastings, "Fears of a Feminized Church," *European Historical Quarterly* 38:1 (2008): 34–65.

38. Modern, *Secularism*, 37.

39. Douglas, *Feminization*, 44.

40. Modern, *Secularism*, 249.

41. Douglas, *Feminization*, 57.

42. Ibid., 10.

43. Modern, *Secularism*, 25.

44. Elizabeth Maddock Dillon, *The Gender of Freedom: Fictions of Liberalism and the Literary Public Sphere* (Stanford, CA: Stanford University Press, 2007), 202.

45. Brian Connolly, "'Hindoo Marriage' and National Sovereignty in the Early Nineteenth-Century United States," in *Warring for America, 1803–1818*, ed. Nicole Eustace and Fredrika J. Teute (Chapel Hill: University of North Carolina Press, 2017), 25 (in MS version). Ironically, proponents of secularism in the Indian nationalist movement in the 1920s took Hinduism to be a rational belief system compatible with secular government, in contrast to "fanatical" Islam—for them the embodiment of religion. See Julia Stephens, "The Politics of Muslim Rage," *History Workshop Journal* 77 (2013): 48.

46. Denise Spellberg, *Thomas Jefferson's Qur'an: Islam and the Founders* (New York: Vintage, 2014). As Spellberg points out, there was great irony in that fact that there *were* Muslims in the United States—but they were slaves, and so seemingly outside Jefferson's consciousness when he talked about what religious groups could enjoy American citizenship!

47. Dagmar Herzog, *Intimacy and Exclusion: Religious Politics in Pre-Revolutionary Baden* (Princeton: Princeton University Press, 1996), 98. See also Todd Weir, *Secularism and Religion in Nineteenth-Century Germany* (Cambridge: Cambridge University Press, 2014).

48. Herzog, *Intimacy and Exclusion*, 99.

49. Wenger, "The God-in-the-Constitution Controversy."

50. Sarah Barringer Gordon, *The Mormon Question: Polygamy and Constitutional Conflict in Nineteenth-Century America* (Chapel Hill: University of North Carolina Press, 2002).

51. Herzog, *Intimacy and Exclusion*, 101–2.

52. Alexis de Tocqueville, *Democracy in America*, trans. Arthur Goldhammer (New York: Library of America, 2004), 706.

53. Modern, *Secularism*, 113.

54. Phyllis Mack, "Religion, Feminism, and the Problem of Agency: Reflections on Eighteenth-Century Quakerism," in *Women, Gender and Enlightenment*, ed. Sarah Knott and Barbara Taylor (Hampshire: Palgrave Macmillan, 2005), 434–59; and Saba Mahmood, *Politics of Piety: The Islamic Revival and the Feminist Subject* (Princeton: Princeton University Press, 2004).

55. Saba Mahmood, *Religious Difference in a Secular Age: A Minority Report* (Princeton: Princeton University Press, 2016), 43.

56. Aziz Al-Azmeh, *Islam and Modernities* (London: Verso, 1993), 12.

57. Joseph Massad, *Colonial Effects: The Making of National Identity in Jordan* (New York: Columbia University Press, 2001), 51.

58. Wael B. Hallaq, *An Introduction to Islamic Law* (Cambridge: Cambridge University Press, 2009), 118.

59. Massad, *Colonial Effects*, 82.

60. Ibid., 82.

61. Hallaq, *An Introduction to Islamic Law*, 85.

62. Ibid., 120.

63. Janet Halley and Kerry Rittich, "Critical Directions in Comparative Family Law: Genealogies and Contemporary Studies of Family Law Exceptionalism." Special issue on Comparative Family Law of the *American Journal of Comparative Law* 58 (2010).

64. Ibid., 753.

65. Indrani Chatterjee, "Monastic Governmentality, Colonial Misogyny, and Postcolonial Amnesia in South Asia," *History of the Present* 3:1 (Spring 2013).

66. Mahmood, *Religious Difference*, 23.

67. Saba Mahmood, "Sexuality and Secularism," in *Religion, the Secular, and the Politics of Sexual Difference*, ed. Linell E. Cady and Tracy Fessenden (New York: Columbia University Press, 2013), 51.

68. Judith Surkis, *Scandalous Subjects: Intimacy and Indecency in France and French Algeria*, forthcoming.

69. Halley and Rittich, "Critical Directions in Comparative Family Law," 772.

70. Beth Baron, "The Making of the Egyptian Nation," in *Gendered Nations: Nationalisms and Gender Order in the Long Nineteenth Century*, ed. Ida Blom, Karen Hagemann, and Catherine Hall (Oxford: Berg, 2000), 138.

71. Mahmood, *Religious Difference*, 32.

72. Massad, *Colonial Effects*, 51.

73. Halley and Rittich, "Critical Directions in Comparative Family Law," 773. See also Pamela Klassen, "Mentality, Fundamentality, and the Colonial Secular," in *The Postsecular Condition*, ed. Rosi Braidotti, Bolette Blaagaard, and Eva Midden (London: Palgrave Macmillan, 2014), 175–94.

74. Frantz Fanon, "Algeria Unveiled," in *A Dying Colonialism*, trans. Haakon Chevalier (New York: Grove Press, 1965), 63.

75. Massad, *Colonial Effects*, 83.

76. Hallaq, *An Introduction to Islamic Law*, 123, citing Ziba Mir-Hosseini, *Marriage on Trial: A Study of Islamic Family Law* (London: I. B. Tauris, 2000).

77. Ibid., 168; Massad, *Colonial Effects*, 85–99.

78. Kumari Jayawardena, *Feminism and Nationalism in the Third World* (London: Zed Books 1986), 4.

79. Ibid., 24.

80. Joseph Massad, *Islam in Liberalism* (Chicago: University of Chicago Press, 2015), 189.

81. Cited in the introduction, note 4.

Chapter Two: Reproductive Futurism

1. Cited in Kevin Floyd, *The Reification of Desire: Toward a Queer Marxism* (Minneapolis: University of Minnesota Press, 2009), 87.

2. Michel Foucault, *Security, Territory, Population: Lectures at the Collège de France, 1977–78*, trans. Graham Burchell (New York: Palgrave, 2007), 42. See also Foucault, *History of Sexuality* (New York: Vintage Books, 1980), 1:139–42.

3. Emile Durkheim, *The Division of Labor in Society*, trans. George Simpson (New York: Free Press, 1964), 60. Durkheim is not the only one to observe this: Rousseau earlier; Freud later.

4. Cited in Susan Kingsley Kent, *Sex and Suffrage in Britain, 1860–1914* (Princeton: Princeton University Press, 1987), 54.

5. Iwan Bloch, *The Sexual Life of Our Time, in Its Relations to Modern Civilisation* (1908), 534, cited by Leela Gandhi, *Affective Communities: Anticolonial Thought, Fin-de-siècle Radicalism and the Politics of Friendship* (Durham, NC: Duke University Press, 2006), 49. Thanks to Sara Pursley for this reference.

6. Stefan Dudink, "Masculinity, Effeminacy, Time," in *Masculinities in Politics and War: Gendering Modern History*, ed. Stefan Dudink, Karen Hagemann, and John Tosh (Manchester: University of Manchester Press, 2009), 78.

7. Cornelia Klinger, "Woman-Landscape-Artwork: Alternative Realms or Patriarchal Reserves?," in *Continental Philosophy in Feminist Perspective: Rereading the Canon in German*, ed. Herta Nagl-Docekal and Cornelia Klinger,

trans. James Dodd (University Park: Pennsylvania State University Press, 2000), 166–67.

8. Robert Nye, *Masculinity and Male Codes of Honor in Modern France* (Berkeley: University of California Press, 1998); Geneviève Fraisse, *Reason's Muse: Sexual Difference and the Birth of Democracy*, trans. Janet Todd (Chicago: University of Chicago Press, 1994).

9. Thomas Laqueur, *Making Sex: Body and Gender from the Greeks to Freud* (Cambridge, MA: Harvard University Press, 1990).

10. G. J. Barker-Benfield, *The Culture of Sensibility: Sex and Society in Eighteenth-Century Britain* (Chicago: University of Chicago Press, 1996), 127.

11. Ibid.

12. Ibid.

13. Jules Michelet, "L'Amour," in *Oeuvres Complètes* (Paris: Flammarion, 1985), 18:61–62.

14. Londa Schiebinger, *The Mind Has No Sex? Women in the Origins of Modern Science* (Cambridge, MA: Harvard University Press, 1989), 189.

15. Jill Conway, "Stereotypes of Femininity in a Theory of Sexual Evolution," in *Suffer and Be Still: Women in the Victorian Age*, ed. Martha Vicinus (Bloomington: Indiana University Press, 1972), 147.

16. Ibid., 141.

17. Patricia Hollis, *Women in Public, 1850–1914: Documents of the Victorian Women's Movement* (London: Routledge, 1979), 30.

18. Schiebinger, *The Mind Has No Sex?*, 209.

19. Isabel Hull, *Sexuality, State, and Civil Society in Germany, 1700–1815* (Ithaca: Cornell University Press, 1997), 249.

20. Ibid.

21. Ibid.

22. Durkheim, *The Division of Labor*, 60.

23. On racial theory in this period, see J. P. Daughton, *An Empire Divided: Religion, Republicanism, and the Making of French Colonialism, 1880–1914* (Oxford: Oxford University Press, 2006) and Sarah A. Curtis, *Civilizing Habits: Women Missionaries and the Revival of French Empire* (Oxford: Oxford University Press, 2010). Anticlericals in this period countenanced missionaries' work in the colonies even as they expelled the Jesuits from teaching orders at home. It was believed that missionaries would provide the moral uplift that colonial subjects needed. See also Schiebinger, *The Mind Has No Sex?*, 211–12; and Robert J. C. Young, *Colonial Desire: Hybridity in Theory, Culture and Race* (New York: Routledge, 1995).

24. Schiebinger, *The Mind Has No Sex?*, 222.

25. Kent, *Sex and Suffrage*, 42.

26. Catherine Hall, "The Sweet Delights of Home," in *A History of Private Life*, vol. 4, *From the Fires of Revolution to the Great War*, ed. Michelle Perrot, trans. Arthur Goldhammer (Cambridge, MA: Harvard University Press, 1990), 50.

27. Cited in John D'Emilio and Estelle B. Freedman, *Intimate Matters: A History of Sexuality in America* (Chicago: University of Chicago Press, [1988] 1997), 146.

28. Jean Borie, "Une gynécologie passionné," in *Misérable et glorieuse: La femme du XIXe siècle*, ed. Jean-Paul Aron (Paris: Fayard, 1980), 157–88.

29. Max Weber, "Science as a Vocation," in *From Max Weber: Essays in Sociology*, ed. Gerth and Mills (New York: Routledge, 1998), 155.

30. Ibid., 139.

31. Weber, "The Social Psychology of the World Religions," in *From Max Weber*, ed. Gerth and Mills, 281.

32. Weber, "Religious Rejections of the World and Their Directions," in ibid., 342.

33. Ibid., 347.

34. Wendy Brown, *Manhood and Politics: A Feminist Reader in Political Theory* (Lanham, MD: Rowman and Littlefield, 1988).

35. Klinger, "Woman-Landscape-Artwork," 159.

36. Weber, "Religious Rejections," 355.

37. Philippe Ariès, *Western Attitudes toward Death* (Baltimore: Johns Hopkins University Press, 1974), 56–57.

38. Weber, "Religious Rejections," 355–56.

39. John Farley and Gerald L. Geison, "Science, Politics and Spontaneous Generation in Nineteenth-Century France: The Pasteur-Pouchet Debate," *Bulletin of the History of Medicine* 48 (1974): 161–98.

40. Foucault, *History of Sexuality*, 1:138.

41. Ariès, *Western Attitudes*, 105.

42. *Densmore et al. v. Evergreen Camp*, No. 147, Supreme Court of Washington, Department Two, 61 Wash.230; 112P. 255; 1910 Wash. Lexis 1320, http://courts.mrsc.org/washreports/061WashReport/061WashReport0230.htm. Many thanks to Ellen Stroud for this reference.

43. Russ Castronovo, *Necro Citizenship: Death, Eroticism, and the Public Sphere in the Nineteenth-Century United States* (Durham, NC: Duke University Press, 2001).

44. Ariès, *Western Attitudes*, 56–57.

45. Weber, "Religious Rejections," 357.

46. A. Karina Kordela, "(Psychoanalytic) Biopolitics and Bioracism," *Umbr(a)* (2011): 19. See also Kordela, "Biopolitics: From Tribes to Commodity Fetishism," *differences* 24:1 (2013): 1–29; and Kordela, *Surplus: Spinoza, Lacan* (Albany: SUNY Press, 2007).

47. Lee Edelman, *No Future: Queer Theory and the Death Drive* (Durham, NC: Duke University Press, 2004), 66.

48. Cited in Nye, *Masculinity*, 55.

49. Ibid., 56.

50. Weber, "Religious Rejections," 347.

51. Foucault, *History of Sexuality*, 1:139–40.

52. Brian Connolly, *Domestic Intimacies: Incest and the Liberal Subject in Nineteenth-Century America* (Philadelphia: University of Pennsylvania Press, 2014), 10.

53. Judith Surkis, *Sexing the Citizen: Morality and Masculinity in France, 1870–1920* (Ithaca: Cornell University Press, 2006).

54. Connolly, *Domestic Intimacies*, 220.

55. Brian Connolly, "'Hindoo Marriage' and National Sovereignty in the Early Nineteenth-Century United States," in *Warring for America, 1803–1818*, ed. Nicole Eustace and Fredrika J. Teute (Chapel Hill: University of North Carolina Press, 2017), 25 (in MS version).

56. Hull, *Sexuality, State and Civil Society*, 318–19.

57. Florence Rochefort, "Laïcité et droits des femmes: Quelques jalons pour une réflexion historique," *Archives de Philosophie du droit* 48 (2005): 100.

58. Michelle Perrot, "Introduction" in *A History of Private Life*, 106.

59. Afsaneh Najmabadi, *Women with Mustaches and Men without Beards*, 59.

60. Hanan Kholoussy, "Talking about a Revolution: Gender and the Politics of Marriage in Early Twentieth-Century Egypt," *Graduate Researcher: Journal for the Arts, Sciences, and Technology* 1:2 (2003): 29.

61. Sara Pursley, all references that follow refer to her 2011 dissertation at the Graduate Center, City University of New York: "A Race against Time: Governing Femininity and Reproducing the Future in Revolutionary Iraq, 1945–1963," 19.

62. Ibid., 10, 20.

63. Hull, *Sexuality, State, and Civil Society*, 295.

64. Dagmar Herzog, *Intimacy and Exclusion: Religious Politics in Pre-Revolutionary Baden* (Princeton: Princeton University Press, 1996), 95–98.

65. Göran Therborn, *Between Sex and Power: Family in the World, 1900–2000* (New York: Routledge 2004), 17.

66. Rochefort, "Laïcité et droits des femmes," 101.

67. On Britain, see Francesca Klug, "Oh to Be in England': The British Case Study," in *Woman-Nation-State*, ed. Nira Yuval-Davis and Floya Anthias (London: Macmillan, 1989). For British influence in Jordan, see Joseph Massad, *Colonial Effects*, 35–38.

68. R. A. Sydie, "Sex and the Sociological Fathers," *Canadian Review of Sociology and Anthropology* 31:2 (1994): 123.

69. Janet Jakobsen, "Sex + Freedom = Regulation. Why?" *Social Text* 84–85 (2005): 294.

70. Philippe Ariès, *Centuries of Childhood: A Social History of Family Life* (New York: Vintage, 1965).

71. Jacques Donzelot, *La police des familles* (Paris: Editions des Minuit, 1977), 15.

72. Edelman, *No Future*, 114, 134.

73. Ibid., 12.

74. Ibid., 34.

75. Pursley, "A Race against Time," 18.

76. Anne Martin-Fugier, "Bourgeois Rituals," in *A History of Private Life*, vol. 4, *From the Fires of Revolution to the Great War*, ed. Michelle Perrot, trans. Arthur Goldhammer (Cambridge, MA: Harvard University Press, 1994), 336.

77. Donzelot, *La police des familles*.

78. G. J. Barker-Benfield, "The Spermatic Economy: A Nineteenth-Century View of Sexuality," *Feminist Studies* 1:1 (1972): 56.

79. Connolly, *Domestic Intimacies*; Andrew Aisenberg, *Contagion: Disease, Government, and the "Social Question" in Nineteenth-Century France* (Stanford, CA: Stanford University Press, 1999).

80. Hugh Ridley, *Images of Imperial Rule* (London: St. Martin's Press; Croom Helm, 1983), 75. See also Ridley, "Germany in the Mirror of Its Colonial Literature," *German Life and Letters* 28 (1974–75): 375–86; and Robbie Aitken, *Exclusion and Inclusion: Gradations of Whiteness and Socio-Economic Engineering in German Southwest Africa, 1884–1914* (Bern: Peter Lang, 2007).

81. Judith Surkis, *Scandalous Subjects: Intimacy and Indecency in France and French Algeria*, forthcoming.

82. A. James Hammerton, "Feminism and Female Emigration, 1861–1886," in *A Widening Sphere: Changing Roles of Victorian Women*, ed. Martha Vicinus (Bloomington: Indiana University Press, 1977), 57.

83. *L'Immigration des femmes aux colonies* [The Immigration of Women to the Colonies], Speech by M. le Comte d'Haussonville and Address by Mr. J. Chailley-Bert, at a conference given on January 12, 1897, by the French Colonial Union (Paris: Colin & Cie, 1897), 23.

84. Ibid., 59.

85. Mark Rifkin, *When Did Indians Become Straight? Kinship, the History of Sexuality, and Native Sovereignty* (Oxford: Oxford University Press, 2011), 149.

86. Ibid., 151.

87. Ibid., 152.

88. Ibid., 153. See also Tiya Miles, *Ties that Bind: The Story of an Afro-Cherokee Family in Slavery and Freedom* (Berkeley: University of California Press, 2005).

89. Andrew Zimmerman, *Alabama in Africa: Booker T. Washington, the German Empire, and the Globalization of the New South* (Princeton: Princeton University Press, 2010), 92.

90. Pursley, "A Race against Time," 162.

91. Ibid., 183–84.

92. Adam Smith, *The Wealth of Nations*, 2nd ed. (Oxford: Clarendon Press, 1880), 1:71.

93. Cited in Thérèse Moreau, *Le sang de l'histoire: Michelet, l'histoire, et l'idée de la femme aux XIXe siècle* (Paris: Flammarion 1982), 74.

94. Eli Zaretsky, *Capitalism, the Family, and Personal Life* (New York: Harper and Row, 1976), 25. See also Friedrich Engels, *The Origin of the Family, Private Property, and the State* (New York: Penguin Classics, 2010).

95. Elizabeth Maddock Dillon, *The Gender of Freedom: Fictions of Liberalism and the Literary Public Sphere* (Stanford, CA: Stanford University Press, 2004), 203.

96. Ibid.

97. Ibid., 40.

98. Cited in Jane Lewis, *Women in England, 1870–1950: Sexual Division and Social Change* (Sussex: Wheatsheaf Books, 1984), 175.

99. Donzelot, *La police des familles*, 38.

100. Cited in Mary Lynn Stewart, *Women, Work and the French State: Labour Protection and Social Patriarchy, 1879–1919* (Montreal: McGill-Queen's University Press, 1989), 175. See also Jules Simon, *L'Ouvière*, 2nd ed. (Paris: Hachette, 1861).

101. Zimmerman, *Alabama in Africa*, 96.

102. Anne McClintock, "Family Feuds: Gender, Nationalism, and the Family," *Feminist Review* 44 (1993): 64.

Chapter Three: Political Emancipation

1. Cited in Jill Lepore, "Comment: The Sovereignty of Women," *New Yorker*, April 18, 2016, 18.

2. Olympe de Gouges, *Déclaration des droits de la femme et de la citoyenne* (Paris, 1791).

3. Eliane Viennot, "De l'Ancien Régime au Nouveau: La masculinité au fondement de la modernité," in *Les défis de la république: Genre, territoires, citoyenneté*, ed. Bruno Perreau and Joan W. Scott (Paris: Presses Sciences Po, 2017).

4. Many factors determined when women got the vote: national independence, constitutional changes, war, revolution, and so on. In some cases there were also age restrictions. Here are some dates: Finland 1906; Norway 1913; USSR 1918; Germany 1919; UK 1928; Spain 1931, Turkey 1934, and Switzerland 1971.

5. Cited in Robert Nye, *Masculinity and Male Codes of Honor in Modern France* (Berkeley: University of California Press, 1998), 156.

6. Cited in *Women in Revolutionary Paris, 1789–1795*, ed. and trans. Darlene Gay Levy, Harriet Branson Applewhite, and Mary Durham Johnson (Urbana: University of Illinois Press, 1979), 215.

7. Thomas Jefferson, letter to Anne Willing Bingham, Paris, May 11, 1788, http://www.let.rug.nl/usa/presidents/thomas-jefferson/letters-of-thomas-jefferson/jefl69.php.

8. Linda Kerber, "The Republic Mother: Women and the Enlightenment—an American Perspective," *American Quarterly* 28:2 (1976): 187–205.

9. Wendy Brown, *Manhood and Politics: A Feminist Reading in Political Theory* (Lanham, MD: Rowman and Littlefield, 1988.

10. Cited in Yvonne Knibiehler, "Les médecins et la 'Nature féminine' au temps du Code civil," *Annales E.S.C. 31* (1976): 835.

11. Brown, *Manhood and Politics*, 180.

12. Hull, *Sexuality, State, and Civil Society*, 335.

13. Ibid., 411.

14. Ibid.

15. Geneviève Fraisse and Michelle Perrot, "Defining the Essence of Femininity," in *Emerging Feminism from Revolution to World War*, vol. 4 of *A History of Women in the West*, ed. Michelle Perrot (Cambridge, MA: Harvard University Press, 1993), 11.

16. Carole Pateman, *The Sexual Contract* (Stanford, CA: Stanford University Press, 1988), 113.

17. Ibid., 181.

18. Alexis de Tocqueville, *Democracy in America*, trans. Arthur Goldhammer (New York: Library of America, 2004), 705–6.

19. Ibid., 706.

20. Hull, *Sexuality, State, Civil Society*, 240.

21. Anne McClintock, *Imperial Leather: Race, Gender, and Sexuality in the Colonial Contest* (New York: Routledge, 1995), 45.

22. Quoted in Pateman, *The Sexual Contract*, 93.

23. Ibid., 97.

24. Sigmund Freud, *Totem and Taboo*, vol. 13 in the standard ed. of *The Complete Psychological Works of Sigmund Freud*, ed. James Strachey (London: Hogarth Press, 1995), 142.

25. Ibid., 146.

26. Ibid., 149.

27. Joan Copjec, *Read My Desire: Lacan against the Historicists* (Cambridge, MA: MIT Press, 1994), 154.

28. Freud, *Totem and Taboo*, 144. See also Jacques Lacan, "The Signification of the Phallus," trans. Alan Sheridan, in Lacan, *Écrits: A Selection*, trans. Bruce Fink (London: Tavistock, 1977).

29. Ernst H. Kantorowicz, *The King's Two Bodies: A Study in Medieval Political Theology* (Princeton: Princeton University Press, 1957).

30. Peter Stallybrass and Allon White, *The Politics and Poetics of Transgression* (Ithaca: Cornell University Press, 1986).

31. Cited in Jules Tixerant, *Le féminisme à l'époque de 1848 dans l'ordre politique et l'ordre économique* (Paris: V. Girard and E. Brière, 1908), 86.

32. J-J. Rousseau, *Emile, or On Education*, trans. Allan Bloom (New York: Basic Books, 1979), 358–59. See also Linda Zerilli, *Signifying Woman: Culture and Chaos in Rousseau, Burke, and Mill* (Ithaca: Cornell University Press, 1994).

33. Pateman, *The Sexual Contract*, 177.

34. Lacan, "The Signification of the Phallus."

35. Judith Surkis, "Carnival Balls and Penal Codes: Body Politics in July Monarchy France," *History of the Present* 1:1 (2011): 77–78.

36. Claude Lefort, *Democracy and Political Theory*, trans. David Macey (Cambridge: Polity Press, 1988), 17.

37. Ibid., 19.

38. Max Weber, "The Social Psychology of the World Religions," in *From Max Weber: Essays in Sociology*, ed. and trans. H. H. Gerth and C. Wright Mills (New York: Routledge, 1998), 299.

39. Copjec, *Read My Desire*, 153.

40. Lefort, *Democracy and Political Theory*, 17.

41. Joan Wallach Scott, "Introduction: Flyers into the Unknown," in *The Fantasy of Feminist History* (Durham, NC: Duke University Press, 2011), 1–22.

42. Françoise Thébaud, "The Great War and the Triumph of Sexual Division," in *A History of Women in the West*, vol. 5, *Toward a Cultural Identity in the Twentieth Century*, trans. Arthur Goldhammer, ed. Françoise Thébaud, gen. ed. Georges Duby and Michelle Perrot (Cambridge, MA: Harvard University Press, 1994), 35.

43. Mary Louise Roberts, *Civilization without Sexes: Reconstructing Gender in Postwar France, 1917–1927* (Chicago: University of Chicago Press, 1994), 4.

44. Marquis de Condorcet, "On the Admission of Women to the Rights of Citizenship (1790)," in *Selected Writings*, ed. Keith Michael Baker (Indianapolis: Bobbs-Merrill, 1976), 98.

45. Levy, Applewhite, and Johnson, *Women in Revolutionary Paris*, 220.

46. Ibid.

47. Cited in Karen Offen, "Ernest Legouvé and the Doctrine of 'Equality in Difference' for Women: A Case Study of Male Feminism in Nineteenth-Century French Thought," *Journal of Modern History* 58:2 (1986): 476.

48. Cited in Christine Fauré, *La démocratie sans les femmes: Essai sur le libéralisme en France* (Paris: Presses Universitaires de France, 1986), 226.

49. Jacques Alary, *Le travail de la femme dans l'imprimerie typographique; Ses conséquences physiques et morales* (Paris, 1883), 15.

50. Joan Wallach Scott, *Only Paradoxes to Offer: French Feminists and the Rights of Man* (Cambridge, MA: Harvard University Press, 1996), 118–19.

51. Eliane Gubin, Catherine Jacques, and Claudine Marissal, "Une citoyenneté différée? Le suffrage féminin en Belgique, 1830–1940," in *Féminismes et identités nationales*, ed. Yolande Cohen and Françoise Thébaud (Programme Rhône-Alpes de recherche en sciences humaines, 1998), 100.

52. Sara Evans, *Born for Liberty: A History of Women in America* (New York: Free Press, 1989), 56.

53. Ibid., 154.

54. Nancy Cott, *The Grounding of Modern Feminism* (New Haven: Yale University Press, 1989), 13.

55. Patricia Hollis, *Women in Public, 1850–1900: Documents of the Victorian Women's Movement* (London: George Allen and Unwin, 1979), 305.

56. Ibid., 307.

57. Ibid., 320.

58. Jill Conway, "Stereotypes of Femininity in a Theory of Sexual Evolution," in *Suffer and Be Still: Women in the Victorian Age*, ed. Martha Vicinus (Bloomington: Indiana University Press, 1972), 144.

59. Ibid., 146.

60. Scott, *Only Paradoxes to Offer*.

61. Denise Riley, *"Am I that Name?"*, see especially 67–69 and 112–13. See also Cott, *The Grounding of Modern Feminism*.

62. Hollis, *Women in Public*, 28–30.

63. Ibid., 312.

64. Ibid., 331.

65. Evans, *Born for Liberty*, 15.

66. Cited in Scott, *Only Paradoxes to Offer*, 77.

67. Riley, *"Am I that Name?,"* 46.

68. Ibid., 48.

69. Ibid., 72–73.

70. Simone de Beauvoir, *The Second Sex*, trans. and ed. H. M. Parshley (New York: Vintage Books, 1974), 150.

71. Ibid., 758.

72. Cott, *The Grounding of Modern Feminism*, 110.

73. Scott, *Parité*, 143.

74. Riley, *"Am I that Name?,"* 112–13.

75. Cott, *The Grounding of Modern Feminism*, 186.

76. Seth Koven and Sonya Michel, "Womanly Duties: Maternalist Politics and the Origins of Welfare States in France, Germany, Great Britain, and the United States," in *Gender and History in Western Europe*, ed. Robert Shoemaker and Mary Vincent (London: Arnold, 1998), 339.

77. Ibid.

78. Madeleine Pelletier, *La Femme en lutte pour ses droits* (Paris, 1907), 37. On Pelletier, see Scott, *Only Paradoxes to Offer*, 125–60.

79. Cott, *The Grounding of Modern Feminism*, 221.

80. Ibid., 174.

81. Hester Eisenstein, *Feminism Seduced: How Global Elites Use Women's Labor and Ideas to Exploit the World* (Boulder, CO: Paradigm, 2009).

82. Rose-Marie Lagrave, "A Supervised Emancipation," in *A History of Women in the West*, vol. 5, *Toward a Cultural Identity in the Twentieth Century*, ed. Françoise Thébaud (Cambridge, MA: Harvard University Press, 1994), 467.

83. Ibid., 488.

84. Nilüfer Göle, "The Gendered Nature of the Public Sphere," *Public Culture* 10:1 (1997): 68. See also Göle, *Islam and Secularity: The Future of Europe's Public Sphere* (Durham, NC: Duke University Press, 2015).

85. Jenny White, "State Feminism, Modernization, and the Turkish Republican Woman," *NWSA Journal* 15:3 (2003): 153–54.

86. Deniz Kandiyoti, "Emancipated but Unliberated? Reflections on the Turkish Case," *Feminist Studies* 13:2 (1987): 324. See also Alev Cinar, "Subversion and Subjugation in the Public Sphere: Secularism and the Islamic Headscarf," *Signs* 33:4 (2008): 891–913; Zehra F. Arat, "Kemalism and Turkish Women," *Women and Politics* 14:4 (1994): 57–80.

87. Sara Pursley, "A Race against Time," 83.

88. Ibid.

89. Elizabeth Thompson, *Colonial Citizens: Republican Rights, Paternal Privilege, and Gender in French Syria and Lebanon* (New York: Columbia University Press, 2000), 143.

90. Mrinalini Sinha, *Specters of Mother India: The Global Restructuring of an Empire* (Durham, NC: Duke University Press, 2006), 235.

91. Ibid.

92. Ibid.

93. Ibid.

94. Ibid., 222.

95. Ibid., 253.

96. Lefort, *Democracy and Political Theory*, 39.

Chapter Four: From the Cold War to the Clash of Civilizations

1. Jacques Maritain referred to it as "theocratic atheism." Cited in Samuel Moyn, "From Communist to Muslim: European Human Rights, the Cold War, and Religious Liberty," *South Atlantic Quarterly* 113:1 (2014): 72.

2. The history of religion under Soviet communism is far more complex than the anticommunist rhetoric suggests. Even though atheism was state policy, religion was not entirely suppressed; indeed, it was sometimes tolerated and even encouraged by officials. On changing Soviet policy toward religion, see S. A. Smith, "Communism and Religion," in *The Cambridge History of Communism*, ed. Juliane Furst, Silvio Pons, and Mark Selden, vol. 3 (Cambridge: Cambridge University Press, 2017).

3. Dianne Kirby, "Harry Truman's Religious Legacy: The Holy Alliance, Containment, and the Cold War," in *Religion and the Cold War*, ed. Kirby (Basingstoke: Palgrave Macmillan, 2003), 78.

4. See Thomas Aiello, "Constructing 'Godless Communism': Religion, Politics, and Popular Culture, 1954–60," *Americana: The Journal of American Popular Culture* 4:1 (2005).

5. Tony Shaw, "'Martyrs, Miracles, and Martians': Religious and Cold War Cinematic Propaganda in the 1950s," in *Religion and the Cold War*, ed. Kirby 214.

6. Michel Foucault, *The Birth of Biopolitics: Lectures at the Collège de France, 1978–1979*, trans. Graham Burchell (New York: Palgrave Macmillan, 2004), 63.

7. Ibid., 65. For an incisive analysis based on these lectures, see Letitia Sabsay, "The Emergence of the Other Sexual Citizen: Orientalism and the Modernisation of Sexuality," *Citizenship Studies* 16:5–6 (2012): 605–23.

8. Dianne Kirby, "Harry Truman's Religious Legacy: The Holy Alliance, Containment and the Cold War," in *Religion and the Cold War*, ed. Kirby, 80.

9. Winston Churchill, "Sinews of Peace," March 5, 1946, http://www.historyguide.org/europe/churchill.html.

10. Cited in Frances Stonor Saunders, *The Cultural Cold War: The CIA and the World of Arts and Letters* (New York: New Press, 1999), 58. See also Dianne Kirby, "Divinely Sanctioned: The Anglo-American Cold War Alliance and the Defence of Western Civilization and Christianity, 1945–48," *Journal of Contemporary History* 35:3 (2000): 412.

11. Moyn, "From Communist to Muslim," 76.

12. Dianne Kirby, "The Religious Cold War," in *The Oxford Handbook of the Cold War*, ed. Richard H. Immerman and Petra Goedde (Oxford: Oxford University Press, 2013), 549.

13. George Egerton, "Between War and Peace: Politics, Religion and Human Rights in Early Cold War Canada, 1945–50," in *Religion and the Cold War*, ed. Kirby, 163.

14. Ibid.

15. United Nations Universal Declaration of Human Rights, 1948, http://www.un.org/en/universal-declaration-human-rights/.

16. Egerton, "Between War and Peace," 175.

17. Moyn "From Communist to Muslim," 76.

18. European Convention on Human Rights, 1950, https://en.wikipedia.org/wiki/European_Convention_on_Human_Rights.

19. Moyn, "From Communist to Muslim," 77.

20. Ibid., 65, 77.

21. Ibid., 72.

22. For example, Moyn reads the Irish delegate to the EC as referring to the "persecutory spirit of political secularism" when it is Eastern Europe and Soviet atheism that is his target (76). He restates Maritain's reference to "theocratic atheism" as "theocratic secularism" (72), and he elides any difference between secularism and atheism when he uses the terms in reference to the Soviets, as if they mean the same thing for those who used the terms *at the time*.

23. Kirby, "The Religious Cold War," 549.

24. Ibid., 549–50.

25. Brenda Gayle Plummer, "Race and the Cold War," in *The Oxford Handbook of the Cold War*, ed. Immerman and Goedde, 503.

26. The poster can be viewed in the article by Vincze Miklós, "Anti-Communist Propaganda Is More Awesome than Any Horror Movie Poster," io9.gizmodo website, November 7, 2013, http://io9.gizmodo.com/anti-communist-propaganda-is-more-awesome-than-any-horr-1460028336.

27. Ibid.

28. Cited in Massad, *Islam in Liberalism*, 55.

29. Dianne Kirby, "The Religious Cold War," 552. See also Massad, *Islam in Liberalism*, 109.

30. Kirby, "The Religious Cold War," 553.

31. The term was originally coined by Bernard Lewis in "The Roots of Muslim Rage," *Atlantic Monthly* 266 (September 1990): 60: "This is no less than a clash of civilizations—the perhaps irrational but surely historic reaction of an ancient rival versus our Judeo-Christian heritage, our secular present, and the worldwide expansion of both."

32. Samuel P. Huntington, "Democracy's Third Wave," *Journal of Democracy* (Spring 1993): 13.

33. Peter Waldman and Hugh Pope, "Updated 'Crusade' Reference Reinforces Fears War on Terrorism Is against Muslims," *Wall Street Journal* online, Sept. 21, 2001, http://www.wsj.com/articles/SB1001020294332922160.

34. Cited in Massad, *Islam in Liberalism*, 14.

35. Cited by Eric Fassin, "National Identities and Transnational Intimacies: Sexual Democracy and the Politics of Immigration in Europe," *Public Culture* 22:3 (2010): 519.

36. Ibid., 521.

37. "German Chancellor Angela Merkel: NWO Has Failed, Germany Returning to Its Christian Roots!," October 18, 2010, https://politicalvelcraft.org/2010/10/18/german-chancellor-angela-merkel-nwo-has-failed-germany-returning-to-its-christian-roots.

38. Joseph Ratzinger and Jürgen Habermas, *The Dialectics of Secularization: On Reason and Religion* (San Francisco: Ignatius Press, 2007).

39. Jürgen Habermas, *Time of Transitions* (Cambridge: Polity, 2006), 150–51.

40. Pope Benedict XVI, "Regensburg address," September 12, 2006, Zenit.org, https://zenit.org/articles/papal-address-at-university-of-regensburg/.

41. George Friedman, "A Net Assessment of the Middle East," *Geopolitical Weekly*, June 9, 2015, https://www.stratfor.com/weekly/net-assessment-middle-east.

42. Harrison E. Salisbury, "Nixon and Khrushchev Argue in Public as U.S. Exhibit Opens; Accuse Each Other of Threats," *New York Times*, July 24, 1959. For this and other coverage of the debate, see http://www.nytimes.com/learning/general/onthisday/big/0724.html#article.

43. Elaine Tyler May, *Homeward Bound: American Families in the Cold War Era* (New York: Basic Books, [1988] 2008), 13.

44. Marga Vicedo, *The Nature and Nurture of Love: From Imprinting to Attachment in Cold War America* (Chicago: University of Chicago Press, 2014), 80.

45. Helen Laville, "Gender and Women's Rights in the Cold War," in *The Oxford Handbook of the Cold War*, ed. Immerman and Goedde, 531.

46. Ibid., 530. Another battleground was, of course, the question of race. See Saunders, *The Cultural Cold War*, 20.

47. Susan Gal and Gail Kligman, *The Politics of Gender after Socialism* (Princeton: Princeton University Press, 2000). See also Celia Donert, "Women's Rights in Cold War Europe: Disentangling Feminist Histories," *Past and Present* Supplement 8 (2013): 178–202.

48. Cited in Laville, "Gender and Women's Rights," 530.

49. In this vein, Leon Trotsky in 1924 saw "new economic relations" as the solution for the religious oppression of "the Eastern [Muslim] woman, in her habits and in creativity, the slave of slaves." Cited in Massad, *Islam in Liberalism*, 120.

50. May, *Homeward Bound*, 22.

51. Ibid., 132.

52. Francisca de Haan, "Continuing Cold War Paradigms in Western Historiography of Transnational Women's Organizations: The Case of the Women's International Democratic Federation (WIDF)," *Women's History Review* 19:4 (2010): 547–73, http://wasi.alexanderstreet.com/help/view/the_womens_international_democratic_federation_widf_history_main_agenda_and_contributions_19451991. See also Donert, "Women's Rights in Cold War Europe."

53. Cited in Kate Weigand, "The Red Menace: The Feminine Mystique and Ohio Un-American Activities Commission," *Journal of Women's History* 3 (1992): 71.

54. May, *Homeward Bound*, 91.

55. Ibid., 95.

56. Emily Rosenberg, "Foreign Affairs after WWII," *Diplomatic History* 18 (1994): 68.

57. Ibid., 70.

58. May, *Homeward Bound*, 99.

59. Dagmar Herzog, *Sexuality in Europe: A Twentieth-Century History* (Cambridge: Cambridge University Press, 2011), 106.

60. May, *Homeward Bound*, 142.

61. Ibid., 142–43.

62. Herzog, *Sexuality in Europe*, 107 and 137–39. Expansion in use of the pill was exponential. By 1969, one in ten Italian women were using it. There are similar figures for Spain and France. In West Germany, by 1968 1.4 million women were using it. "By 1975–77, one third of all fertile women in W[est] Germany were relying on the pill; among younger women, the rates were even higher—close to 80% of young women under age 20" (139).

63. Francisca de Haan offers several examples of feminist activism in the 1940s and '50s, including the Congress of American Women, founded in 1946 as a branch of the Women's International Democratic Federation (1945), and Women Strike for Peace (1961), another US group. See de Haan, "Continuing Cold War Paradigms in Western Historiography of Transnational Women's Organisations."

64. Jocelyn Olcott, "Cold War Conflicts and Cheap Cabaret: Sexual Politics at the 1975 United Nations International Women's Year Conference," *Gender and History* 22:3 (2010): 733–54.

65. Gisela Bock, "Poverty and Mothers' Rights in the Emerging Welfare States," in *A History of Women in the West*, vol. 5, *Toward a Cultural Identity in the Twentieth Century*, ed. Françoise Thébaud (Cambridge, MA: Harvard University Press, 1994), 405.

66. Abortion rights in the West were extended in the UK (1967), Canada (1969), the United States (1973), France (1975), Italy (1978), the Netherlands (1980), and Belgium (1990).

67. C. Alison McIntosh and Jason L. Finkle, "The Cairo Conference on Population and Development: A New Paradigm?," *Population and Development Review* 21:2 (1995): 227.

68. Samuel Moyn, *The Last Utopia: Human Rights in History* (Cambridge, MA: Harvard University Press, 2010), 12.

69. Kristen Ghodsee, "Revisiting the United Nations Decade for Women: Brief Reflections on Feminism, Capitalism and Cold War Politics in the Early Years of the International Women's Movement," *Women's Studies International Forum*, Special Issue: "Compliance without Commitment? The EU's Gender Equality Agenda in the Central and Eastern Europe States," *ScienceDirect* 33 (1): 3–12, January–February 2010.

70. Herzog, *Sexuality in Europe*, 1–3.

71. Eli Zaretsky, *Capitalism, the Family, and Personal Life* (New York: Harper and Row, 1976).

72. Herzog, *Sexuality in Europe*, 133.

73. Ibid., 146.

74. Alfred C. Kinsey et al., *Sexual Behavior in the Human Male* (Philadelphia: W. B. Saunders, [1948] 1998); Bloomington: Indiana University Press, [1953] 1998); Alfred C. Kinsey et al., *Sexual Behavior in the Human Female* (Philadelphia: W. B. Saunders, [1953] 1998; Bloomington: Indiana University Press); W. H. Masters and V. Johnson, *Human Sexual Behavior* (New York: Bantam Books, [1966] 1994).

75. Bonnie Smith, ed., *Global Feminisms since 1945: A Survey of Issues and Controversies* (New York: Routledge, 2000); Ruth Rosen, *The World Split Open: How the Modern Women's Movement Changed America* (New York: Penguin, 2006); Nancy Holmstrom, *The Socialist Feminist Project: A Contemporary Reader in Theory and Politics* (New York: Monthly Review Press, 2004); Lillian Faderman, *The Gay Revolution: The Story of the Struggle* (New York: Simon and Schuster, 2015); Barry D. Adam, *The Rise of a Gay and Lesbian Movement*, rev. ed. (New York: Twayne, 1995); David Paternotte and Marion Tremblay, eds., *The Ashgate Research Companion to Lesbian and Gay Activism* (Abingdon: Ashgate, 2015).

76. Ann Snitow, Christine Stansell, and Sharon Thompson, *Powers of Desire: The Politics of Sexuality* (New York: Monthly Review Press, 1983), 41.

77. Catharine A. MacKinnon, "Feminism, Marxism, Method, and the State: An Agenda for Theory," in *Feminism and Sexuality: A Reader*, ed. Stevi Jackson and Mary McIntosh (New York: Columbia University Press, 1996), 182–90.

78. Monique Wittig, "One Is Not Born a Woman," in *The Norton Anthology of Theory and Criticism*, ed. Vincent B. Letich (New York: W. W. Norton, 2010).

79. Shulamith Firestone, *The Dialectic of Sex: The Case for Feminist Revolution* (New York: Bantam, 1970).

80. Jessica Spector, *Prostitution and Pornography: Philosophical Debate about the Sex Industry* (Stanford, CA: Stanford University Press, 2006).

81. Marianne Hirsch and Evelyn Fox Keller, eds., *Conflicts in Feminism* (New York: Routledge, 1990).

82. A good overview is "Feminist Perspectives on Class and Work," *Stanford Encyclopedia of Philosophy* online, https://plato.stanford.edu/entries/feminism-class/.

83. Snitow et al., *Powers of Desire*, 35.

84. Ibid., 41–42.

85. Emily Martin, "The End of the Body?," *American Ethnologist* (1992): 121.

86. Sabsay, "The Emergence of the Other Sexual Citizen," 608.

87. Massad, *Islam in Liberalism*, 217.

88. Sabsay, "The Emergence of the Other Sexual Citizen," 610.

89. Massad, *Islam in Liberalism*, 132–33.

90. Elizabeth Bernstein, "Introduction: Sexual Economies and New Regimes of Governance," *Social Politics* 21:3 (2014): 345–54. See also her *Brokered Subjects: Sex, Trafficking, and the Politics of Freedom* (Chicago: University of Chicago Press, 2017).

91. Massad, *Islam in Liberalism*, 145.

92. Inderpal Grewal, *Transnational America* (Durham, NC: Duke University Press, 2005), 157. See also the discussion of these issues in Massad, *Islam in Liberalism*, 135–45.

93. Fassin, "National Identities and Transnational Intimacies," 513.

94. Joanna Goven, "Gender Politics in Hungary: Autonomy and Antifeminism," in *Gender Politics and Post-Communism: Reflections from Eastern Europe and the Former Soviet Union*, ed. Nanette Funk and Magda Mueller (New York: Routledge, 1993), 227.

95. Gal and Kligman, *The Politics of Gender*, 69.

96. Roman Kuhar, "Playing with Science: Sexual Citizenship and the Roman Catholic Counter-Narratives in Slovenia and Croatia," *Women's Studies International Forum* online, August 14, 2014.

97. Gal and Kligman, *The Politics of Gender*, 29.

98. Ibid., 69.

99. Ibid.

100. Katalin Fabian, *Contemporary Women's Movements in Hungary: Globalization, Democracy, and Gender Equality* (Washington, DC: Woodrow Wilson Center Press and Johns Hopkins University Press, 2009).

101. On this history, see the important work of Ioana Cirstocea, "La fin du Deuxième Monde et la seconde vie de la femme rouge: Sociologie politique des constructions transnationales du genre en contexte postsocialiste," *Mémoire de Recherche Original*, Dossier pour l'habilitation à diriger des recherches, Université du Paris 1, Panthéon Sorbonne, January 2017.

102. Doina Psca Harsanyi, "Women in Romania," in Funk and Mueller, *Gender Politics and Post-Communism*, 49.

103. Ewa Hauser, Barbara Heyns, and Jane Mansbridge, "Feminism in the Interstices of Politics and Culture: Poland in Transition," in Funk and Mueller, *Gender Politics and Post-Communism*, 267.

104. Slavenka Drakulic, "Women and the New Democracy in the Former Yugoslavia," in Funk and Mueller, *Gender Politics and Post-Communism*, 127.

105. Irene Dölling, "'But the Pictures Stay the Same . . .' The Image of Women in the Journal *Für Dich* before and after the 'Turning Point,'" in Funk and Mueller, *Gender Politics and Post-Communism*, 177.

106. Larissa Lissyutkina, "Soviet Women at the Crossroads of Perestroika," in Funk and Mueller, *Gender Politics and Post-Communism*, 284.

107. Elizabeth Waters, "Finding a Voice: The Emergence of a Women's Movement," Interview with Anastasya Posadskaya and Valentina Konstantinova of the Center for Gender Studies in Moscow, in Funk and Mueller, *Gender Politics and Post-Communism*, 295.

108. Ibid., 296–97.

109. See Goven, "Gender Politics in Hungary," in Funk and Mueller, *Gender Politics and Post-Communism*, 224–40.

110. Gal and Kligman, *The Politics of Gender*, 83.

111. See the long discussion of this from many scholars in the forum edited by Francisca de Haan, "Ten Years After: Communism and Feminism Revisited," *Aspasia* 10 (2016): 102–68.

Chapter Five: Sexual Emancipation

1. *Le Nouvel observateur*, November 2, 1989.

2. Inglehart and Norris, "The True Clash of Civilizations," 65.

3. Ibid., 68.

4. Martha Nussbaum, *Women and Human Development: The Capabilities Approach* (Cambridge: Cambridge University Press, 2001), 78–79.

5. Cited in Mayanthi Fernando, *The Republic Unsettled: Muslim French and the Contradictions of Secularism* (Durham, NC: Duke University Press, 2014), 210.

6. Ibid.

7. Ibid., 211.

8. See, for one example, Dan Bilefsky, "Ordered to Wear Heels, She Ignited a Rebellion," *New York Times*, January 26, 2017, A9.

9. Hester Eisenstein, *Feminism Seduced: How Global Elites Use Women's Labor and Ideas to Exploit the World* (Boulder, CO: 2009), viii–ix.

10. Nicolas Sarkozy, "Convention sur l'immigration—Une immigration choisie, une intégration réussie," Address to the Convention of the Union for a Popular Movement (UMP), June 9, 2005. I am grateful to Eric Fassin for this reference. See also Fassin, "La démocratie sexuelle et le conflit des civilisations," *Multitudes* 26 (Fall 2006): 123–31.

11. Dina M. Siddiqi, "Solidarity, Sexuality and Saving Muslim Women in Neoliberal Times," *Women's Studies Quarterly* 42:3/4 (2014): 292–306. For an article about the ad, see http://www.elle.com/news/culture/american-apparel-bangladesh-ad. A similar argument about the equation of nude women's bodies with sexual liberation comes from two scholars who interpreted Ayaan Hirsi Ali's film *Submission* (made with Theo van Gogh) in these terms: "Female nakedness signifies the rights of an autonomous woman's body"—even though that body is being presented for men to see. Marc de Leeuw and Sonja van Wichelen, "Please, Go Wake Up: Submission, Hirsi Ali and the 'War on Terror" in the Netherlands," *Feminist Media Studies* 5:3 (2005): 332.

12. Eric Fassin, "National Identities and Transnational Intimacies: Sexual Democracy and the Politics of Immigration in Europe," *Public Culture* 22:3 (Fall 2010): 513.

13. Anne Norton, *On the Muslim Question* (Princeton: Princeton University Press, 2013).

14. Michel Foucault, "The Confession of the Flesh," in *Power/Knowledge: Selected Interviews and Other Writings, 1972–1977*, by Foucault, ed. Colin Gordon (New York: Pantheon Books, 1970), 219.

15. Foucault, *History of Sexuality* (New York: Vintage Books, 1980), 1: 103.

16. Ibid., 1:26.

17. Ibid., 1:146.

18. Ibid., 1:78.

19. Ibid., 1:57.

20. Foucault, "The Confession of the Flesh," in *Power/Knowledge*, 220.

21. It is ironic that Foucault's critique itself provided inspiration for the churning out of more and more studies of sex and sexuality, themselves fueling the notion of the centrality of sex as a natural phenomenon.

22. See, for example, Elizabeth Bernstein, "The Sexual Politics of the 'New Abolitionism,'" *differences* 18:3 (2007): 128–51 and *Temporarily Yours: Intimacy, Authenticity, and the Commerce of Sex* (Chicago: University of Chicago Press, 2007); Dagmar Herzog, *Sex in Crisis: The New Sexual Revolution and the Future of American Politics* (New York: Basic Books, 2008); Carole S. Vance, "States of Contradiction: Twelve Ways to Do Nothing about Trafficking while Pretending to," *Social Research* 78:3 (Fall 2011): 933–45 and "Innocence and Experience: Melodramatic Narratives of Sex Trafficking and Their Consequences for Law and Policy," *History of the Present* 2:2 (2012): 200–218.

23. Peter van der Veer, "Pim Fortuyn, Theo van Gogh, and the Politics of Tolerance in the Netherlands," *Public Culture* 18 (2006): 120.

24. Sarah Schulman, "Israel and 'Pinkwashing,'" *New York Times*, November 22, 2011.

25. Norton, *On the Muslim Question*, 57.

26. Saba Mahmood, *The Politics of Piety* (Princeton: Princeton University Press, 2004), 17. The classic work on this is Judith Butler, *The Psychic Life of Power* (Stanford, CA: Stanford University Press, 1997).

27. Ibid., 32.

28. Ibid., 28.

29. Nilüfer Göle, "Manifestations of the Religious-Secular Divide: Self-State and the Public Sphere," in *Comparative Secularisms in a Global Age*, ed. Linell E. Cady and Elizabeth Shakman Hurd (New York: Palgrave Macmillan, 2010), 49–50.

30. Ibid., 48.

31. Ibid., 49.

32. Ibid., 50.

33. Sara Farris, "Femonationalism and the 'Regular' Army of Labor Called Migrant Women," *History of the Present* 2:2 (Fall 2012): 196.

34. Alexandra Chasin, *Selling Out: The Gay and Lesbian Movement Goes to Market* (New York: Palgrave, 2000); David Harvey, "Neoliberalism as Creative Destruction," *Annals of the American Academy of Political and Social Science* 610 (March 2007): 31. See also Lisa Rofel, *Desiring China: Experiments in Neoliberalism, Sexuality, and Public Culture* (Durham, NC: Duke University Press, 2007). She writes, "If socialist power operated on the terrain of 'consciousness,' postsocialist power operates on the site of 'desire'" (6). In the new China, as elsewhere, toleration includes "the 'right' of homosexuality to exist along with the right of all desires to flourish" (24).

35. A. Kiarina Kordela, "(Psychoanalytic) Biopolitics and Bioracism," in *Umbr(a)* (2011): 19. See also her "Consent beyond Ideology: (Marxian-Psychoanalytic) Biopolitics," *differences* 24:1 (Spring 2013).

36. Ibid.

37. Comte Stanislas de Clermont-Tonnerre, cited in Esther Benbassa, *The Jews of France: A History from Antiquity to the Present*, trans. M. B. DeBevoise (Princeton: Princeton University Press, 1999), 81.

38. Norton, *On the Muslim Question* (Princeton: Princeton University Press, 2013), 171.

39. Wendy Brown, *States of Injury: Power and Freedom in Late Modernity* (Princeton: Princeton University Press, 1995), 133–34.

40. Saidiya V. Hartman, *Scenes of Subjection: Terror, Slavery, and Self-Making in Nineteenth-Century America* (New York: Oxford University Press, 1997), 6.

41. Scott, *Only Paradoxes to Offer*.

42. Ayaan Hirsi Ali, *Infidel* (New York: Free Press, 2007).

43. André Glucksmann, *L'Exprès* (1994), cited in Thomas Deltombe, *L'Islam imaginaire: La construction médiatique de l'Islamophobie en France, 1975–2005* (Paris: La Découverte, 2005). Jacques Chirac, cited in Deltombe, ibid., 347.

44. Anne Vigerie and Anne Zelensky, "Laïcardes' pusique féministes," *Pro-Choix* 25 (Summer 2003): 12.

45. Here Norton's comments on the Jewish Question are pertinent: "It was characteristic of the Jewish Question in its practical and historical form that Jews were marked out as a political threat even as they were subject to political assaults; marked as evil even as conduct toward them testified to the failure of the ethical system that had abandoned them." *On the Muslim Question*, 2.

46. Karl Marx, "On the Jewish Question," in *The Marx-Engels Reader*, ed. Robert Tucker (New York: Norton, 1978), 29–30.

47. *The Compact Edition of the Oxford English Dictionary* (New York: Oxford University Press, 1971), 1:848.

48. Ibid.

49. Hartman, *Scenes of Subjection*, 57.

50. Marx, "On the Jewish Question," 33.

51. Ibid.

52. Karl Marx, *Capital*, ed. Frederick Engels, trans. Samuel Moore and Edward Aveling (New York: Modern Library, 1947), 69.

53. Wendy Brown, *Undoing the Demos: Neoliberalism's Stealth Revolution* (Cambridge, MA: Zone Books, 2015).

54. Ibid.

55. E. Deci and R. Ryan, eds., *Handbook of Self-Determination Research* (Rochester, NY: University of Rochester Press, 2002); Bald de Vries and Lyana Francot, "Information, Decision and Self-Determination: Euthanasia as a Case Study," *SCRIPTed* 6:3 (2009): 558. See also the entry in Wikipedia for "self-determination theory," http://en.wikipedia.org/wiki/self-determination_theory.

56. Kevin Lloyd, *The Reification of Desire: Toward a Queer Marxism* (Minneapolis: University of Minnesota Press, 2009).

57. Eli Zaretsky, *Capitalism, the Family, and Personal Life* (New York: Harper and Row, 1976), 111.

58. Foucault lecture (January 25, 1978) in Foucault, *Security, Territory, Population: Lectures at the Collège de France, 1977–78*, trans. Graham Burchell (New York: Palgrave, 2007), 74.

59. Viviana A. Zelizer, *The Purchase of Intimacy* (Princeton: Princeton University Press, 2005).

60. Norton, *On the Muslim Question*, 56.

61. The classic study is, of course, Judith Butler, *Gender Trouble: Feminism and the Subversion of Identity* (New York: Routledge, 1990).

62. Joan Wallach Scott, "The Veil and the Political Unconscious of French Republicanism," *OrientXXI*, April 27, 2016, http://orientxxi.info/magazine/the-veil-and-the-political-unconscious-of-french-republicanism,1310,1310.

BIBLIOGRAPHY

Adam, Barry D. *The Rise of a Gay and Lesbian Movement*. Rev. ed. New York: Twayne, 1995.

Agulhon, Maurice. *Marianne au combat: L'imagerie et la symbolique républicaine de 1789 à 1880*. Paris: Flammarion, 1992.

Aisenberg, Andrew. *Contagion: Disease, Government, and the "Social Question" in Nineteenth-Century France*. Stanford, CA: Stanford University Press, 1999.

Aitken, Robbie. *Exclusion and Inclusion: Gradations of Whiteness and Socio-Economic Engineering in German Southwest Africa, 1884–1914*. Bern: Peter Lang, 2007.

Anidjar, Gil. "Secularism." *Critical Inquiry* 33 (2006): 52–77.

Arat, Zehra F. "Kemalism and Turkish Women." *Women and Politics* 14:4 (1994): 57–80.

Ariès, Philippe. *Centuries of Childhood: A Social History of Family Life*. New York: Vintage, 1965.

———. *Western Attitudes toward Death*. Baltimore: Johns Hopkins University Press, 1974.

Armstrong, Nancy. *Desire and Domestic Fiction: A Political History of the Novel*. New York: Oxford University Press, 1987.

Asad, Talal. *Formations of the Secular: Christianity, Islam, Modernity*. Stanford, CA: Stanford University Press, 2003.

———. *Genealogies of Religion: Disciplines and Reasons of Power in Christianity and Islam*. Baltimore: Johns Hopkins University Press, 2009.

Ashton, Trevor, ed. *Crisis in Europe, 1560–1660*. New York: Basic Books, 1965.

Auclert, Hubertine. *Les femmes arabes en Algérie*. Paris, 1900.

———. *Le vote des femmes*. Paris, 1908.

Azmeh, Aziz al-. *Islam and Modernities*. London: Verso, 1993.

Barker-Benfield, G. J. *The Culture of Sensibility: Sex and Society in Eighteenth-Century Britain*. Chicago: University of Chicago Press, 1996.

———. "The Spermatic Economy: A Nineteenth Century View of Sexuality." *Feminist Studies* 1:1 (1972): 45–74.

Baron, Beth. "The Making of the Egyptian Nation." In *Gendered Nations: Nationalisms and Gender Order in the Long Nineteenth Century*, ed. Ida Blom, Karen Hagemann, and Catherine Hall, 138. Oxford: Berg, 2000.

Barthes, Roland. *Michelet*. New York: Hill and Wang, 1987.

Beauvoir, Simone de. *The Second Sex*. Trans and ed. H. M. Parshley. New York: Vintage Books, 1974.

Benbassa, Esther. *The Jews of France: A History from Antiquity to the Present*. Trans. M. B. DeBevoise. Princeton: Princeton University Press, 1999.

Bernstein, Elizabeth. *Brokered Subjects: Sex, Trafficking, and the Politics of Freedom*. Chicago: University of Chicago Press, 2017.

———. "Introduction: Sexual Economies and New Regimes of Governance." *Social Politics* 21:3 (2014): 345–54.

———. "The Sexual Politics of the 'New Abolitionism.'" *differences* 18:3 (2007): 128–51.

———. *Temporarily Yours: Intimacy, Authenticity, and the Commerce of Sex*. Chicago: University of Chicago Press, 2007.

Bhargava, Rajeev, ed. *Secularism and Its Critics*. New Delhi: Oxford University Press, 1998.

Bock, Gisela. "Poverty and Mothers' Rights in the Emerging Welfare States." In *A History of Women in the West*, gen. ed. Georges Duby and Michelle Perrot. Vol. 5, *Toward a Cultural Identity in the Twentieth Century*, ed. Françoise Thébaud. Cambridge, MA: Harvard University Press, 1994.

Borie, Jean. "Une gynécologie passionné." In *Misérable et glorieuse: La femme du XIXe siècle*, ed. Jean-Paul Aron. Paris: Fayard, 1980.

Brown, Wendy. *Manhood and Politics: A Feminist Reader in Political Theory*. Lanham, MD: Rowman and Littlefield, 1988.

———. *States of Injury: Power and Freedom in Late Modernity*. Princeton: Princeton University Press, 1995.

———. *Undoing the Demos: Liberalism's Stealth Revolution*. Cambridge, MA: Zone Books, 2015.

Butler, Judith. *Gender Trouble: Feminism and the Subversion of Identity*. New York: Routledge, 1990.

———. *The Psychic Life of Power*. Stanford, CA: Stanford University Press, 1997.

Cady, Linell E., and Elizabeth Shakman Hurd, eds. *Comparative Secularisms in a Global Age*. New York: Palgrave Macmillan, 2010.

———. *Religion, the Secular, and the Politics of Sexual Difference*. New York: Columbia University Press, 2013.

Casanova, José. "Secularization." In *International Encyclopedia of the Social and Behavioral Sciences*, ed. Neil Smelser and Paul B. Baltes. Amsterdam: Elsevier, 2001.

Castronovo, Russ. *Necro Citizenship: Death, Eroticism, and the Public Sphere in the Nineteenth-Century United States*. Durham, NC: Duke University Press, 2001.

Chadwick, Owen. *The Secularization of the European Mind in the Nineteenth Century*. Cambridge: Cambridge University Press, 1975.

Chasin, Alexandra. *Selling Out: The Gay and Lesbian Movement Goes to Market*. New York: Palgrave, 2000.

Chatterjee, Indrani. "Monastic Governmentality, Colonial Misogyny, and Postcolonial Amnesia in South Asia." *History of the Present* 3:1 (Spring 2013): 57–98.

Cinar, Alev. "Subversion and Subjugation in the Public Sphere: Secularism and the Islamic Headscarf." *Signs* 33:4 (2008): 891–913.

Cirstocea, Ioana. "La fin du *Deuxième Monde* et la seconde vie de la *femme rouge*: Sociologie politique des constructions transnationales du genre en contexte postsocialiste." *Mémoire de Recherche Original.* Dossier pour l'habilitation à diriger des recherches. Université de Paris 1—Panthéon-Sorbonne, January 2017.

Clark, Linda. *Schooling the Daughters of Marianne: Textbooks and the Socialization of Girls in Modern French Primary Schools.* Albany: SUNY Press, 1986.

Cobb, Richard. *Les armées révolutionnaires: Instrument de la terreur dans les départements, avril 1793-Floréal an II.* Paris: Mouton, 1961–63.

Connolly, Brian. *Domestic Intimacies: Incest and the Liberal Subject in Nineteenth-Century America.* Philadelphia: University of Pennsylvania Press, 2014.

———. "'Hindoo Marriage' and National Sovereignty in the Early Nineteenth-Century United States." In *Warring for America, 1803–1818,* ed. Nicole Eustace and Fredrika J. Teute. Chapel Hill: University of North Carolina Press, 2017.

Conway, Jill. "Stereotypes of Femininity in a Theory of Sexual Evolution." In *Suffer and Be Still: Women in the Victorian Age,* ed. Martha Vicinus. Bloomington: Indiana University Press, 1972.

Copjec, Joan. *Read My Desire: Lacan against the Historicists.* Cambridge, MA: MIT Press, 1994.

Cott, Nancy. *The Grounding of Modern Feminism.* New Haven: Yale University Press, 1989.

Coviello, Peter, and Jared Hickman. "Introduction: After the Postsecular." *American Literature* 86:4 (December 2014): 645–54.

Curtis, Sarah A. "Charitable Ladies: Gender, Class and Religion in Mid-Nineteenth-Century Paris." *Past and Present* 177 (2002): 121–56.

———. *Civilizing Habits: Women Missionaries and the Revival of French Empire.* Oxford: Oxford University Press, 2010.

Daughton, J. P. *An Empire Divided: Religion, Republicanism, and the Making of French Colonialism, 1880–1914.* Oxford: Oxford University Press, 2006.

Davis, Kathleen. *Periodization and Sovereignty: How Ideas of Feudalism and Secularization Govern the Politics of Time.* Philadelphia: University of Pennsylvania Press, 2008.

Deltombe, Thomas. *L'Islam imaginaire: La construction médiatique de l'Islamophobie en France, 1975–2005.* Paris: La Découverte, 2005.

D'Emilio, John, and Estelle B. Freedman. *Intimate Matters: A History of Sexuality in America.* Chicago: University of Chicago Press, [1988] 1997.

Di Giorgio, Michela. "The Catholic Model." In *A History of Women in the West,* gen. ed. Georges Duby and Michelle Perrot. Vol. 4, *Emerging Feminism from Revolution to World War,* trans. Arthur Goldhammer. Cambridge, MA: Harvard University Press, 1993.

Dillon, Elizabeth Maddock. *The Gender of Freedom: Fictions of Liberalism and the Literary Public Sphere.* Stanford, CA: Stanford University Press, 2004.

Donert, Celia. "Women's Rights in Cold War Europe: Disentangling Feminist Histories." *Past and Present* Supplement 8 (2013): 178–202.

Donzelot, Jacques. *La police des familles*. Paris: Editions des Minuit, 1977.

Douglas, Ann. *The Feminization of American Culture*. New York: Knopf, 1977.

Dudink, Stefan. "Masculinity, Effeminacy, Time." In *Masculinities in Politics and War: Gendering Modern History*, ed. Stefan Dudink, Karen Hagemann, and John Tosh, 78. Manchester: University of Manchester Press, 2009.

Durkheim, Emile. *The Division of Labor in Society*. Trans. George Simpson. New York: Free Press, 1964.

Edelman, Lee. *No Future: Queer Theory and the Death Drive*. Durham, NC: Duke University Press, 2004.

Eisenstein, Hester. *Feminism Seduced: How Global Elites Use Women's Labor and Ideas to Exploit the World*. Boulder, CO: Paradigm, 2009.

Engels, Friedrich. *The Origin of the Family, Private Property, and the State*. New York: Penguin Classics, 2010.

Evans, Sara. *Born for Liberty: A History of Women in America*. New York: Free Press, 1989.

Fabian, Katalin. *Contemporary Women's Movements in Hungary: Globalization, Democracy, and Gender Equality*. Washington, DC: Woodrow Wilson Center Press and Johns Hopkins University Press, 2009.

Faderman, Lillian. *The Gay Revolution: The Story of the Struggle*. New York: Simon and Schuster, 2015.

Fanon, Frantz. "Algeria Unveiled." In *A Dying Colonialism*, trans. Haakon Chevalier. New York: Grove Press, 1965.

Farris, Sara. "Femonationalism and the 'Regular' Army of Labor Called Migrant Women." *History of the Present* 2:2 (2012): 184–99.

———. *In the Name of Women's Rights: The Rise of Femonationalism*. Durham, NC: Duke University Press, 2017.

Fassin, Eric. "La démocratie sexuelle et le conflit des civilisations." *Multitudes* 26 (Fall 2006): 123–31.

———. "National Identities and Transnational Intimacies: Sexual Democracy and the Politics of Immigration in Europe." *Public Culture* 22:3 (2010): 507–29.

Fauré, Christine. *La démocratie sans les femmes: Essai sur le libéralisme en France*. Paris: Presses Universitaires de France, 1986.

Fernando, Mayanthi. *The Republic Unsettled: Muslim French and the Contradictions of Secularism*. Durham, NC: Duke University Press, 2014.

Firestone, Shulamith. *The Dialectic of Sex: The Case for Feminist Revolution*. New York: Bantam, 1970.

Floyd, Kevin. *The Reification of Desire: Toward a Queer Marxism*. Minneapolis: University of Minnesota Press, 2009.

Foucault, Michel. *The Birth of Biopolitics: Lectures at the Collège de France, 1978–1979*. Trans. Graham Burchell. New York: Palgrave Macmillan, 2004.

———. "The Confession of the Flesh." In *Power/Knowledge: Selected Interviews and Other Writings, 1972–1977*, ed. Colin Gordon. New York: Pantheon Books, 1970.

———. *History of Sexuality*. Vol. 1. New York: Vintage Books, 1980.

———. *Security, Territory, Population: Lectures at the Collège de France, 1977–78*. Trans. Graham Burchell. New York: Palgrave, 2007.

Fraisse, Geneviève. *Reason's Muse: Sexual Difference and the Birth of Democracy*. Trans. Janet Todd. Chicago: University of Chicago Press, 1994.

Freud, Sigmund. *Totem and Taboo*. Vol. 13 in the standard ed. of *The Complete Psychological Works of Sigmund Freud*, ed. James Strachey. London: Hogarth Press, 1995.

Funk, Nanette, and Magda Mueller, eds. *Gender Politics and Post-Communism: Reflections from Eastern Europe and the Former Soviet Union*. New York: Routledge, 1993.

Gal, Susan, and Gail Kligman. *The Politics of Gender after Socialism*. Princeton: Princeton University Press, 2000.

Ghodsee, Kristen. "Revisiting the United Nations Decade for Women: Brief Reflections on Feminism, Capitalism and Cold War Politics in the Early Years of the International Women's Movement." *Women's Studies International Forum*, Special Issue: "Compliance without Commitment? The EU's Gender Equality Agenda in the Central and Eastern Europe States," *ScienceDirect* 33 (1): 3–12. January–February 2010.

Gibson, Ralph. "Le catholicisme et les femmes en France au XIXe siècle." *Revue d'histoire de l'église de France* 79 (1993): 63–94.

Göle, Nilüfer. "The Gendered Nature of the Public Sphere." *Public Culture* 10:1 (1997): 61–81.

———. *Islam and Secularity: The Future of Europe's Public Sphere*. Durham, NC: Duke University Press, 2015.

Gordon, Sarah Barringer. *The Mormon Question: Polygamy and Constitutional Conflict in Nineteenth-Century America*. Chapel Hill: University of North Carolina Press, 2002.

Gouges, Olympe de. *Déclaration des droits de la femme et de la citoyenne*. Paris, 1791.

Goven, Joanna. "Gender Politics in Hungary: Autonomy and Antifeminism." In *Gender Politics and Post-Communism: Reflections from Eastern Europe and the Former Soviet Union*, ed. Nanette Funk and Magda Mueller. New York: Routledge, 1993.

Grewal, Inderpal. *Transnational America*. Durham, NC: Duke University Press, 2005.

Gubin, Eliane, Catherine Jacques, and Claudine Marissal. "Une citoyenneté différée? Le suffrage féminin en Belgique, 1830–1940." In *Féminismes et identités nationales*, ed. Yolande Cohen and Françoise Thébaud. Programme Rhône-Alpes de recherche en sciences humaines, 1998.

Haan, Francisca de. "Continuing Cold War Paradigms in Western Historiography of Transnational Women's Organizations: The Case of the Women's

International Democratic Federation (WIDF)." *Women's History Review* 19:4 (2010): 547–73.

———. "Ten Years After: Communism and Feminism Revisited." *Aspasia* 10 (2016): 102–68.

Hall, Catherine. "The Sweet Delights of Home." In *A History of Private Life*. Vol. 4, ed. Michelle Perrot. Trans. Arthur Goldhammer. Cambridge, MA: Harvard University Press, 1990.

Hallaq, Wael B. *An Introduction to Islamic Law*. Cambridge: Cambridge University Press, 2009.

Halley, Janet, and Kerry Rittich. "Critical Directions in Comparative Family Law: Genealogies and Contemporary Studies of Family Law Exceptionalism." Special issue on Comparative Family Law of the *American Journal of Comparative Law* 58 (2010).

Hartman, Saidiya V. *Scenes of Subjection: Terror, Slavery, and Self-Making in Nineteenth-Century America*. New York: Oxford University Press, 1997.

Harvey, David. "Neoliberalism as Creative Destruction." *Annals of the American Academy of Political and Social Science* 610 (March 2007): 22–44.

Hastings, Derek K. "Fears of a Feminized Church." *European Historical Quarterly* 38:1 (2008): 34–65.

Hause, Steven C., with Anne R. Kenny. *Women's Suffrage and Social Politics in the French Third Republic*. Princeton: Princeton University Press, 1984.

Herzog, Dagmar. *Intimacy and Exclusion: Religious Politics in Pre-Revolutionary Baden*. Princeton: Princeton University Press, 1996.

———. *Sex in Crisis: The New Sexual Revolution and the Future of American Politics*. New York: Basic Books, 2008.

———. *Sexuality in Europe: A Twentieth-Century History*. Cambridge: Cambridge University Press, 2011.

Hirsch, Marianne, and Evelyn Fox Keller, eds. *Conflicts in Feminism*. New York: Routledge, 1990.

Hollis, Patricia. *Women in Public, 1850–1914: Documents of the Victorian Women's Movement*. London: Routledge, 1979.

Holmstrom, Nancy. *The Socialist Feminist Project: A Contemporary Reader in Theory and Politics*. New York: Monthly Review Press, 2004.

Hufton, Olwen. "Women in Revolution." *French Politics and Society* 7:3 (Summer 1989): 65–81.

Hull, Isabel. *Sexuality, State, and Civil Society in Germany, 1700–1815*. Ithaca: Cornell University Press, 1997.

Huntington, Samuel. "The Clash of Civilizations?" *Foreign Affairs* 72:3 (1993): 22–49.

Hurd, Elizabeth Shakman. *The Politics of Secularism in International Relations*. Princeton: Princeton University Press, 2008.

Hyatt, Vera Lawrence, and Rex Nettleford, eds. *Race, Discourse, and the Origin of the Americas: A New World View*. Washington, DC: Smithsonian Institution Press, 1995.

Immerman, Richard H., and Petra Goedde, eds. *The Oxford Handbook of the Cold War*. Oxford: Oxford University Press, 2013.

Inglehart, Ronald, and Pippa Norris. *Sacred and Secular: Religion and Politics Worldwide*. Cambridge: Cambridge University Press, 2004.

———. "The True Clash of Civilizations." *Foreign Policy* 135 (2003): 62–70.

Jakobsen, Janet R. "Sex + Freedom = Regulation. Why?" *Social Text* 84–85 (2005): 285–308.

Jakobsen, Janet R., and Ann Pellegrini, eds. *Secularisms*. Durham, NC: Duke University Press, 2008.

Jayawardena, Kumari. *Feminism and Nationalism in the Third World*. London: Zed Books 1986.

Juster, Susan. *Disorderly Women: Sexual Politics and Evangelicalism in Revolutionary New England*. Ithaca: Cornell University Press, 1996.

———. *Doomsayers: Anglo-American Prophecy in the Age of Revolution*. Philadelphia: University of Pennsylvania Press, 2003.

Kandiyoti, Deniz. "Emancipated but Unliberated? Reflections on the Turkish Case." *Feminist Studies* 13:2 (1987): 317–38.

Kantorowicz, Ernst H. *The King's Two Bodies: A Study in Medieval Political Theology*. Princeton: Princeton University Press, 1957.

Kent, Susan Kingsley. *Sex and Suffrage in Britain, 1860–1914*. Princeton: Princeton University Press, 1987.

Kerber, Linda. "The Republican Mother: Women and the Enlightenment—an American Perspective." *American Quarterly* 28:2 (1976): 187–205.

Kholoussy, Hanan. "Talking about a Revolution: Gender and the Politics of Marriage in Early Twentieth-Century Egypt." *Graduate Researcher: Journal for the Arts, Sciences, and Technology* 1:2 (2003): 25–34.

Kirby, Dianne. "Divinely Sanctioned: The Anglo-American Cold War Alliance and the Defence of Western Civilization and Christianity, 1945–48." *Journal of Contemporary History* 35:3 (2000): 385–412.

———. "Harry Truman's Religious Legacy: The Holy Alliance, Containment, and the Cold War." In *Religion and the Cold War*, ed. Kirby. Basingstoke: Palgrave Macmillan, 2003.

———, ed. *Religion and the Cold War*. Basingstoke: Palgrave Macmillan, 2003.

———. "The Religious Cold War." In *The Oxford Handbook of the Cold War*, ed. Richard H. Immerman and Petra Goedde. Oxford: Oxford University Press, 2013.

Klassen, Pamela. "Christianity as a Polemical Concept." In *The Companion to the Anthropology of Religion*, ed. Janice Boddy and Michael Lambek. Chichester, UK: Wiley-Blackwell, 2013.

———. "Mentality, Fundamentality, and the Colonial Secular." In *The Postsecular Condition*, ed. Rosi Braidotti, Bolette Blaagaard, and Eva Midden. London: Palgrave MacMillan, 2014.

Klinger, Cornelia. "Woman-Landscape-Artwork: Alternative Realms or Patriarchal Reserves?" In *Continental Philosophy in Feminist Perspective:*

Re-Reading the Canon in German, ed. Herta Nagl-Docekal and Cornelia Klinger, trans. James Dodd. University Park: Pennsylvania State University Press, 2000.

Klug, Francesca. "'Oh to Be in England': The British Case Study." In *Woman-Nation-State*, ed. Nira Yuval-Davis and Floya Anthias. London: Macmillan, 1989.

Knibiehler, Yvonne. "Les médecins et la 'Nature féminine' au temps du Code civil." *Annales E.S.C. 31* (1976): 835.

Kordela, A. Kiarina. "Biopolitics: From Tribes to Commodity Fetishism." *differences* 24:1 (2013): 1–29.

———. "Consent beyond Ideology: (Marxian-Psychoanalytic) Biopolitics." *differences* 24:1 (Spring 2013).

———. "(Psychoanalytic) Biopolitics and Bioracism." *Umbr(a)* 2011.

———. *Surplus: Spinoza, Lacan*. Albany: SUNY Press, 2007.

Koselleck, Reinhart. *The Practice of Conceptual History: Timing History, Spacing Concept*. Trans. Todd Presen, Kersten Behnke, and Jobst Welge. Stanford, CA: Stanford University Press, 2002.

Koven, Seth, and Sonya Michel. "Womanly Duties: Maternalist Politics and the Origins of Welfare States in France, Germany, Great Britain, and the United States." In *Gender and History in Western Europe*, ed. Robert Shoemaker and Mary Vincent. London: Arnold, 1998.

Kuhar, Roman. "Playing with Science: Sexual Citizenship and the Roman Catholic Counter-Narratives in Slovenia and Croatia." *Women's Studies International Forum* online, August 14, 2014.

Lacan, Jacques. "The Signification of the Phallus." Trans. Alan Sheridan. In Lacan, *Écrits: A Selection*, trans. Bruce Fink. London: Tavistock, 1977.

Lagrave, Rose-Marie. "A Supervised Emancipation." In *A History of Women in the West*, gen. ed. Georges Duby and Michelle Perrot. Vol. 5, *Toward a Cultural Identity in the Twentieth Century*, ed. Françoise Thébaud. Cambridge, MA: Harvard University Press, 1994.

Laqueur, Thomas. *Making Sex: Body and Gender from the Greeks to Freud*. Cambridge, MA: Harvard University Press, 1990.

Laville, Helen. "Gender and Women's Rights in the Cold War." In *The Oxford Handbook of the Cold War*, ed. Immerman and Goedde. Oxford: Oxford University Press, 2013.

Leeuw, Marc de, and Sonja van Wichelen. "Please, Go Wake Up: Submission, Hirsi Ali and the 'War on Terror' in the Netherlands." *Feminist Media Studies* 5:3 (2005): 325–40.

Lefort, Claude. *Democracy and Political Theory*. Trans. David Macey. Cambridge: Polity Press, 1988.

Levy, Darlene Gay, Harriet Branson Applewhite, and Mary Durham Johnson, eds. and trans. *Women in Revolutionary Paris, 1789–1795*. Urbana: University of Illinois Press, 1979.

Lewis, Jane. *Women in England, 1870–1950: Sexual Division and Social Change*. Sussex: Wheatsheaf Books, 1984.

Lloyd, Kevin. *The Reification of Desire: Toward a Queer Marxism*. Minneapolis: University of Minnesota Press, 2009.

Mack, Phyllis. "Religion, Feminism, and the Problem of Agency: Reflections on Eighteenth-Century Quakerism." In *Women, Gender and Enlightenment*, ed. Sarah Knott and Barbara Taylor. Hampshire: Palgrave Macmillan, 2005.

MacKinnon, Catharine A. "Feminism, Marxism, Method, and the State: An Agenda for Theory." In *Feminism and Sexuality: A Reader*, ed. Stevi Jackson and Mary McIntosh. New York: Columbia University Press, 1996.

Mahmood, Saba. *The Politics of Piety: The Islamic Revival and the Feminist Subject*. Princeton: Princeton University Press, 2004.

———. *Religious Difference in a Secular Age: A Minority Report*. Princeton: Princeton University Press, 2016.

———. "Sexuality and Secularism." In *Religion, the Secular, and the Politics of Sexual Difference*, ed. Linell E. Cady and Tracy Fessenden, 51. New York: Columbia University Press, 2013.

Mallette, Karla. *European Modernity and the Arab Mediterranean: Toward a New Philology and a Counter-Orientalism*. Philadelphia: University of Pennsylvania Press, 2010.

Martin, Emily. "The End of the Body?" *American Ethnologist* (1992): 121–40.

Martin-Fugier, Anne. "Bourgeois Rituals." In *A History of Private Life*. Vol. 4, *From the Fires of Revolution to the Great War*, ed. Michelle Perrot, trans. Arthur Goldhammer. Cambridge, MA: Harvard University Press, 1994.

Marx, Karl. *Capital*. Ed. Frederick Engels. Trans. Samuel Moore and Edward Aveling. New York: Modern Library, 1947.

———. "On the Jewish Question." In *The Marx-Engels Reader*, ed. Robert Tucker. New York: Norton, 1978.

Massad, Joseph. *Colonial Effects: The Making of National Identity in Jordan*. New York: Columbia University Press, 2001.

———. *Islam in Liberalism*. Chicago: University of Chicago Press, 2015.

Masuzawa, Tomoko. *The Invention of World Religions, or How European Universalism Was Preserved in the Language of Pluralism*. Chicago: University of Chicago Press, 2005.

May, Elaine Tyler. *Homeward Bound: American Families in the Cold War Era*. New York: Basic Books, [1988] 2008.

Mayeur, Françoise. "The Secular Model of Girls' Education." In *A History of Women in the West*, gen. ed. Georges Duby and Michelle Perrot. Vol. 4, *Emerging Feminism from Revolution to World War*, trans. Arthur Goldhammer. Cambridge, MA: Harvard University Press, 1993.

McClintock, Anne. "Family Feuds: Gender, Nationalism, and the Family." *Feminist Review* 44 (1993): 61–80.

———. *Imperial Leather: Race, Gender, and Sexuality in the Colonial Contest*. New York: Routledge, 1995.

McGoldrick, Dominic. *Human Rights and Religion: The Islamic Debate in Europe*. Portland, OR: Hart, 2006.

Michelet, Jules. *Du Prêtre, de la femme, de la famille*. 3rd ed. Paris: Hachette, 1845.
———. *L'Amour*. In *Oeuvres Complètes*. Vol. 18. Paris: Flammarion, [1858] 1985.
———. *La Femme*. In *Oeuvres Complètes*. Vol. 18. Paris: Flammarion, [1859] 1985.
Miles, Tiya. *Ties that Bind: The Story of an Afro-Cherokee Family in Slavery and Freedom*. Berkeley: University of California Press, 2005.
Mitchell, Timothy. *Colonizing Egypt*. Berkeley: University of California Press, 1991.
Modern, John Lardas. *Secularism in Antebellum America*. Chicago: University of Chicago Press, 2011.
Moglen, Seth. "Excess and Utopia: Meditations on Moravian Bethlehem." *History of the Present* 2:2 (2012): 122–47.
Moreau, Thérèse. *Le sang de l'histoire: Michelet, l'histoire, et l'idée de la femme aux XIXe siècle*. Paris: Flammarion, 1982.
Moyn, Samuel. "From Communist to Muslim: European Human Rights, the Cold War, and Religious Liberty." *South Atlantic Quarterly* 113:1 (2014): 63–86.
———. *The Last Utopia: Human Rights in History*. Cambridge, MA: Harvard University Press, 2010.
Najmabadi, Afsaneh. *Women with Mustaches and Men without Beards: Gender and Sexual Anxieties of Iranian Modernity*. Berkeley: University of California Press, 2005.
Norton, Anne. *On the Muslim Question*. Princeton: Princeton University Press, 2013.
Nye, Robert. *Masculinity and Male Codes of Honor in Modern France*. Berkeley: University of California Press, 1998.
Olcott, Jocelyn. "Cold War Conflicts and Cheap Cabaret: Sexual Politics at the 1975 United Nations International Women's Year Conference." *Gender and History* 22:3 (2010): 733–54.
Parker, Andrew, Mary Russo, Doris Sommer, and Patricia Yaeger, eds. *Nationalisms and Sexualities*. New York: Routledge, 1992.
Pateman, Carole. *The Sexual Contract*. Stanford, CA: Stanford University Press, 1988.
Paternotte, David, and Marion Tremblay, eds. *The Ashgate Research Companion to Lesbian and Gay Activism*. Abingdon: Ashgate, 2015.
Perrot, Michelle. *A History of Private Life*. Vol. 4, *From the Fires of Revolution to the Great War*, ed. Michelle Perrot. Trans. Arthur Goldhammer. Cambridge, MA: Harvard University Press, 1994.
Pursley, Sara. "A Race against Time: Governing Femininity and Reproducing the Future in Revolutionary Iraq, 1945–1963." PhD diss., Graduate Center, City University of New York, 2011.
Ratzinger, Joseph, and Jürgen Habermas. *The Dialectics of Secularization: On Reason and Religion*. San Francisco: Ignatius Press, 2007.

Renan, Ernest. *De la part des peuples sémitiques dans l'histoire de la civilization* (1862).

———. "L'Islamisme et la Science" (1883). In *Discours et Conférences*. Paris: Calmann-Lévy, 1887.

Ridley, Hugh. "Germany in the Mirror of Its Colonial Literature." *German Life and Letters* 28 (1974–75): 375–86.

———. *Images of Imperial Rule*. London: St. Martin's Press; Croom Helm, 1983.

Rifkin, Mark. *When Did Indians Become Straight? Kinship, the History of Sexuality, and Native Sovereignty*. Oxford: Oxford University Press, 2011.

Riley, Denise. *"Am I that Name?" Feminism and the Category of "Women" in History*. London: Macmillan, 1988.

Roberts, Mary Louise. *Civilization without Sexes: Reconstructing Gender in Postwar France, 1917–1927*. Chicago: University of Chicago Press, 1994.

Rochefort, Florence. "Laïcité et droits des femmes: Quelques jalons pour une réflexion historique." *Archives de Philosophie du droit* 48 (2005): 95–107.

Rofel, Lisa. *Desiring China: Experiments in Neoliberalism, Sexuality, and Public Culture*. Durham, NC: Duke University Press, 2007.

Rosen, Ruth. *The World Split Open: How the Modern Women's Movement Changed America*. New York: Penguin, 2006.

Rosenberg, Emily. "Foreign Affairs after WWII." *Diplomatic History* 18 (1994): 59–70.

Rousseau, J-J. *Emile, or On Education*. Trans. Allan Bloom. New York: Basic Books, 1979.

Sabsay, Letitia. "The Emergence of the Other Sexual Citizen: Orientalism and the Modernisation of Sexuality." *Citizenship Studies* 16:5–6 (2012): 605–23.

Said, Edward. *Orientalism*. New York: Vintage Books, [1978] 1994.

Saunders, Frances Stonor. *The Cultural Cold War: The CIA and the World of Arts and Letters*. New York: New Press, 1999.

Schiebinger, Londa. *The Mind Has No Sex? Women in the Origins of Modern Science*. Cambridge, MA: Harvard University Press, 1989.

Schulman, Sarah. "Israel and 'Pinkwashing.'" *New York Times*, November 22, 2011.

Schwartz, Laura. *Infidel Feminism: Secularism, Religion and Women's Emancipation, England, 1830–1914*. Manchester: Manchester University Press, 2015.

Scott, Joan Wallach. "Introduction: Flyers into the Unknown." In *The Fantasy of Feminist History*. Durham, NC: Duke University Press, 2011.

———. *Only Paradoxes to Offer: French Feminists and the Rights of Man*. Cambridge, MA: Harvard University Press, 1996.

———. *Parité: Sexual Equality and the Crisis of French Universalism*. Chicago: University of Chicago Press, 2005.

———. "The Veil and the Political Unconscious of French Republicanism." *OrientXXI*, April 27, 2016. http://orientxxi.info/magazine/the-veil-and-the-political-unconscious-of-french-republicanism,1310,1310.

Seeley, Paul. "Ô Sainte Mère: Liberalism and the Socialization of Catholic Men in Nineteenth-Century France." *Journal of Modern History* 70:4 (December 1998): 862–91.

Siddiqi, Dina M. "Solidarity, Sexuality and Saving Muslim Women in Neoliberal Times." *Women's Studies Quarterly* 42:3/4 (2014): 292–306.

Sinha, Mrinalini. *Specters of Mother India: The Global Restructuring of an Empire*. Durham, NC: Duke University Press, 2006.

Smith, Bonnie, ed. *Global Feminisms since 1945: A Survey of Issues and Controversies*. New York: Routledge, 2000.

Smith, S. A. "Communism and Religion." In *The Cambridge History of Communism*, ed. Juliane Furst, Silvio Pons, and Mark Selden. Vol. 3. Cambridge: Cambridge University Press, 2017.

Snitow, Ann, Christine Stansell, and Sharon Thompson. *Powers of Desire: The Politics of Sexuality*. New York: Monthly Review Press, 1983.

Spector, Jessica. *Prostitution and Pornography: Philosophical Debate about the Sex Industry*. Stanford, CA: Stanford University Press, 2006.

Spellberg, Denise. *Thomas Jefferson's Qur'an: Islam and the Founders*. New York: Vintage, 2014.

Stahuljak, Zrinka. *Pornographic Archaeology: Medicine, Medievalism, and the Invention of the French Nation*. Philadelphia: University of Pennsylvania Press, 2012.

Stallybrass, Peter, and Allon White. *The Politics and Poetics of Transgression*. Ithaca: Cornell University Press, 1986.

Stein, Jordan Alexander. "Angels in (Mexican) America." *American Literature* 86:4 (December 2014): 683–711.

Stephens, Julia. "The Politics of Muslim Rage." *History Workshop Journal* 77 (2013): 45–64.

Stevens, Jacqueline. *Reproducing the State*. Princeton: Princeton University Press, 1999.

Stoler, Ann Laura. *Carnal Knowledge and Imperial Power: Race and the Intimate in Colonial Rule*. Berkeley: University of California Press, 2002.

Stone, Judith. "Anticlericals and Bonnes Soeurs: The Rhetoric of the 1901 Law of Association." *French Historical Studies* 23:1 (Winter 2000): 211–14.

Surkis, Judith. "Carnival Balls and Penal Codes: Body Politics in July Monarchy France." *History of the Present* 1:1 (2011): 59–83.

———. *Scandalous Subjects: Intimacy and Indecency in France and French Algeria*. Forthcoming.

———. *Sexing the Citizen: Morality and Masculinity in France, 1870–1920*. Ithaca: Cornell University Press, 2006.

Tallett, Frank. "Dechristianizing France." In *Religion, Society, and Politics in France since 1789*, ed. Frank Tallett and Nicholas Atkin. London: Hambledon Press, 1991.

Taylor, Barbara. *Eve and the New Jerusalem: Socialism and Feminism in the Nineteenth Century*. New York: Pantheon, 1982.

Taylor, Charles. *A Secular Age*. Cambridge, MA: Harvard University Press, 2007.

Thébaud, Françoise. "The Great War and the Triumph of Sexual Division." In *A History of Women in the West*, gen. ed. Georges Duby and Michelle Perrot. Vol. 5, *Toward a Cultural Identity in the Twentieth Century*, trans. Arthur Goldhammer, ed. Françoise Thébaud. Cambridge, MA: Harvard University Press, 1994.

Therborn, Göran. *Between Sex and Power: Family in the World, 1900–2000*. New York: Routledge, 2004.

Thomas, Keith. "Women in the Civil War Sects." In *Crisis in Europe, 1560–1660*, ed. Trevor Ashton. New York: Basic Books, 1965.

Thompson, Elizabeth. *Colonial Citizens: Republican Rights, Paternal Privilege, and Gender in French Syria and Lebanon*. New York: Columbia University Press, 2000.

Thompson, E. P. *The Making of the English Working Class*. New York: Vintage, 1966.

Tocqueville, Alexis de. *Democracy in America*. Trans. Arthur Goldhammer. New York: Library of America, 2004.

Vance, Carole. "Innocence and Experience: Melodramatic Narratives of Sex Trafficking and Their Consequences for Law and Policy." *History of the Present* 2:2 (2012): 200–218.

———. "States of Contradiction: Twelve Ways to Do Nothing about Trafficking while Pretending to." *Social Research* 78:3 (Fall 2011): 933–48.

van der Veer, Peter. "Pim Fortuyn, Theo van Gogh, and the Politics of Tolerance in the Netherlands." *Public Culture* 18 (2006): 111–24.

Verhoeven, Timothy. "Neither Male nor Female: The Jesuit as Androgyne, 1843–70." *Modern and Contemporary France* 16:1 (2008): 103–27.

Viennot, Eliane. "De l'Ancien Régime au Nouveau: La masculinité au fondement de la modernité." In *Les défis de la république: Genre, territoires, citoyenneté*, ed. Bruno Perreau and Joan W. Scott. Paris: Presses Sciences Po, 2017.

Weber, Max. "Science as a Vocation." In *From Max Weber: Essays in Sociology*, ed. H. H. Gerth and C. Wright Mills. New York: Routledge, 1998.

———. "The Social Psychology of the World Religions." In *From Max Weber: Essays in Sociology*, ed. and trans. H. H. Gerth and C. Wright Mills. New York: Routledge, 1998.

Weir, Todd. *Secularism and Religion in Nineteenth-Century Germany*. Cambridge: Cambridge University Press, 2014.

Wenger, Lisa. "The God-in-the-Constitution Controversy: American Secularisms in Historical Perspective." In *Comparative Secularisms in a Global Age*, ed. Linell E. Cady and Elizabeth Shakman Hurd. New York: Palgrave Macmillan, 2010.

White, Jenny. "State Feminism, Modernization, and the Turkish Republican Woman." *NWSA Journal* 15:3 (2003): 145–59.

Wittig, Monique. "One Is Not Born a Woman." In *The Norton Anthology of Theory and Criticism*, ed. Vincent B. Letich. New York: W. W. Norton, 2010.

Wynter, Sylvia. "1492: A New World View." In *Race, Discourse, and the Origin of the Americas: A New World View*, ed. Vera Lawrence Hyatt and Rex Nettleford. Washington, DC: Smithsonian Institution Press, 1995.

Young, Robert J. C. *Colonial Desire: Hybridity in Theory, Culture and Race*. New York: Routledge, 1995.

Zaretsky, Eli. *Capitalism, the Family, and Personal Life*. New York: Harper and Row, 1976.

Zelizer, Viviana A. *The Purchase of Intimacy*. Princeton: Princeton University Press, 2005.

Zerilli, Linda. *Signifying Woman: Culture and Chaos in Rousseau, Burke, and Mill*. Ithaca: Cornell University Press, 1994.

Zimmerman, Andrew. *Alabama in Africa: Booker T. Washington, the German Empire, and the Globalization of the New South*. Princeton: Princeton University Press, 2010.

Zupančič, Alenka. *Why Psychoanalysis?* Summertalk series. Natchitoches, LA: Northwestern State University Press, 2008.

INDEX

THE PUBLIC SQUARE BOOK SERIES

PRINCETON UNIVERSITY PRESS

Uncouth Nation: Why Europe Dislikes America
by Andrei S. Markovits

The Politics of the Veil by Joan Wallach Scott

Hidden in Plain Sight: The Tragedy of Children's Rights from Ben Franklin to Lionel Tate by Barbara Bennett Woodhouse

The Case for Big Government by Jeff Madrick

The Posthuman Dada Guide: tzara and lenin play chess
by Andrei Codrescu

Not for Profit: Why Democracy Needs the Humanities
by Martha C. Nussbaum

The Whites of Their Eyes: The Tea Party's Revolution and the Battle over American History by Jill Lepore

The End of the West: The Once and Future Europe
by David Marquand

On the Muslim Question by Anne Norton

Sex and Secularism by Joan Wallach Scott

A NOTE ON THE TYPE

THIS BOOK has been composed in Miller, a Scotch Roman typeface designed by Matthew Carter and first released by Font Bureau in 1997. It resembles Monticello, the typeface developed for The Papers of Thomas Jefferson in the 1940s by C. H. Griffith and P. J. Conkwright and reinterpreted in digital form by Carter in 2003.

Pleasant Jefferson ("P. J.") Conkwright (1905–1986) was Typographer at Princeton University Press from 1939 to 1970. He was an acclaimed book designer and AIGA Medalist.

The ornament used throughout this book was designed by Pierre Simon Fournier (1712–1768) and was a favorite of Conkwright's, used in his design of the *Princeton University Library Chronicle.*